"Richard Osmer has written the de[ ]
likely for years to come. It is biblica[ ]
cidly written, and often quite moving[ ]
Seminary have taught him how to think about the good news in ways that
are full of profound hope. And now that crucible of learning is available to
us between these covers. This is essential reading for anyone in practical
theology, Scripture, Barth studies, soteriology, or anyone who wants to share
good news with their neighbor without coming off as a creep, or just to be a
human being in love with God and others."

— **Jason Byassee**
coauthor of *Following: Embodied Discipleship in a Digital Age*

"In this significant, scholarly, and accessible study, Richard Osmer unpacks the inherited church's practice of evangelism as conversionism, with
its accompanying limitations. He then offers a robust theology of evangelism as invitation, grounded in Scripture and theology. This volume offers
a timely and deeply thoughtful contribution to the study and practice of
evangelism. Highly recommended for seminary students and ministry
practitioners."

— **Elaine A. Heath**
author of *The Mystic Way of Evangelism:*
A Contemplative Vision for Christian Outreach

"Richard Osmer has done Christians a great service by examining the cultural and theological toolkits with which conversionist approaches to evangelism operate, placing them in dialogue with the gospels and the theology
of Karl Barth. While respectful of conversionist approaches, he demonstrates the way they rely heavily on cultural ideas and habits, such as individualism, that are incongruous with the scriptural witness and the church's
calling by Christ to be a missional community in the world, empowered by
the Holy Spirit. Osmer's use of case studies gives to his examination a con-
creteness and liveliness from which readers will gain insight, clarity, and
motivation."

— **Bryan Stone**
author of *Evangelism after Pluralism: The Ethics of Christian Witness*

"Evangelism has long been a topic that causes Christians to squirm. Varying
understandings and practices tend to be murky if not conflicting. Osmer provides a beautiful reimagining of evangelism that is deeply rooted in theology

and Scripture. He manages to untangle the complexities found in various traditions and provides the reader with a hope-filled understanding of this invitation to the gospel message. It can be difficult to appeal to both the academic guild and the local church, but Osmer does this brilliantly. This is practical theology at its very best."

— Amanda J. Drury
associate professor of practical theology at Indiana Wesleyan University

"With biblical and theological depth, pastoral sensitivity, and attentiveness to real contexts where Christian faith is lived out, Osmer takes on the hallowed American tradition of 'evangelism as conversionism.' Bringing his students' case studies into nuanced conversation with Scripture and the theology of Karl Barth, Osmer exposes the many weaknesses attending approaches to evangelism centered in human agency, i.e., 'making a decision for Christ.' As one of the leading practical theologians of our time, Osmer reconstructs evangelism around Barth's theme of 'Christ in our place,' encouraging a re-centering of the church's evangelical calling in divine agency and the startling invitation of God, who, in Jesus Christ and the power of the Holy Spirit, accomplishes for us what we can never accomplish for ourselves."

— Thomas John Hastings
executive director of the Overseas Ministries Study Center at
Princeton Theological Seminary

The Invitation

A Theology of Evangelism

Richard R. Osmer

Merry Christmas!
Love you,
Michael Paul
Xmas 2021

WILLIAM B. EERDMANS PUBLISHING COMPANY
GRAND RAPIDS, MICHIGAN

Wm. B. Eerdmans Publishing Co.
4035 Park East Court SE, Grand Rapids, Michigan 49546
www.eerdmans.com

Published 2021
Printed in the United States of America

27 26 25 24 23 22 21   1 2 3 4 5 6 7

ISBN 978-0-8028-7622-5

Library of Congress Cataloging-in-Publication Data

Names: Osmer, Richard Robert, 1950– author.
Title: The invitation : a theology of evangelism / Richard R. Osmer.
Description: Grand Rapids, Michigan : Wm. B. Eerdmans Publishing Co.,
    2021. | Includes bibliographical references and index. | Summary: "A book
    advancing an invitational model of evangelism, helping the church move
    beyond older approaches of proselytization"—Provided by publisher.
Identifiers: LCCN 2021013983 | ISBN 9780802876225 (paperback)
Subjects: LCSH: Evangelistic work.
Classification: LCC BV3790 .O78 2021 | DDC 269/.201—dc23
LC record available at https://lccn.loc.gov/2021013983

To
George Hunsinger and Darrell L. Guder
Colleagues, mentors in Karl Barth, and longtime friends

CONTENTS

CONTENTS

PREFACE

Special thanks to Craig Barnes, president of Princeton Theological Seminary. Shortly after Craig's arrival at PTS, we discussed the possibility of me teaching courses in mission and evangelism. No one had been teaching in this area since the retirement of John Stuart. Craig immediately saw the gap this left in the curriculum and helped make it possible for me to begin teaching courses in this area. I gave up the Thomas W. Synnott Chair in Christian Education and was appointed to the Ralph B. and Helen S. Ashenfelter Chair in Mission and Evangelism. Craig's support came from his deep love for the church and his equally deep love for the academy, as a graduate of the University of Chicago doctoral program in the history of Christianity. Thank you, Craig, for making the teaching and research going into this book possible and making it possible to teach mission and evangelism while I was at Princeton Theological Seminary

I also want to thank my editor, David Bratt, and the editor-in-chief of Eerdmans, James Ernest, for their support, patience, and helpful insight. In am honored to publish this book with their help. I am also grateful to Jenny Hoffman and Jeff Gifford who contributed much to the final form of this book. The manuscript was improved because of their work.

This book grew out of many wonderful years at PTS with colleagues in the Bible department like Beverly Gaventa, Lisa Bowens, Clifton Black, Pat Miller, Don Juel, Chris Becker, Jacqueline Lapsley, Dennis Olson, Joel Marcus, Jimmy Jack Roberts, and George Parsenios. Lisa Bowens and I worked closely in establishing the Center for Church Planting and Revitalization at PTS. She was a wonderful colleague and friend. I also had equally amazing colleagues in the theology department: Wentzel van Huyssteen, Bruce McCormack, George Hunsinger, Daniel Migliore, and Darrell Guder (mission and ecumenics). All but Wentzel had interest in the theology of Karl Barth and were the backdrop for establishing the Center for Barth

Studies at PTS. Their support in various ways made my time at PTS a journey of learning and intellectual growth. Wentzel was my closest dialogue partner in interdisciplinary thinking, especially the relationship between science and theology. We regularly team-taught doctoral seminars on this topic. The dialogue I undertake between practical theology, biblical studies, and dogmatic theology in this book is the fruition of many conversations and recommendations from these departmental colleagues across three decades.

Over the years, I have learned a great deal from PTS students. They are represented here in the form of case studies presented in classes on evangelism and church planting. Learning through teaching has always been important to me. Typically, I have first taught in an area of research and only then written about it. Doctoral students also were catalytic in my intellectual growth at PTS. When it came to Barth, dissertations by Nathan Stucky and Blair Bertrand under my supervision drew heavily on him. We formed a Barth reading group that focused on our own writing as well as writings from *Church Dogmatics*. Tom Hastings, the assistant director for the Center for Theological Inquiry at that time, was also a member of this reading group. He recently has returned to PTS as the executive director of the Overseas Ministries Study Center at Princeton Theological Seminary and editor of the *International Bulletin of Mission Research*.

As always, my closest colleagues at PTS were a lifeline of support and learning. Thank you, Kenda Creasy Dean, Bo Karen Lee, Gordon Mikoski, and Margarita Mooney. Though not in my area in the department of practical theology, Sally Brown and Deborah van Deusen Hunsinger have been amazing colleagues and friends. Most important of all, John Stuart and I were very close while he was teaching evangelism at PTS, and I have learned much about this field from him. He is a wise interpreter of mainline churches and writer on evangelism and a gifted preacher and church leader.

While I was at PTS I helped explore the possibility of establishing a Center for Church Planting and Revitalization with Lisa Bowens and Darrell Guder. This was a joint student and faculty initiative. The key students were Sarah Ann Bixler, Carlos Corro, Daniel Perez, Alison Fraser Kling, David Kling, Daniel Levy, and Kelsey Lambright. Their vision and passion on behalf of this project were truly amazing. It is the journey, not the destination, that really matters.

Finally, this book is dedicated to George Hunsinger and Darrell Guder. Both shaped my understanding of Barth as a theologian and dialogue partner for my own constructive work in practical theology. George and I have been friends since I was a student at Yale Divinity School. My wife, Sally, and I became friends with his wife, Deborah, and him while at YDS. We learned from each other the pleasures of reading J. R. R. Tolkien aloud. George was a precept leader (while a doctoral student) for my favorite course at Yale, Christian Doctrine 1. David Kelsey was a brilliant teacher, and George was an equally brilliant interpreter of Barth, whom we studied in the course. Thus began my interest in Barth and a longstanding friendship with George. I have learned from George's amazing understanding of Barth and been mentored by him. I admire his commitment to radical politics as a necessary dimension of Christian discipleship, his leadership in establishing the National Religious Campaign Against Torture, and his longstanding willingness to take personal risks in order to witness to the gospel. He is truly a theologian of the church—not as it is but as it should be in living obedience to the Word of God. His influence on my thinking is readily apparent throughout this book.

Darrell and I were acquaintances before he joined the faculty, but when he was appointed to a position at PTS we became good friends and colleagues. Eventually, he even became my next-door neighbor! Darrell and I team-taught a course on Lesslie Newbigin and an innovative course for students interested in church planting. The latter attempted to help students integrate their calling, seminary learning, and spirituality. It was one of my favorite courses at PTS. I consistently used Darrell's books in my classes. He has written some of the best books on evangelism and mission over the last fifty years. As a leader of the missional church trajectory of contemporary theology and church life, he has inaugurated innovative thinking about the church that reaches across North America. I admire greatly Darrell's ability to teach a broad cross section of students and his commitment to bringing the church and academy together.

Finally, I thank my partner in life and love, Sally. We have been married for forty-eight years, and she has been my trusted companion every step of our journey through life. My daughter, Sarah, and her husband, Gabriel, are wonderful parents to our two grandchildren, Anabel and Samuel, who bring laughter and joy into our lives every day. Finally, our son, Richard, has become a fantastic cook in recent years and tempts us with much-too-fattening food almost every evening. What more could we ask for? Great food, wonderful family, and many fond memories.

One matter of translation practice should be mentioned. The available version of *Church Dogmatics* has not been retranslated in many years. It still uses masculine pronouns to translate words that refer to humanity, humankind, and so forth. I have retranslated these terms myself in the passages quoted in order to eliminate the highly offensive, inaccurate, and out-of-date practice of using masculine terms to refer to the human race as a whole.

RICHARD R. OSMER
Chapel Hill, NC

INTRODUCTION

Evangelism as Invitation

Throughout this book, we use parts of case studies written by my students at Princeton Theological Seminary in classes on evangelism and church planting. These were presented for discussion in "precepts," groups of around ten students who met weekly in addition to the plenary meeting of the course. In part III, I explain why case studies are such a powerful way of learning in courses on evangelism. To put it in a nutshell, they bring practice and reflection together in ways that prepare students for their future ministries. What is presented in the book is only the opening vignette and some initial thoughts by the presenting students about the contexts. These were discussed in the precepts while other students took notes, which were subsequently sent to the presenters. The final projects involved much longer write-ups of the cases.

In addition to case studies, we also will reflect on the traditions of evangelism that shape our understanding of this ministry today. Often, we take these traditions for granted. Part of what I hope to accomplish in this book is to consider new ways of thinking about evangelism by turning to Scripture and theology anew. As practical theology often does, we begin with present practice. What are our traditions of evangelistic practice?

Starting Where We Are: Traditions of Evangelistic Practice

Jesse Parker drove his truck down the short gravel road to my home in the mountains of western North Carolina. I had met Jesse several times over the years. He works for Terminix and services the contract on my home. He is a thin man with an easy smile. I trust him to come into my home when I am back in Princeton, and more than once he has given me good advice about how to keep mice and spiders out of my house and about the best way to get rid of yellow jackets in the backyard. One time he even helped me make sense of a large gash on the front bank. "That's a bear cleaning out a honey nest," he said.

Jesse works for Terminix during the week, but on weekends he is a preacher for a Missionary Baptist Church in a small town in the next county. He is very open about his faith—not pushy but comfortable talking about his experience in biblical terms. The first time I met Jesse we walked out to my back porch and looked out at the beautiful Smoky Mountains, which we could see clearly in the distance from the vantage point of the home's 4,400-foot elevation. "When I look at those mountains I can't help but think of Psalm 121," I shared, "I lift up my eyes to the hills—from where will my help come?" (NRSV). Jesse responded immediately, "My help cometh from the Lord, which made heaven and earth" (KJV). Ever since then, Jesse seemed to take it for granted that I was a Christian and felt comfortable talking to me about his faith. That was why I was pretty sure that he would be willing to talk to me about evangelism. I reached out to shake hands with Jesse as he stepped out of his truck.

"Hey," I said, "Long time no see. How have you been?"

"I'm doing good," he said, "God's been good to me."

"How's your family?" I asked.

"My son's growin' like a weed. I swear that boy's gonna be taller than me before he's thirteen. Pretty good pitcher for his Little League team."

Our small talk continued for a while, and I finally asked him: "Jesse, I was wondering if you'd be willing to talk to me about evangelism, how you think about it and how your church does it. I'm doing some writing about this and wanted to get your perspective."

"Sure," he responded. "Now or later? I got a little time before my next call."

"Now is good," I said.

"Well, let me take care of your house first."

After Jesse had done his work, we made ourselves comfortable in rockers on the back porch and talked about evangelism over glasses of sweet iced tea. During our forty-five-minute conversation, Jesse used the language of "bringing people to Christ" and "sharing the Word so people will know the Lord from the heart" to describe the purpose of evangelism. He talked about revivals his church hosts periodically where they bring in outside preachers and spread the word around the community that everyone is welcome. He has preached during revivals at other churches in the past. He spoke of regional gatherings of youth with nightly preaching that invites the young people to make decisions for Christ. The youth would break up into small groups and share their personal testimonies. "Of course, they do a lot of fun things too," he added. He had been on a prayer team for one of these conferences several years earlier. He also told me about "missions" he had gone on with friends in his prayer group. They traveled 125 miles to Charlotte and set up tables with literature on a street. They engaged people who walked by. "You'd be surprised how willing people are to talk," he said.

Near the end of our conversation Jesse said, "You know, all these things are important, but in the end, to me, evangelism is about the way you live your faith every day and being willing to talk about it. I do that all the time on my job. Sometimes people respond. Sometimes you can tell that they're not comfortable. I'm praying silently and follow the leading of the Lord when that happens. Jesus told us to go and make disciples. I think evangelism is something every Christian should do. There are a lot of Christians who don't really know Jesus, and there are a lot of Christians who have fallen by the way. You have to be ready and willing to share your faith and trust God will lead you. You have to have confidence that they will make a decision to follow Christ."

"Do you think the purpose of evangelism is to convert people," I asked.

"Yes, I do—those who don't know Jesus or have fallen away," he answered. "They need to hear the gospel and trust in God with all their heart. I've got a cousin who was married to a guy who treated her pretty rough. We started praying for him, and I started visiting him. He really wasn't a bad guy. He was just frustrated with his job, and he took it out on his family. I brought him to Christ, and it changed everything. He comes to church with his family now. He treats them right. I'd have to say he's a changed man. That's what happens when people come to know the Lord."

In his own words, Jesse Parker does a good job of starting where we are. He describes the way many Christians in the United States think about evangelism. It involves sharing the gospel with unbelievers or people who have "fallen away" from the faith so they can enter into a relationship with Jesus Christ "from the heart." This notion of evangelism focuses on conversion, making "a decision to follow Christ" and "knowing the Lord." It is closely associated with many of the practices mentioned by Jesse: revivals, street missions, and sharing the faith in everyday life and personal relationships.

This understanding of evangelism is deeply rooted in the cultural DNA of American life. It was first planted on these shores by Christian missionaries. Pietists settled in Pennsylvania and Baptists in the South. Evangelism in our country took paradigmatic shape during the First and Second Great Awakenings. These were revival and spiritual awakening movements that resulted in the renewal and conversion of the early settlers of the American frontier. The great evangelists George Whitefield and John Wesley participated in these early missions. As the Methodist and Baptist movements began to spread, evangelistic preaching became an important way of converting people and establishing new churches in the American South and West. The Methodist movement was known for establishing small groups, which helped new converts grow in holiness and provided the unconverted with an opportunity to encounter Christ through the testimonies and mutual support of class meetings.

Most Americans continue to think of evangelism in terms of conversion experiences associated with revivals, evangelistic preaching, church missions, and personal relationships seeking to bring people to Christ. This long tradition of evangelistic practice in America shapes our thinking about evangelism in ways that are almost taken for granted. When we read the New Testament, we naturally associate certain Bible stories and passages with evangelism.

We gravitate toward Jesus's call to the disciples—especially his call to the fisherman Simon Peter, whom he tells, "Don't be afraid; from now on you will fish for people" (Luke 5:10). We recall that Jesus "appointed twelve that they might be with him and that he might send them out to preach" (Mark 3:14). We remember the "practice missions" on which Jesus sent the disciples and others (Matt. 10:5-15; Luke 10:1-24). We notice that, as he nears the end of his earthly ministry, Jesus appears to intensify his preparation of the disciples for the mission of evangelism, telling them they are to be his witnesses (John 15:27). He promises to send them the Holy Spirit who will help them remember and communicate his words (John 14:25-26; 16:7-11). We are drawn to accounts of post-resurrection appearances where Jesus commands his followers to proclaim his name "to all nations" and "to the ends of the earth" (Luke 24:47; Acts 1:8). We especially remember the passage commonly known as the Great Commission:

> Then the eleven disciples went to Galilee, to the mountain where Jesus had told them to go. When they saw him, they worshiped him; but some doubted. Then Jesus came to them and said, "All authority in heaven and on earth has been given to me. Therefore, go and make disciples of all nations, baptizing them in the name of the Father and of the Son and of the Holy Spirit, and teaching them to obey everything I have com-

manded you. And surely I am with you always, to the very end of the age." (Matt. 28:16-20)

We also approach the book of Acts as the story of the early church's evangelistic mission, recalling the dramatic outpouring of the Spirit on Pentecost, the street preaching of the apostles, and their testimonies before Roman and Jewish authorities. We are drawn especially to the story of Paul's dramatic conversion on the road to Damascus (Acts 9:1-9). This appears to be paradigmatic of the kind of conversion we associate with evangelism. Saul, the persecutor of the church, is converted by a mighty intervention of God and becomes Paul, the most powerful proponent of the gentile mission in early Christianity. We think of the mission trips taken by Paul and his companions around the Mediterranean, spreading the gospel and planting churches.

While I did not have the time to ask Jesse Parker to share the biblical stories he associates with evangelism, I imagine that he would resonate with the passages shared above. The traditions of evangelistic practice in American Christianity evoke them again and again. We know what evangelism is because we have been shaped by these traditions. It involves spreading the gospel and converting people.

In contrast to Jesse Parker, at the other end of the theological and educational spectrum stands Everett Vernon Smith—EV to his friends. EV went to an Ivy League divinity school and then earned a PhD in church history. He now is the pastor of a large, predominantly white Presbyterian congregation in a suburb of a mid-sized city in the northeast. He too knows the traditions of evangelistic practice shaping Jesse Parker, but he is deeply critical of them.

Sitting across from him in his office at church, I asked EV to share his understanding of evangelism. "We have stopped using the term 'evangelism' in my church," EV said. "It carries too much baggage. It calls up images of people knocking on your door or stopping you on the street in a very aggressive way. It smacks of coercion and manipulation, keeping kids up late at night until they finally break down and have a tear-filled, emotional experience. We don't have an evangelism committee. We have a hospitality committee. We work at making newcomers to our church and community feel welcome. We try to *show* God's love, not just *talk* about God's love. We want all people to feel welcome—divorced or married, straight or gay, young or old, black or white, Asian or Hispanic."

When I asked EV what parts of the Bible he draws on for this understanding of hospitality, he picked up a Bible and said, "Well, you know, it's not just about the Bible. It is about our social context too. Our society today is more pluralistic. You can't assault people from other religions trying to convert them. What kind of welcome is that? A lot of them are immigrants. And young people today are leaving the church in droves because they believe the church is too self-righteous, too much 'Our way or the highway.' In our context, we need to rethink evangelism. Too often, evangelism has sent the message, 'Convert and become like us.'"

EV continued: "But if you want the biblical basis of our understanding of hospitality, that's easy. Almost every page of the Gospels shows Jesus reaching out to people outside the religious establishment: the Samaritan woman, the demon-possessed, the tax-collectors and sinners. Jesus was constantly crossing boundaries to bring healing, freedom, and forgiveness to outsiders. He pretty much says this directly in his response to John the Baptist's disciples [he turned to Matthew 11:2-6 and read]: 'Go and tell John what you have seen and heard: the blind receive their sight, the lame walk, the lepers are cleansed, the deaf hear, and the dead are raised, the poor have good news brought to them. And blessed is anyone who takes no offense at me.' And we see social boundaries broken in the early church [he turned to Galatians 3:28 and read]: 'There is no longer Jew or Greek, there is no longer slave or free, there is no longer male and female; for all of you are one in Christ Jesus.' This same kind of language appears at other points in the Epistles, and some scholars even think it was part of the baptismal formula in Paul's churches. You can't find any other community in the first century that brought people of all classes and genders and ethnicities together with this kind of equality. It was only later in the Pastoral Epistles that you see the hierarchies and divisions of the surrounding culture beginning to creep into the church. We want to be like the earliest Christians—welcoming all into the welcoming love of God. To me that's the heart of the gospel. And there's a lot in the Bible to support it."

Everett Smith and Jesse Parker represent nicely two attitudes toward inherited traditions of evangelistic practice among American Protestants today.[1] Jesse represents the dominant tradition of evangelicalism stretching back to the American frontier when evangelism was closely associated with revivalism and itinerant preaching. Here, the accent is on conversion

1. For what is meant by practices here, see Richard Osmer, *Confirmation: Presbyterian Practices in Ecumenical Perspective* (Louisville: Geneva Press, 1996), 29-32; *The Teaching Ministry of Congregations* (Louisville: Westminster John Knox, 2005), 62-66, 87-112.

and spiritual awakening. EV represents the progressive wing of American Protestantism, which has long been suspicious of conversionistic practices of evangelism.[2] Progressive Protestantism emerged in the final decades of the nineteenth century and the first decades of the twentieth. During this era, America was starting to industrialize and urbanize. Waves of immigrants were making the tapestry of American culture more pluralistic, eliciting a nativist response from the Ku Klux Klan and mainline politicians. During this period, modern biblical studies, the social gospel, and liberal theology began to make their way into mainline Protestant seminaries and denominations.[3] EV's focus on inclusive hospitality and God's welcome stands in this tradition.

Traditions of practice, like those described above, shape our contemporary understandings of evangelism. They orient us to the present. They help us understand what evangelism is and how to carry out this ministry (or not!). Directly or implicitly, they embed certain normative claims in the practices and theological language, images, and narratives they use. We cannot do without such traditions, yet they also can be limiting. At times they result in tunnel vision. Like a horse wearing blinders, we only see what is immediately in front of us, keeping out of view other possibilities in our context or Scripture. This is why Christian theology must reflect critically on its traditions of practice. This is an important task for practical theology—especially with regard to evangelism.

Evangelism as Conversionism: A Hypothesis

Over the course of this book, I will argue that traditions of evangelistic practice in American Protestantism are dominated by a particular way of thinking about evangelism. I will call this *evangelism as conversionism*. This particular understanding of evangelism emerged after the Reformation of the sixteenth century among the renewal movements and new churches that followed the Reformation. These include German Lutheran Pietists in their

2. On the longstanding tension between traditions of pastoral guidance and care in America, see E. Brooks Holifield, *A History of Pastoral Care in America: From Salvation to Self-Realization* (Nashville: Abingdon, 1983).

3. In spite of the influence of these theological trends in mainline theological education, many mainline congregations continued to identify with evangelical or Reformation Protestantism, resulting in numerous splits and internal fights over the course of the twentieth century and continuing into the twenty-first.

various forms, Anabaptists (from whom the Amish, Mennonites, and Hutterites are descended), Baptists, some of the Puritans, and the Methodist renewal movement.[4]

While these groups are different in terms of their origins, histories, and specific beliefs, they share certain features that proved important to religion in the context of modernity. These include the importance of personal faith before baptism; great emphasis on individual religious experience, including conversion; and the separation of church and state as a bedrock of religious liberty.

Not every prominent leader or theologian in these movements placed equal emphasis on all of these. John Wesley, for example, allowed infant baptism and viewed the Eucharist as a converting ordinance. But he also emphasized the importance of a conscious turning toward Christ and growth in personal and social holiness.[5] His itinerant ministers were well-known for supporting established congregations on the frontier and also for carrying out various forms of evangelism through revivals, family visits, small groups, and one-on-one relationships.

My primary purpose in this book is to encourage new thinking about evangelism in dialogue with Scripture and dogmatic theology. But I want to offer at least a hypothesis about why evangelism as conversionism became dominant across a broad and diverse swath of modern Christianity. I do not intend to prove this hypothesis in this book. That would take extensive historical and social scientific research. Rather, my goal here is simply to suggest a possible explanation of why evangelism came to be viewed in terms of conversionism. In order to do so we must step briefly into social science.

As contemporary sociology has explored the role of culture in human communities, one line of thinking that has emerged in the work of Ann Swidler, Christian Smith, Michael Emerson, and others is called a cultural toolkit approach.[6] Rather than viewing culture as monolithic and unified, it recognizes

---

4. At the end of this chapter, I have included some resources for further reading on each of these.

5. Marlon D. De Deblasio, "Conversion, Justification, and the Experience of Grace: The Post-Aldersgate Wesley: Towards an Understanding of Who Is a 'Child of God,'" *The Asbury Journal* 66, no. 2 (2011): 18–34.

6. For an introduction to culture and sociology, see Robert Wuthnow, *Meaning and Moral Order: Explorations in Cultural Analysis* (Berkley: University of California Press, 1987); Christian Smith, *Moral Believing Animals: Human Personhood and Culture* (Oxford: Oxford University Press, 2003); Ann Swidler, *Talk of Love: How Culture Matters* (Chicago: University of Chicago Press, 2001).

that culture is diverse and often filled with conflicting perspectives. Even members of the same church, for example, often draw on different religious cultures (for example, older, long-term members versus younger or newer members who grew up elsewhere). The toolkit model also is less deterministic than older approaches to culture. It acknowledges that human beings draw on culture for different purposes in different situations.

Just as a toolbox may contain a hammer, screwdrivers, a tape measure, a small level, and other tools, so too a cultural toolkit contains a repertoire of ideas, methods, habits, skills, and styles. Different tools are used in different situations. Together, they help a person frame situations and construct strategies of action. Moreover, toolkits are transposable. They can be extended to settings beyond those in which they were originally learned.

The most interesting and timely work on religious toolkits is that of Michael Emerson and Christian Smith in *Divided by Faith: Evangelical Religion and the Problem of Race in America*.[7] They explore the ways the cultural toolkit of white evangelical Christians shapes their engagement of racism and the constraints it places on their ability to view it in systemic terms. Evangelicals are highly diverse and belong to many different traditions and independent churches. But the authors say that white evangelicals tend to make use of a common toolkit that includes (1) accountable freewill individualism, (2) relationalism (attaching central importance to interpersonal relationships), and (3) antistructuralism (downplaying the influence of social structures on human behavior).[8]

These core features of the evangelical toolkit can be accommodated to different theological positions. Southern Baptists and Disciples of Christ do not share the same theology, yet they share the basic features, or toolkit, of evangelical religious culture. I suspect mainline evangelicals share some version of this toolkit as well, though they may explain and justify some of its ideas on different theological grounds. Wesley, for example, developed his understanding of prevenient grace to explain how God could be involved in the human acceptance of the gift of salvation and still affirm that this is an act of human freedom or cooperation. Prevenient grace "enables" but does not "guarantee" that individuals will cooperate with saving grace. Likewise, while Jonathan Edwards, Gilbert Tennent, and George Whitefield played important roles in the Great Awakening and preached many sermons calling

---

7. Michael Emerson and Christian Smith, *Divided by Faith: Evangelical Religion and the Problem of Race in America* (Oxford: Oxford University Press, 2000); see especially ch. 4.

8. Emerson and Smith, *Divided by Faith*, 76.

on people who were already church members to repent, these prominent figures remained Calvinists theologically.

From the perspective of the sociology of culture, toolkits work on a different level than theology. The latter is an explicit system of religious beliefs. Toolkits are the religious cultures that ground and grant plausibility to theologies. Just as different crops can grow in the soil of the same field, so too different theologies can emerge from similar cultural toolkits.

The toolkit approach to culture provides us a plausible hypothesis about why evangelism as conversionism came to dominate different Christian traditions across the modern period.[9] The religious cultures of renewal movements and new Protestant churches during the post-Reformation period shared many elements in their religious cultural toolkits. The core ideas in the toolkit of evangelism as conversionism overlap those identified by Emerson and Smith and can be summarized as follows:

1. *People are saved when they convert.* Once people convert, they are no longer among the "lost." They are now among the "saved." The contrast between lost and saved is a very important part of conversionism. The nineteenth-century evangelist Dwight Moody put it like this: "I look upon this world as a wrecked vessel. God has given me a life-boat and said, 'Moody, save all you can.'"[10] More recently, a Baptist professor summarized nicely this core conviction of evangelism as conversionism: "*Men and women are lost until they receive salvation through Jesus.* Therefore, we must evangelize *urgently.* People apart from Christ are lost (Luke 15), dead in sins (Eph. 2:1), under sin (Rom. 3:9), and under condemnation (John 3:18)."[11]

2. *Individuals have the freedom to decide whether they will convert or not.* Human beings face a choice: They can either give their lives to Christ or continue to live in sin and death. The former brings eternal life; the latter eternal damnation. This choice is set before every individual who hears the gospel. God is involved in conversion, to be sure. But ul-

---

9. I do not claim to have proved this thesis, though it does dovetail with Smith and Emerson's research. Rather, I am offering this as a plausible hypothesis to explain how evangelism as conversionism could be found among traditions and theologians with such different theologies, from Baptist to Reformed.

10. Paul W. Chilcote and Laceye C. Warner, eds., *The Study of Evangelism: Exploring a Missional Practice of the Church* (Grand Rapids: Eerdmans, 2008), 5.

11. Alvin Reed, *Introduction to Evangelism* (Nashville: Broadman & Holman, 1998), Kindle edition, loc. 105. Italics in the original.

timately individuals must decide to turn away from sin, cooperate with God's grace, and give their lives to Christ. When this decision occurs, they are saved. It is no accident that some Christian traditions speak of evangelism in terms of decision. Evangelistic preaching is often called "preaching for decision." Billy Graham was part of a television show for many years called *The Hour of Decision*.

3. *Conversion is life-changing and accompanied by a dramatic experience at a particular moment (or short period) of time.* Being saved through evangelism is marked off by a "before" and "after." Paul's conversion on the road to Damascus is the paradigm case of conversion, and evangelism as conversionism seeks to replicate this. It is "a sudden, point-in-time transformation based on an encounter with Jesus. Thus evangelism has focused on a single issue: accepting Jesus as Lord and Savior—now, at this moment in time."[12] We speak of Damascus road experiences to this very day.

Over time, these three elements of evangelism as conversionism became so dominant that most Christians could hardly think of evangelism in any other way. Many Christian denominations or communions today do not practice evangelism because one or more of these ideas seem incompatible with core beliefs of their tradition. Only the most evangelical members of their congregations are interested in evangelism, and they often came into these congregations from more conservative churches or parachurch organizations. The problem with this situation is the neglect of evangelism altogether. Yet this is the reality in many mainline congregations today. Increasingly, it also is the reality of evangelical congregations whose members believe they should evangelize but do not.[13]

Moreover, evangelical leaders are beginning to raise questions about evangelism as conversionism, especially the traditional methods associated with instantaneous conversions. Old-timers may be complaining that people are less willing to share their faith today than in the past or that altar calls are no longer the norm or that door-to-door evangelism has declined, but many leaders realize these methods no longer work, especially with young people. In 2016, the Southern Baptist Convention had its lowest number of

12. Richard Peace, *Conversion in the New Testament: Paul and the Twelve* (Grand Rapids: Eerdmans, 1999), 4.
13. See Robert Wuthnow, *America and the Challenges of Religious Diversity* (Princeton: Princeton University Press, 2005), 178–79.

baptisms since 1946.[14] Some of the most creative and searching books on evangelism are coming from evangelicals who are encouraging the church to move beyond conversionism.[15] I hope to join people across the theological spectrum in working together to reimagine evangelism.

The Dialogue with Scripture: Evangelism as Invitation

I have come to believe that practical theology's dialogue with biblical and dogmatic theology is more important than its dialogue with the social sciences.[16] I will share my reasons for this in the final chapter. As a practical theologian in the Reformed tradition, I affirm Scripture and tradition as the preeminent sources of authority in theology, though I also engage experience and reason in certain ways. The social sciences can help us grasp the "phenomenon" of the Christian life through empirical research and interpretation. But they do not (and cannot) adopt the perspective of God's self-revelation in Jesus Christ that I believe is the starting point of Christian scholarship.

We start thus with a simple introductory definition of evangelism through an initial dialogue with Scripture. My claim is straightforward and quite general at this point. It will be challenged and added to as the book unfolds:

> Evangelism is the invitation to respond to the gospel, the good news of God's salvation of the world in Jesus Christ, which is offered to others as part of the witness of the church under the guidance and persuasive power of the Holy Spirit.

The Gospels tell the story of Jesus in different ways. So too the letters of the New Testament raise different issues and rely on different theological images, concepts, and stories. Yet a theme presupposed throughout the New Testament is Jesus's calling of disciples to follow him and the gathering

14. Tobin Perry, "What Every Southern Baptist Must Do to Reverse the Evangelism Crisis," https://pushpay.com/blog/baptist-evangelism-crisis/, accessed April 2019.

15. Peace, *Conversion in the New Testament*; Rick Richardson, *Reimagining Evangelism: Inviting Friends on a Spiritual Journey* (Downers Grove, IL: InterVarsity, 2006); Brian D. McLaren, *More Ready Than You Realize: The Power of Everyday Conversations* (Grand Rapids: Zondervan, 2006).

16. See my entry "Barth and Practical Theology," in *The Wiley Blackwell Companion to Karl Barth*, vol. 2, *Barth in Dialogue*, ed. George Hunsinger and Keith L. Johnson (Hoboken, NJ: John Wiley and Sons, 2020).

of a community of disciples. From Matthew to Revelation, communities of people following Jesus are addressed. In all of the verses cited below, I have italicized variants of *call* for the sake of emphasis.

A key term used to describe the calling and community of people who follow Jesus is *kaleō* (verb), meaning to call, invite, or name. Other closely related terms are *klēsis* (noun), meaning a calling or invitation, and *klētos* (adjective), meaning called or invited. A term commonly used to describe the community of disciples is *ekklēsia*, from *ek* (out of) and *kaleō* (to call).[17] The congregation and worldwide church are communities "called out" from society into an assembly of those who follow Jesus.

These terms were part of the everyday language of the Greco-Roman world. Yet "call" and "calling" acquired special meaning in the early Christian movement. Christians believed that Jesus had called them to come and follow him as part of a community of disciples. We see this, for example, in Matthew 4:21–22 (compare Mark 1:19–20):

> Going on from there, he saw two other brothers, James son of Zebedee and his brother John. They were in a boat with their father Zebedee, preparing their nets. Jesus called them, and immediately they left the boat and their father and followed him.

Elsewhere, Jesus describes the purpose of his mission in terms of calling, as in Matthew 9:13: "But go and learn what this means: 'I desire mercy, not sacrifice.' For I have not come *to call* the righteous, but sinners" (compare Mark 2:17 and Luke 5:32).

In several of Jesus's parables, *kaleō* and *klēsis* appear in stories about guests invited to a wedding feast or great banquet. The invited guests give excuses, and others are invited in their place (Matt. 22:1–14; Luke 14:16–24). These parables draw on imagery of the messianic feast associated with the arrival of the promised Messiah. In calling people to follow him, Jesus is inviting them to reorient their lives around the good news that God's promises were being fulfilled and that the kingdom of God was breaking in through his ministry. The people who might be expected to respond do not. This results in the invitation of unexpected guests to the feast.

---

17. *Ekklēsia* was used among the Greeks to refer to an assembly of citizens gathered together to discuss the affairs of the state. In the Greek translation of Hebrew Scripture, it was used to designate the gathering of Israel or its representatives for any particular purpose.

The language of calling, called, and call appears in a wide range of New Testament writings beyond the Gospels. Yet it is Paul and his coworkers who develop this language most extensively. Again and again in the Pauline material, God is referred to as the *one who calls*:[18]

God is faithful, who has *called* you into fellowship with his Son, Jesus Christ our Lord. (1 Cor. 1:9)

He [God] *called* you to this through our gospel, that you might share in the glory of our Lord Jesus Christ. (2 Thess. 2:14)

I am amazed that you are so quickly deserting *him who called you* by the grace of Christ, for a different gospel. (Gal. 1:6)

Paul refers to his mission to the Gentiles as a calling to which God has appointed him:

Paul, a servant of Christ Jesus, *called* to be an apostle and set apart for the gospel of God. . . . Through him we received grace and apostleship *to call* all the Gentiles to the obedience that comes from faith for his name's sake. (Rom. 1:1, 5)

Paul, *called* to be an apostle of Christ Jesus by the will of God. (1 Cor. 1:1)

Paul also refers to the congregations to which he is writing as *ekklēsia*, as called-out people. He emphasizes their calling, as we see in the salutations of his letters: "To all in Rome who are loved by God and called to be his holy people" (Rom. 1:7); "To the church of God in Corinth, to those sanctified in Christ Jesus and called to be his holy people" (1 Cor. 1:2). Paul exhorts his readers to "live a life worthy of the calling you have received" (Eph. 4:1). He says that "we constantly pray for you, that our God may make you worthy of his calling" (2 Thess. 1:11).

As we reflect on this brief examination of the theme of calling, several points emerge. They serve as the port of entry to our understanding of evangelism as invitation.

---

18. In each quotation, italics are added for emphasis. Cf. Rom. 4:17; 8:30; 9:11; 9:24; Gal. 1:15; 5:8; 1 Thess. 5:24.

1. It is God who calls. It is very important to grasp the relationship between divine and human action in evangelism. In the Gospels, it is Jesus, God's Son, who calls disciples and invites the crowds to respond to the good news of the kingdom of God. In the Pauline material, God is described as the one who calls. It always is a mistake when evangelism confuses human action with divine action. It is God who calls, not us. We deliver an invitation on behalf of another to come to their party.

2. God's call comes through the gospel. The gospel is the good news of God's salvation of the world in Jesus Christ. It is the message of salvation. Evangelism always must give pride of place to the "Yes!" of God. Divine judgment—God's "No!"—is in the service of God's grace. In evangelism we are inviting people to respond to the story of God's love of the world in Christ Jesus. We are not shaming, berating, or threatening people in the name of God.

3. Those people who respond to God's call through the gospel receive a new identity: They become God's called people and followers of Jesus. There are corporate and personal dimensions to this new identity. Those who respond to the invitation of the gospel become part of the church, a called-out people who follow Jesus. Their personal identities are transformed as they participate in this community and respond to the gospel in faith, hope, and love. Evangelism is never exclusively about the conversion of individuals. It is about inviting people to become participants in the *ekklēsia*. It is an invitation to community.

4. The community of disciples and its individual members have a common mission: to bear witness to the gospel of God. In all the church says and does it bears witness to the good news of God's love of the world in Jesus Christ. As Paul puts it: "We are therefore Christ's ambassadors, as though God were making his appeal through us" (2 Cor. 5:20). This is true of the church's life as a gathered community of worship, fellowship, teaching, and mutual care. This also is true of the church as a sent community, one that serves others in love, supports the common good of public life, and invites others to respond to the gospel. These are the inward and outward dimensions of the church's witness—the witness of a community that embodies a particular way of life as God's called-out people and the witness of a sent community that loves and serves the world as God does.

5. The mission of witness encompasses saying, doing, and being the gospel.[19] The gospel is communicated verbally through words in personal relationships, social media, literature, and other ways that are appropriate to different cultural settings. The gospel also is communicated through actions that show God's love in acts of healing, compassion, service, justice seeking, and kindness. Likewise, the gospel is embodied in the being of the witnesses—the spirituality, ethos, and character of the community and its individual members.

6. Evangelism is the ministry of inviting others to hear Christ's call to come and follow him. Within the mission of the church as witness, evangelism plays a special role. It focuses on communicating the gospel verbally in ways that help particular individuals or groups hear God's call. This is not a matter of techniques, models, or traditions of evangelistic practice that are effective in all times and places. Wedding invitations take many different forms and likewise the invitations of evangelism must fit the persons, circumstances, and cultural settings. They always are personal and contextual. Moreover, the Holy Spirit is at work in evangelism, persuading people to accept the invitation and come to the wedding feast. The Holy Spirit is not under human control.

Looking Ahead

This is the understanding of evangelism with which we begin. We hope to deepen, elaborate, and change this framework as we move through the coming chapters. For practical theology to reimagine evangelism, it must engage Scripture and theology anew. Our relationship to these resources is direct. I do not follow those who believe that we start first with Scripture, then move to church doctrine, and finally ask practical theology to apply it all to the church. The movement must be one of dialogue, back-and-forth conversation all along the way. Biblical scholars and dogmatic theologians have a great deal to offer practical theology. As I hope to show, they can help us rethink the purpose of evangelism as it currently exists.

19. For an excellent discussion of these three dimensions, see Darrell Guder, *Be My Witnesses: The Church's Mission, Message, and Messengers* (Grand Rapids: Eerdmans, 1985), especially chs. 6–9.

But biblical scholars and dogmatic theologians cannot do scholarship as if the church did not exist. The pressing issues of the contemporary church in a particular time and place comprise the primary subject matter of practical theology. Dialogue between the other theological disciplines and practical theology must be face-to-face at every point, not just when they get to the so-called moment of application. If we do not engage in dialogue as we move along, who will biblical scholars and theologians be writing for? No one but their academic guilds, I fear.

For Further Reading

Bosch, David. *Transforming Mission: Paradigm Shifts in Theology of Mission.* Maryknoll, NY: Orbis, 1991. A foundational text in missional theology that explores the history of mission and its relationship to evangelism.

Estep, William R. *The Anabaptist Story: An Introduction to Sixteenth-Century Anabaptism.* 3rd ed. Grand Rapids: Eerdmans, 1996.

Gourley, Bruce T. *A Capsule History of Baptists.* Atlanta: The Baptist History and Heritage Society, 2010.

Green, Michael. *Evangelism in the Early Church.* Grand Rapids: Eerdmans, 2004. An excellent overview of evangelism in the first centuries of the church that explores the pathways and obstacles facing the spread of the gospel.

Guder, Darrell. *The Continuing Conversion of the Church.* Grand Rapids: Eerdmans, 2000. A foundational text in evangelism that explores the relationship between evangelism and mission and the renewal of the church through evangelism.

Jones, Scott. *The Evangelistic Love of God and Neighbor: A Theology of Witness and Discipleship.* Nashville: Abingdon, 2003. Offers a comprehensive theology of evangelism grounded in the incarnation of God's love in Jesus Christ.

Newbigin, Lesslie. *The Gospel in a Pluralist Society.* Grand Rapids: Eerdmans, 1989. A former missionary to India returns home to England. Shocked by the changes he sees, he offers a compelling theology of mission and evangelism for a pluralistic and increasingly secular context.

Richardson, Rick. *Reimagining Evangelism: Inviting Friends on a Spiritual Journey.* Downers Grove, IL: InterVarsity, 2006. A short, well-written book that effectively invites readers to put aside stereotypical understandings of evangelism to imagine this ministry in new ways.

Shantz, Douglass H. *An Introduction to German Pietism: Protestant Renewal at the Dawn of Modern Europe.* Baltimore: Johns Hopkins University Press, 2013. An excellent historical overview of the history of pietism. The introduction by Peter C. Erb outlines various lines of interpretation emerging over the past fifty years.

PART I

Evangelism in Dialogue with Scripture

From the beginning, Christianity has been a missionary movement seeking to spread the gospel of Jesus Christ to the ends of the known world. The sociologist Rodney Stark estimates that in AD 40 Christianity had approximately 1,000 adherents, representing about .00017 percent of the Roman Empire.[1] By AD 300, this stood at around 6,299,832, approximately 10.5 percent. N. T. Wright comments on the success of the Christian mission: "The single most striking thing about early Christianity is its speed of growth.... Why then did early Christianity spread? Because early Christians believed that what they had found to be true was true for the whole world. The impetus to mission sprang from the very heart of early Christian conviction."[2]

Over the centuries, Christians have rarely used the term "evangelism" to describe sharing the gospel with others in the context of the church's mission. Once the church was legalized and given favor under Constantine in the fourth century, it spread more by "diffusion" than evangelism—through conquest, socialization, and cultural acceptance.[3] When "conversion" did take place, it often was at the point of a sword. Four hundred years later Charlemagne (742-814), for example, compelled border tribes conquered

1. Rodney Stark, *The Rise of Christianity: How the Obscure, Marginal Jesus Movement Became the Dominant Religious Force in the Western World in a Few Centuries* (Princeton: Princeton University Press, 1996), 5-6.

2. N. T. Wright, *The New Testament and the People of God*, vol. 1 (Minneapolis: Fortress, 1992), 359-60.

3. Lamin Sanneh, *Translating the Message: The Missionary Impact on Culture* (Maryknoll, NY: Orbis, 1989). For a more detailed discussion of the history summarized here, see also Milton Rudnick, *Speaking the Gospel Through the Ages: A History of Evangelism* (St. Louis: Concordia, 1984); David Bosch, *Transforming Mission: Paradigm Shifts in Theology of Mission* (Maryknoll, NY: Orbis, 1991); and Kenneth Scott Latourette, *The Thousand Years of Uncertainty*, vol. 2, *A History of the Expansion of Christianity* (Grand Rapids: Zondervan, 1970).

by his armies to be baptized *en masse* to integrate them into the Holy Roman Empire. The spread of Christianity and the spread of Latin Western culture went hand in hand.

While mission by cultural diffusion was the norm in the West, what we would call evangelism today was carried out by Irish, Roman, and English missionary-evangelists from the eighth century forward. In the thirteenth century, orders of friars committed to social service also offered evangelistic preaching, especially the Franciscans and Dominicans. The dominant understanding of evangelism, however, was sharing the gospel through cultural diffusion.

This impacted the way the Bible was interpreted. The New Testament uses a variety of terms to describe communication of the gospel, like *kēryssein* (to announce news like a herald) and *euangelizein* (to announce glad tidings). Throughout this period, these terms were consistently translated "to preach" and "to proclaim." Darrell Guder points to the underlying assumptions:

> Such language demonstrates one of the basic assumptions of the Western Christian civilization, the *corpus Christianum*, which evolved from Constantine onward: the apostolic commission of the early church had been fulfilled with the Christianization of the West. The church's ongoing task was to proclaim this word within the Christianized world, to expand its boundaries by diffusion, and very importantly, to ensure that everyone within these boundaries thought and acted in accordance with the church's dogma and structures.[4]

Since priests and bishops were the ones who preached and proclaimed, the task of sharing the gospel with others was reduced to practices of preaching by ordained leaders and mission-minded monastics.[5] It was not a task of the entire Christian community or its individual members.

While the Protestant Reformation of the sixteenth century brought many changes to the theology and practice of the Western church, it largely maintained the stance of mission through diffusion in established geographical areas. Thus, biblical texts that might have been viewed as commissioning the entire church to share the gospel with others continued to be interpreted in

4. Darrell L. Guder, *The Continuing Conversion of the Church* (Grand Rapids: Eerdmans, 2000), 11.

5. There were some exceptions to this tendency. See George G. Hunter III, *The Celtic Way of Evangelism: How Christians Can Reach the West . . . Again* (Nashville: Abingdon, 2000).

terms of proclamation by pastors in the gathered community. Both in theology and practice, emphasis fell on preaching and teaching, which were viewed as essential to reforming the church according to the word of God.[6] It was not until after the Reformation that new ways of thinking about evangelism and mission began to emerge.

The catalyst of new theologies and practices of evangelism and mission emerged among German Lutheran Pietists, Baptists, and Anabaptists. Church renewal and overseas missions became priorities among these movements and the communities they established.[7] They influenced the rise of the Methodist movement and American evangelicalism.[8] It is from these post-Reformation developments that the modern missionary movement emerged, and it is in the context of this movement that the language and practices we commonly associate with evangelism and mission today began to take shape. Evangelism was viewed as converting non-Christians, renewing the faith of nominal Christians, and establishing congregations on the home front and the frontier. Mission was viewed as spreading the gospel and planting churches beyond North America and Europe.

Across the theological spectrum today, it is widely acknowledged that this way of viewing evangelism and mission is problematic on many levels. Viewing mission as something done "over there" in the non-Western world distorts the missionary calling of every congregation to bear witness to the gospel in its own community. Moreover, the missionary movement was compromised by its ties with Western colonialism. Too often, the spread of the gospel was confused with the diffusion of Western culture, and Christianity was used to legitimate the political control and economic exploitation

---

6. It is no accident that John Calvin's favorite descriptive word for the Holy Spirit was "Teacher." See Jaroslav Pelikan, *The Christian Tradition: A History of the Development of Doctrine*, vol. 4, *The Reformation of Church and Dogma (1300-1700)* (Chicago: University of Chicago Press, 1984), 187.

7. Douglas Shantz, *An Introduction to German Pietism: Protestant Renewal at the Dawn of Modern Europe* (Baltimore: Johns Hopkins University Press, 2013); Peter Erb, ed., *Pietists: Selected Writings*, The Classics of Western Spirituality (Mahwah, NJ: Paulist, 1983); Katherine Carté Engle, *Religion and Profit: Moravians in Early America* (Philadelphia: University of Pennsylvania Press, 2009); J. E. Hutton, *History of the Moravian Missions* (London: Moravian Publishing House, 2011).

8. Mark Noll, *The Rise of Evangelicalism: The Age of Edwards, Whitefield and the Wesleys*, History of Evangelicalism Series (Downers Grove, IL: InterVarsity, 2003); David Hempton, *Methodism: Empire of the Spirit* (New Haven: Yale University Press, 2005); *John and Charles Wesley: Selected Writings and Hymns*, ed. Frank Whaling, The Classics of Western Spirituality (Mahwah, NJ: Paulist, 1981).

of countries that were colonized. Though the story of Western missions is complex and filled with light as well as darkness, the shadow side is a deeply troubling legacy. This has been analyzed in depth by a range of scholars.[9]

The inherited distinction between evangelism at home and mission overseas has proved problematic for an additional reason. The secularization and de-Christianization of the West have turned Europe and North America into mission fields. Lesslie Newbigin, David Bosch, Darrell Guder, and many others have begun to describe the West as a post-Christendom context. They have challenged the Western church to rethink its understanding of evangelism and mission, posing fundamental questions: What is the relationship between the mission of God and the missions of congregations? What is the relationship between congregational mission and evangelism? Is mission broader than evangelism or are they identical? To what extent are evangelistic practices of one context transferrable to another? If contextualization is necessary for effective evangelism, how might this be done while remaining faithful to the apostolic mandate of the New Testament?

These questions are basic. They invite us to reflect critically on the language and practices emerging during the era following the Reformation. They encourage us to look anew at the biblical and theological foundations of evangelism and mission. In the following chapter, our exploration begins with two cases from an American context. We then turn to biblical resources that might help us think anew about evangelism in our own time and place.

9. Andrew F. Walls, *The Missionary Movement in Christian History: Studies in the Transmission of Faith* (Maryknoll, NY: Orbis, 1996); Wolfgang Reinhard, *A Short History of Colonialism* (Manchester: Manchester University Press, 1996).

CHAPTER 1

Evangelism and the Apostle Paul

Paul was the missionary and evangelist par excellence in early Christianity. He was a church planter who cared for his congregations like a long-term pastor. He shared the gospel with politicians and jailers, Jews and Gentiles, in the forum and the synagogue. He debated Greek philosophers and Jewish leaders on the significance of Jesus Christ. He confronted Jewish Christian leaders who he believed were leading his churches astray. He even was willing to take on established Christian leaders, like Peter and Barnabas, when their actions or judgments contradicted what he believed was best for the spread of the gospel.

Paul appears to have followed a clear strategy in his work as a missionary and evangelist. He concentrated on cities that were centers of Roman administration and commerce. They often had synagogues and religious temples.[1] Sea and land routes to these centers made travel much easier and safer than to rural areas. Paul sometimes used them as hubs of missionary activity to nearby regions. He planted a congregation, provided initial teaching and training of leaders and then turned over the church and its mission to the local community. The strategy of establishing a new community and moving on while allowing indigenous leadership to take charge seems to have been crucial to the spread of Christianity.

When Paul wrote to the Christians in Rome, he appeared to be planning a new phase of his missionary work, which involved traveling to Spain (Rom. 15:24). In his letter to the Roman Christians, he likely was laying the groundwork for this future mission in hopes that the church in Rome would support

1. This is Michael Green's summary of insights offered by Roland Allen in *Missionary Methods: St. Paul's or Ours? A Study of the Church in the Four Provinces* (London: R. Scott, 1912). See Green, *Evangelism in the Early Church* (Grand Rapids: Eerdmans, 2003), 362.

him. Clearly, Paul was a planner and strategist who thought ahead. But it never was just a matter of his own reasoning or desire for success. He had an extremely strong sense of his calling as an apostle sent to the gentiles, the nations. He continually prayed for God's guidance and was willing to change plans at a moment's notice when directed to do so by the Spirit.[2] He worked as part of a team of missionaries and evangelists.

It is fitting, thus, that we turn first to Paul in our dialogue with Scripture. We enter this conversation after examining two case studies written by students in classes on evangelism at Princeton Theological Seminary. At the very end of the chapter, we bring the case material and our study of Paul into conversation.

Cases of Evangelistic Practice

"From Scratch" Evangelism

The first case was shared by a student named Bob. He told his precept group of ten students that the case represented his understanding of evangelism before coming to seminary. Back home in Colorado he became friends with a Jewish convert to Christianity, Bruce, who invited him to join in "from scratch" evangelism several evenings a week. Together, they would go to a large upscale mall called the Citadel, which had a variety of shops and outdoor rides. They chose this setting "because it was a place where a lot of people hung out and were sometimes willing to talk to strangers like us." The following is a reconstructed verbatim of Bob and Bruce's conversation with one man:

> **Bruce:** Hi, my name is Bruce, and this is my friend, Bob.
> **Bob:** Hi, what's your name?
> **Francisco:** My name is Francisco.
> **Bruce:** Hi Francisco, it is a pleasure to meet you. May we ask you some questions?
> **Francisco:** Yes, that will be fine.
> **Bruce:** Do you believe in God?
> **Francisco:** Yes, I believe in God. I was raised Catholic in Honduras, my homeland.

2. See, for example, Acts 13:1-3; 14:23; 16:25; 20:36; 21:5; 22:17.

Bob: Do you still practice your Catholic faith?

Francisco: No. I haven't been to church since I left Honduras. That was twenty years ago. I didn't really look for a church once I moved to Colorado.

Bob: Yeah, it was probably enough of a transition just to move to Colorado.

Francisco: Well yeah, but I was also not very interested in going to church anymore.

Bob: So even though you don't go to church, you believe in God. What do you believe about God?

Francisco: Oh, I don't know. I've always believed in God. I guess I believe in Jesus.

Bruce: Yes, I'm glad you brought up Jesus. Bob and I believe that Jesus is God's Son. And many years ago Jesus died on a cross to forgive all of humanity for all of their sins. Then he rose from the dead three days later. He wants to forgive you your sins and give you a new life. Would you like to have this?

Francisco: Yes, I would.

Bob: Well, can we pray that you would receive forgiveness for your sins and a new relationship with God?

Francisco: Yes, that would be good. I want to be closer to God.

Bob: That is wonderful, Francisco. Let's pray together then. Bruce is going to lead. Follow Bruce, and say what he tells you to say. May we each lay our hand on your shoulder as we pray with you? That is how they pray in the Bible.

Francisco: Yes, that is okay.

Bruce: Heavenly Father, we thank you for Francisco and his willing heart to receive you. Francisco, please repeat after me, okay?

Francisco: Okay.

Bruce: Dear God . . .

Francisco: Dear God . . .

Bruce: I know that I am a sinner and that my sin has separated me from you. (Francisco repeats after Bruce, word for word.)

Bruce: Thank you for sending your Son Jesus to die on the cross and rise from the dead so that my sin no longer separates me from you. (Francisco repeats.)

Bruce: I believe that you, God, forgive me of my sins. (Francisco repeats.)

Bruce: And give me a new life. I put my faith and trust in you. (Francisco repeats.)

Bruce: I thank you, God, and I love you. (Francisco repeats.)

Bruce and Bob: Amen! (Francisco repeats.)

Bob: Okay Francisco, you have just given your life to Christ. This is very exciting.

Francisco: Yes, this is good. Okay, thank you. I have to go now. (As he says this, he is looking at people walking out of a store.)

Bob: Okay, just remember that you have now started a new relationship with God.

Francisco: Yes, thank you. Goodbye. (He leaves quickly and joins his friends.)

Bruce and Bob: Goodbye, Francisco.

Let's turn to another case before reflecting on this example of evangelistic practice. It was presented in the same precept a week later.

Tongues of Healing and Unity

Ariana Diaz met Paula Arrowsmith when Paula's family moved into their new home two doors away. Located in a suburb north of Atlanta, their homes were part of a neighborhood graced with many large trees, beautiful yards, and a swimming pool complex managed by the neighborhood association. When Ariana arrived ten years earlier, she had been pleasantly surprised by the welcome her family received, especially given that they are Hispanic. Their children quickly made friends at the pool, and their family met others at the neighborhood association's Friday evening cookouts. Ariana decided that she would make a special effort to extend hospitality to other new families.

As was her custom, thus, Ariana took the Arrowsmith family some food several days after they moved in. She followed up with phone calls to see if she could help in any way. The Arrowsmiths soon joined the neighborhood association, and Ariana and Paula began to see each other regularly. Ariana soon discovered that Paula's husband was a surgeon at the hospital where she worked as a nurse and that Paula had decided to stay at home with the kids until they started school. Ariana's husband was a lawyer who worked for a firm in downtown Atlanta.

The Diaz family was very involved in a large, multiracial Pentecostal church. According to Ariana, "This is, by far, the best church we've ever been a part of. My daughters (13 and 16) love it. The worship is incredibly powerful—great preaching, great music, passionate speech in the tongues of angels. The Holy Spirit is present and real. In our church, the Spirit unites all people of all races and backgrounds and nations. Lots of immigrants attend. We are drawn together. We're one in the Spirit, and we are committed to ministries of service and healing and justice. Pastor Chris teaches the new members' class. He taught us that glossolalia is a foretaste of the ultimate destiny of heaven and earth. It creates the *koinōnia* of all people from all nations. When we speak the tongues of angels here on earth, the spiritual world and material world come together, and the Spirit empowers us to live as a redeemed community. You know, I had been a Pentecostal all my life, but I never really understood what this meant until I started coming to this church."

Ariana and Paula were little more than friendly acquaintances until Paula was diagnosed with an aggressive form of breast cancer. She had a double mastectomy followed by reconstructive surgery. Throughout this period, Ariana helped organize neighbors to provide meals for the family. She visited Paula while she was in the hospital and then at home during Paula's recovery. With Paula's permission, she prayed for her when they were together.

While Paula's body healed nicely in the months following surgery, she slowly sank into a deep depression. Ariana noticed that Paula started deflecting her visits and was quiet and listless when they got together. Finally, she asked her what was going on. This is a reconstructed verbatim of part of their conversation:

Ariana: So, Paula, what's going on? You don't seem like yourself.

Paula: Yes, John [Paula's husband] has noticed that too. He says I'm depressed and it's normal. But he's gone so much—you know, being a doctor and all. We really haven't talked about it much.

Ariana: What are you experiencing?

Paula: I can't sleep well. I worry about my kids. What if the cancer comes back? What if I die? (Paula grows tearful and shares more.)

Ariana: I can see why that would worry you. It must feel very scary.

Paula: Yes, it does.

Ariana: How might I help you?

Paula: Would you pray for me? I've never heard anyone pray like you do. It's like you're really talking to God, like God is right here with us. Sometimes my body tingles.

Ariana: Yes, I will pray for you. Would you like me to ask God to take away your troubling thoughts? At our church, we believe the Holy Spirit can heal people.

Paula: Yes, please do that. I'd like to feel better.

Ariana: (Kneels next to Paula and holds her hands.) Holy Spirit, lover and giver of new life, we ask you to be with us today. We praise you and through you we glorify our heavenly Father. We ask your healing presence to come upon Paula. Take her troubling thoughts away. Let her know the love of Jesus Christ, who offers us the forgiveness of sins. Take Paula's burdens away and heal her body and soul. (Continues in a quiet voice.)

Paula: I felt my body warmed. I felt God was with us. Thank you.

(The two talk for a while longer, and then Ariana leaves.)

Ariana continued to visit Paula in the weeks that followed. She was not surprised when Paula shared that her depression had lifted. Paula began to ask Ariana about her church, and Ariana invited her to come. The next week Paula and her two children accompanied the Diaz family for a Sunday worship service. After the service Paula asked if she could go with them again the following week, saying, "I grew up in a Methodist church, but I haven't really been since I left for college. That's where I met John, and he's not much of a churchgoer. But this is different than anything I've ever experienced before. Here we are in the South, and people from all races and countries are worshiping together and hugging each other and working together. I'm quite impressed."

Reflection on Evangelistic Practice

These cases portray very different approaches to evangelism. In the "from scratch" case, we see a form of the sinner's prayer being used in evangelism. This is a prayer offered by individuals to confess their sins to God and accept the forgiveness offered through the death of Jesus Christ. It represents the first step of a personal relationship with God through Christ. Some believe the sinner's prayer emerged out the widespread use of the mourner's seat and altar call in revivalism. These were popularized by Charles Finney, Dwight Moody, and Billy Sunday. It was not until the 1950s, however, that the sinner's prayer was placed in a standard form in the writings of Bill Bright and Billy Graham.[3] Subsequently, it appeared on tracts handed out by street evangelists and became central to the evangelistic practices of Campus Crusade for Christ, founded by Bright.

3. Paul Chitwood, "The Sinner's Prayer: A Historical and Theological Analysis" (PhD dissertation, Southern Baptist Theological Seminary, 2001). Chitwood argues that Billy Graham's *Steps to Peace with God* and Bill Bright's *The Four Spiritual Laws*, both written in the 1950s, were crucial in popularizing this approach to evangelism.

Some evangelicals are critical of this evangelistic practice.[4] They argue that the sinner's prayer does not appear in the Bible and worry that it may promote superficial conversions. Real evangelism, they contend, invites people to genuine conversion. This involves a change of heart that is the starting point of a life of discipleship, which leads to moral and spiritual transformation within a community of disciples. As these critics sometimes put it, Christ wants disciples, not just converts.

The student who presented this case, Bob, prefaced the class discussion by sharing that he was no longer comfortable with "from scratch" evangelism, but he said he was not sure what he would do instead. A sizable number of students were familiar with the sinner's prayer, having used it themselves in the past or having been approached by others who used it. In general, they were critical of this approach in ways that echoed the issues raised by many evangelicals. Approaching someone "from scratch" with the goal of asking him or her to repeat the sinner's prayer seemed mechanical and superficial to them. As one person put it:

Getting them to "repeat after me" and then sending them on their way is not really evangelism. What about connecting them with a church? What about finding out who they are and their life circumstances? Francisco was from Honduras. We don't learn anything about his legal status in the US, how he is making a living, his family situation, nothing! This is totally decontextualized and nonrelational.

Another student responded that in his experience the sinner's prayer usually was a part of relational evangelism in which Christians get to know people and have many conversations about faith over time. It is only used when a person expresses a readiness to make a commitment to Christ.

In general, most students in the precept agreed with the criticisms raised above. They wondered whether using a set formula is a helpful way of sharing the gospel with others and inviting them to a life of Christian discipleship. No real relational context was established in this case, either before or after the sinner's prayer. They wondered whether evangelism should include gathering more of Francisco's story. They also wondered about the

---

4. See, for example, David P. Gushee, "Jesus and the Sinner's Prayer: What Jesus Says Doesn't Match What We Usually Say," *Christianity Today*, March 6, 2007, accessed online July 2016, http://www.christianitytoday.com/ct/2007/march/29.72.htm.

importance of staying involved with Francisco and getting him involved in a congregation.

In contrast, the response of most students to the second case was very positive. They were especially drawn to what was missing in the previous case: the kind of relationship Ariana formed with Paula. It started with hospitality when the Arrowsmith family moved to the neighborhood. Ariana then offered care and support for Paula in her struggle with breast cancer. She did not try to convert her in the midst of this crisis. But she prayed for her, shared her faith, and was open about her love for her congregation. When Paula experienced depression, Ariana prayed for God's healing after asking Paula's permission. Paula's depression lifted, according to what she shared with Ariana. Later, Paula and her two children accompanied Ariana to church.

In addition, students drew attention to the initial impact of the church on Paula. She was impressed by its racial and ethnic diversity and by the ways people seemed to love each other amid this diversity. She asked to come back the following week. Some students wondered about Dr. Arrowsmith, a surgeon whom Paula characterized as "not much of a churchgoer." What was his reaction going to be if his wife and children began going to a Pentecostal church on a regular basis?

During class discussion, Ariana shared that she believed praying with Paula was the key to renewing her interest in church, especially the prayer for the healing of depression. She pointed out that healing and evangelism often go hand in hand in the Pentecostal community—a trend documented by the historian Gaston Espinosa and other scholars.[5] Ariana believes it is the actual experience of God's power that makes God real. She also added: "I trust the Holy Spirit in everything. The Spirit brought Paula and me together, and the Spirit was using me to renew her faith. I just try to follow the Spirit's lead. I try to stay out of the way."

While a number of questions and insights emerge from these two cases, three topics are particularly important: salvation, the gospel, and evangelism's relationship to the gospel. Clusters of questions emerge around each of these topics:

5. Gaston Espinosa, "'El Azteca': Francisco Olazábal and Latino Pentecostal Charisma, Power, and Healing in the Borderlands," *Journal of the American Academy of Religion* 67, no. 3 (September 1999): 597–616, and "Latino Pentecostal Healing in the North American Borderlands," in *Global Pentecostal and Charismatic Healing*, ed. Candy Gunther Brown (Oxford: Oxford University Press, 2010). For an overview, see Cecil M. Robeck Jr., *The Azusa Street Mission and Revival: The Birth of the Global Pentecostal Movement* (Nashville: Thomas Nelson, 2006), chs. 5–6.

What is salvation? What is the relationship between our understanding of salvation and evangelism? What is the gospel? Our understanding of salvation, the gospel, and evangelism go hand in hand. How we understand salvation and the gospel is basic to how we think of evangelism. Both of the above cases highlight Jesus's role in the forgiveness of sin(s). In the first case, Francisco is asked to repeat, "Thank you for sending your Son Jesus to die on the cross and rise from the dead so that my sin no longer separates me from you." In the second, Ariana prays for Paula: "Let her know the love of Jesus Christ, who offers us the forgiveness of sins." Does the emphasis on the cross and forgiveness of sin in both cases give adequate expression to the gospel?

How should we invite people to respond to the gospel? The first case concentrates on verbal testimony in an encounter with a stranger at the mall. The second includes offering hospitality, building a relationship, caring and praying, and bringing a family to church. Can evangelism take place in a variety of ways or are some forms of invitation to the gospel inherently better than others?

What sort of response do we hope for in evangelism: conversion, renewal, acknowledgement of God's grace with faith, participation in a community of disciples, or something else? Clearly, in the example of "from scratch" evangelism, conversion is the hoped-for response. It takes the form of confessing sin and trusting Jesus as the one who forgives sin. If we put aside the role of the sinner's prayer in this particular case, we see here a much wider tradition of evangelistic practice in which salvation and conversion are closely related. Salvation is viewed as taking place at a moment in time—an event—in which individuals make some sort of decision or commitment to Christ. This is the moment of salvation, the "soteriological moment" when a person moves from the status of sinner to the status of saved, the moment when a person is converted or born again. Does this soteriology really pass the test of Scripture?

On the basis of the available information, we do not know if this is how Ariana and her church think about evangelism. But we do know that her case raises issues that are worth considering. What are we to make of Ariana's use of the language of "renewal" to describe what is taking place through her relationship with Paula? Paula grew up a Methodist. Presumably, she was baptized as an infant. She stopped going to church when she met her husband. Does Paula need to be converted or to have her faith renewed? Does evangelism encompass both?

This case also invites us to think about evangelism as an invitation to community. Ariana walks with Paula through a process that unfolds over time. In the end, she invites Paula to her church, not to Christ. Perhaps she assumes that her ethnically diverse congregation embodies the gospel in ways that go far beyond what she could communicate in a one-with-one conversation. There are good reasons to think belonging before believing is an effective form of evangelism in some instances.[6]

Moreover, the case invites us to reflect on the goal of evangelism. Where do we hope people end up? Do we hope they will acknowledge Christ as the Savior and Lord of the world? How much of this do they need to understand when they become disciples of Jesus? Should evangelism include an initial process of catechesis and spiritual formation as persons enter the Christian community?[7] If so, how does this impact our understanding of the goal of evangelism?

These questions are not easy to answer. They challenge each of us to think through our theology of evangelism: What is salvation? What is the gospel? How do we invite people to respond to the gospel? What sort of response do we hope for? I believe the best way to begin forming our answers is by turning to Scripture. Stories of practice raise many issues, but they alone cannot offer us the insight we need. For this, we must turn to Christian Scripture and theology.

Biblical Dialogue Partner: Paul the Apostle

Background

The most obvious place to begin our investigation of the relationship between salvation, the gospel, and evangelism is with terms used widely in the Greek New Testament to signify the announcement of good news: (1) *kēryssein* (to proclaim or announce news like a herald) and *kērygma* (the content of this announcement), (2) *euangelizein* (to announce glad tidings) and *to euangelion* (the gospel, good news, glad tidings), and (3) *martyrein* (to bear witness) and *martys* (one who bears witness to the gospel, even to the point of death). It is not unusual for these terms to appear together in different combinations. In

---

6. Brian McLaren was one of the first to think about the implications of this insight. See his *A New Kind of Christian: A Tale of Two Friends on a Spiritual Journey* (Minneapolis: Fortress, 2019).

7. See William Abraham's potent argument for catechesis as a part of evangelism in *The Logic of Evangelism* (Grand Rapids: Eerdmans, 1989).

Mark 16:15, for example, Jesus tells his disciples, "Go into all the world and preach (*kēryssō*) the gospel (*euangelion*) to all creation."

Obviously, word studies are not enough, for the same word can have various meanings in different contexts. But it is also true that words have overlapping meanings in different contexts. They are part of a common discourse shared in a community. This is the case, I believe, with these important terms in the early Christian movement. *Euangelizō* and *euangelion* are especially important for our purposes because they are the terms from which "evangelism," "evangelize," and "evangelization" are derived. Their linguistic roots are *eu* (good) and *angellein* (to share or proclaim).[8] At the heart of evangelism is sharing good news!

In the literature of the Greco-Roman world, terms with the word stem *euangel* were used for sacrifices offered in thanksgiving for good news. They also signified the announcement of good news of special events like a victory in battle, the birth of a child, a benefactor's gift to a city, or the beginning of a political leader's reign. A famous calendar inscription, for example, celebrates Caesar Augustus "as universal benefactor, peacemaker, and 'savior'" and concludes: "The birthday of the god (Caesar Augustus) has been for the whole world the beginning of the good news."[9]

Some New Testament scholars believe that the acknowledgement of Caesar as divine in the imperial cult was an important backdrop to Christian usage of gospel language.[10] Under pressure to acknowledge the emperor as divine, Christians resisted, sometimes to the point of martyrdom. They believed they had been commissioned by God to announce a different gospel: the good news of the sovereign reign of the one true God and the redemption of his Son, Jesus Christ. They worshiped God, not Caesar.

The Hebrew Bible and the Septuagint (the Greek translation of the Old Testament) also served as background for the Christian use of gospel language.[11] The Hebrew word-stem *bsr*, from which words translated "to announce" or "to proclaim" are derived, appears in contexts in which good news of a military victory (for example, 2 Sam 4:10; 18:22) or of divine deliverance is announced (for example, Pss. 40:10; 68:12; 96:2). Most important of

---

8. For a detailed discussion of these terms, see David Barrett, *Evangelize! A Historical Survey of the Concept* (Birmingham: New Hope, 1987), chs. 1–5.

9. Brendan Byrne, "Gospel," in *The Oxford Encyclopedia of the Bible and Theology*, vol. 1, ed. Samuel Balentine et al. (Oxford: Oxford University Press, 2015), 432–33.

10. See, for example, Graham N. Stanton, *Jesus and Gospel* (Cambridge: University of Cambridge Press, 2004), 35–46.

11. For discussion, see Byrne, "Gospel," 433.

all are a number of passages in Second Isaiah that announce the good news of the coming salvation of Israel from captivity in exile (Isa. 40:9; 41:27; 52:7; 60:6; 61:1). In Isaiah 61:1-2, the prophet portrays a figure who is "anointed" by the Spirit "to proclaim good news to the poor" and "freedom for the captives" and to announce "the year of the Lord's favor." While these texts originally announced the glad tidings of Israel's imminent return from captivity in Babylon, they came to be associated with the messianic hopes of Israel up through the time of Jesus.[12]

The Beginning of Gospel Language in the Christian Community

Gospel language appears quite early among Christians.[13] In 1 Corinthians 15:1 and 3, Paul writes:

> Now, brothers, I want to remind you of the *gospel* I preached to you, which you received and on which you have taken your stand. . . . For what I received I passed on to you as of first importance: that Christ died for our sins according to the Scriptures, that he was buried, that he was raised on the third day according to the Scriptures, and that he appeared to Peter and the Twelve.

This is one of several places in Paul's letters where the language of handing on (*paradidōmi*) and receiving (*paralambanō*) is used.[14] Sometimes, these terms are used to refer to the transmission of communal traditions, as they are in this passage. Paul is portraying the content of his gospel as consistent with the communal traditions he received and handed on. The appearance of gospel language in the early Christian community thus seems to predate his conversion.[15]

---

12. For example, *Psalm of Solomon* 11:1 states: "Announce in Jerusalem the voice of one bringing good news" (*euangelizomenou*). Several texts from Qumran, likewise, refer to a messianic figure who will "make the dead alive" and "proclaim good news to the poor." See Byrne, "Gospel," 434.

13. In this paragraph, I follow Byrne, "Gospel," 434. I italicize the term "gospel" to make it easier for readers to locate it in various passages.

14. 1 Thess. 4:1-2; 1 Cor. 11:2, 23-26.

15. For further discussion, see my book *The Teaching Ministry of Congregations* (Louisville: Westminster John Knox, 2005), 29-30; Martin Hengel, *The Atonement: The Origins of the Doctrine in the New Testament* (Eugene, OR: Wipf & Stock, 1981), 37-39.

This interpretation receives support in Galatians 2:1–10, where Paul reports a meeting with church leaders in Jerusalem "to set before them the *gospel* that I preach among the Gentiles." According to Paul, these leaders "added nothing to my message" and affirmed that "I had been given the task of preaching the *gospel* to the Gentiles, just as Peter had been given the task of preaching the *gospel* to the Jews." Here again, gospel language appears to be used by a variety of church leaders and not Paul alone.

Paul also uses gospel language twice in the introduction of Romans (1:1, 16). In this letter he is writing to a community he did not found and has not visited. But he assumes the Roman Christians are familiar with this term.

Taken together, this evidence seems to indicate that gospel language is not something initiated by Paul alone. As Brendan Byrne puts it, the use of gospel language "must, then, have been a feature of the pre-Pauline, Greek-speaking communities of believers, either in Jerusalem or in Antioch, little more than three or four years after the death of Jesus."[16]

Why did gospel language appear so quickly in the early Christian community? While scholars debate this point, I am persuaded that it emerged from Jesus's reliance on "good news" language in Isaiah to proclaim his message and interpret his mission.[17] Passages citing or alluding to this Isaiah material appear across the New Testament.[18] The synoptic Gospels incorporate it into their narratives. Luke 4:16–21, for example, portrays Jesus as reading Isaiah 61:1–2 at the outset of his public ministry:

He stood up to read, and the scroll of the prophet Isaiah was handed to him. Unrolling it, he found the place where it is written: The Spirit of

---

16. Byrne, "Gospel," 434.

17. There is no question that the early church engaged in messianic exegesis of Israel's Scripture to make sense of Jesus's life, death, and resurrection. See Donald Juel's fine summary in *Messianic Exegesis: Christological Interpretation of the Old Testament in Early Christianity* (Minneapolis: Augsburg Fortress, 2009). Without contradicting this point, Arland Hultgren traces the continuity between the words and deeds of Jesus and the early church's interpretation of his mission and message, including his suffering and death. See *The Rise of Normative Christianity* (Minneapolis: Augsburg Fortress, 1994). See also Graham Stanton's discussion of texts from Qumran that make it clear that the Isaiah passages discussed in that community were used during Jesus's day to refer to a messianic prophet. See his *Gospels and Jesus*, 2nd ed. (Oxford: Oxford University Press, 2002), 253–54. See also James D. G. Dunn, *Theology of Paul the Apostle* (Grand Rapids: Eerdmans, 1998), 26.

18. See Dunn, who points to Acts 4:27; 10:36, 38; Eph. 2:17; 6:15; Rev. 1:6; 5:10 in *Theology of Paul*, 168. Scholars do not all agree that Jesus himself relied on Isaiah.

the Lord is on me, because he has anointed me to proclaim *good news* to the poor. He has sent me to proclaim freedom for the prisoners and recovery of sight for the blind, to set the oppressed free, to proclaim the year of the Lord's favor. Then he rolled up the scroll, and gave it back to the attendant and sat down. The eyes of everyone in the synagogue were fastened on him. He began by saying to them, "Today this scripture is fulfilled in your hearing."

In Luke's narrative, this is a pivotal event. Jesus portrays his mission as the messianic fulfillment of Yahweh's promises to Israel as announced by Isaiah.

In Luke, Jesus also is depicted as alluding to Isaiah in response to the disciples of John the Baptist who ask him: "Are you the one who is to come, or should we expect someone else?" Jesus replies:

Go back and report to John what you have seen and heard: The blind receive sight, the lame walk, those who have leprosy are cleansed, the deaf hear, and the dead are raised, and the *good news* is proclaimed to the poor. Blessed is anyone who does not stumble on account of me. (Luke 7:22–23; cf. Matt. 11:4–5)

Here Jesus draws on passages from Isaiah that depict salvation at the advent of God's kingly rule.[19] When salvation comes, sorrow is ended, the afflicted are healed, captives are set free, and the poor receive good news. This is precisely what is taking place in the healings, actions, teaching, and preaching of Jesus. In effect, Jesus is telling John's disciples that he is the promised one, the long-awaited Messiah who will free the people from captivity and restore them to a right relationship with God. The kingly rule of God has drawn near in his person and work. Salvation has arrived. This is good news.

Paul's Understanding of the Gospel

While gospel language predates Paul in the early church, it is developed extensively in his letters and those of the Pauline school.[20] *Euangelizō* appears

19. Isa. 35:5–7; 29:18–19; and 61:1–2.
20. By Pauline school, scholars commonly mean leaders who worked closely with

twenty-two times and *euangelion* fifty-six. It is a consistent theme in all of Paul's letters, from 1 Thessalonians to Philippians. Indeed, Paul uses a variety of terms to describe sharing the gospel.[21] The gospel is spoken (1 Thess. 1:5; 2:2), preached (Gal. 2:2; 1 Thess. 2:9), proclaimed (1 Cor. 9:14), and evangelized (1 Cor. 9:18, 15:1; 2 Cor. 11:7; Gal. 1:11).[22]

For Paul, the gospel primarily is *the message of salvation* that is shared through face-to-face communication. It is the good news about Jesus that is spoken to individuals or groups in particular times and places. Paul challenges us to think in terms of specific acts of face-to-face communication, which include preaching and teaching as well as conversations in homes, after work, with friends and family members, and in other ways.[23]

Yet Paul does not view the gospel as shared exclusively through face-to-face communication. It also is communicated through the actions and attitudes of Paul, his coworkers, and the communities he establishes. Paul makes this clear in many places in his letters. First Thessalonians 1:5–10 is a good example:

> Our *gospel* came to you not simply with words but also with power, with the Holy Spirit and deep conviction. You know how we lived among you for your sake. You became imitators of us and of the Lord, for you welcomed the message in the midst of severe suffering with the joy given by the Holy Spirit. And so you became a model to all the believers in Macedonia and Achaia. The Lord's message rang out from you not only in Macedonia and Achaia—your faith in God has become known everywhere.

Paul and his coworkers came to the Thessalonians after being treated "outrageously" in Philippi, but they persisted in sharing the gospel

---

Paul, drew on traditions he established, and sometimes wrote letters under his name, a common practice during that period. Some scholars believe that these letters may have been based on fragments of earlier letters written by Paul. Paul's undisputed epistles are 1 Thessalonians, Galatians, 1 and 2 Corinthians, Romans, Philippians, and Philemon. The so-called disputed letters written in Paul's name are Ephesians, Colossians, 2 Thessalonians, 1 Timothy, 2 Timothy, and Titus.

21. Francis Watson, *The Fourfold Gospel* (Grand Rapids: Baker Academic, 2016), Kindle edition, loc. 310.

22. Cf. Watson, *The Fourfold Gospel*, note 24.

23. Abraham J. Malherbe, *Paul and the Thessalonians: The Philosophic Tradition of Pastoral Care* (Eugene, OR: Wipf & Stock, 1987).

(1 Thess. 2:2). In turn, the Thessalonians remained joyful in spite of their own suffering. First Thessalonians offers glimpses of the way Paul lived among this community (for example, as a nursing mother caring for her children, 1 Thess. 2:7), and the way the Thessalonians subsequently became a "model" for believers throughout the region.[24] Actions often speak louder than words. This was evident in the second case study we examined above.

Paul also developed ways of sharing the gospel beyond face-to-face communication and actions. The most important of these were his pastoral letters. These letters represented Paul's apostolic presence to his congregations in his absence, reminding, encouraging, and explaining the meaning of the gospel. His letters were read aloud to the communities for whom they were written. They typically were delivered by an emissary who could explain further what Paul had written.

Paul signals the relationship of his letters to the gospel at various points. For example, while he desires to come to the Christians in Rome in order "to preach the gospel" in person (Rom. 1:15), his letter offers an exposition of the gospel in advance to gather support for his future mission in Spain (Rom. 15:16, 24). He portrays his letters to the Corinthians as a "reminder" of the gospel he originally preached (1 Cor. 15:1). In Galatians, he even seems to "reevangelize" the community because some members have come to believe a "different gospel" (Gal. 1:6).[25]

Paul's letters, thus, were a way of communicating the gospel in written form, which allowed him to continue to guide his congregations. This is an important reminder that evangelism, teaching, and the spiritual formation of the community overlap. It is not enough to "convert" people and send them on their way, as in the case of "from scratch" evangelism. I am doubtful that this has anything to do with conversion in the New Testament. Paul seeks to establish communities of faith and continues to engage in community formation even when he cannot be present in person. His letters invite his congregations to encounter the gospel anew as they face new issues. Paul believes congregations play a crucial role in equipping individuals to share

24. Beverly Roberts Gaventa, *First and Second Thessalonians*, Interpretation: A Bible Commentary for Preaching and Teaching (Louisville: Westminster John Knox, 1998).

25. J. Louis Martyn, "The Apocalyptic Gospel in Galatians," *Interpretation* 34, no. 3 (July 2000): 247. In his commentary, Martyn describes this as "repreaching the gospel"; *Galatians: A New Translation with Introduction and Commentary*, The Anchor Bible, vol. 33A (New York: Doubleday, 1997), 23, 117.

the gospel with others and in witnessing to the gospel in their relations with one another and their neighbors.

This brings us to an all-important question emerging from our two cases: *If evangelism is inviting people to respond to the gospel, what is the gospel?* Paul provides a succinct answer at various points. It is the message of God's salvation of the world in Jesus Christ. Thus, he speaks of the "gospel of God," for God is the primary agent of salvation.[26] He also describes the gospel as "the power of God that brings salvation to everyone who believes" and "the message I proclaim about Jesus Christ" (Rom. 16:25).[27] Francis Watson expresses well the centrality of Christ to the gospel Paul shares: "It is Christ who has sent him to preach it, Christ who speaks through it, and Christ who is its content."[28] While Paul develops his understanding of the gospel in a variety of ways in his letters, we focus on four key elements embodied in representative texts. They constitute the heart of Paul's understanding of the gospel.

The Gospel Is in Accordance with Israel's Scripture

The gospel he promised beforehand through his prophets in the Holy Scriptures regarding his Son. (Rom. 1:2-3)

Paul portrays the good news of God's salvation of the world in Jesus Christ as the fulfillment of God's promises to Israel. In the passage from 1 Corinthians 15:1-3, cited above, he describes Christ's death and resurrection as taking place "according to the Scriptures." Paul also claims that "Scripture foresaw that God would justify the Gentiles by faith and announced the gospel in advance to Abraham: 'All nations will be blessed through you'" (Gal. 3:8). Paul "reads" Christ in light of Israel's Scripture, and he reinterprets Israel's Scripture (as well as events unfolding in the early church) in light of Christ.[29]

Paul's appeal to Scripture was a good strategy when he preached and taught the gospel in synagogues, addressing an audience familiar with Is-

---

26. Rom. 1:1; 15:16; 2 Cor. 11:7; 1 Thess. 2:2, 8, 9.
27. Cf. Rom. 15:19; 1 Cor. 9:12; 2 Cor. 2:12; 9:13; 10:14; Gal. 1:7; Phil. 1:27; 1 Thess. 3:2.
28. Watson, *The Fourfold Gospel*, loc. 319.
29. See Richard Hays, *Echoes of Scripture in the Letters of Paul* (New Haven: Yale University Press, 1989).

rael's story.[30] It also was a good strategy in his polemics against Jewish Christian opponents who opposed his understanding of the gospel and sought to maintain markers of Jewish identity such as circumcision and dietary regulations.[31] By drawing on Israel's Scripture, he meets them on their own ground. But most important of all, Paul portrays the gospel as the fulfillment of Scripture so his fledgling congregations will see that their identity and mission stand in continuity with the identity and mission of Israel, God's covenant people. The good news of God's salvation of the world in Jesus Christ is the fulfillment of God's promises to Israel. It is not an unexpected turn.

Indeed, Paul and his school take the logic of promise and fulfillment one step further. They use apocalyptic language of *mystery* to portray the gospel as fulfilling and unveiling the purposes of God from eternity:

> We declare God's wisdom, a *mystery* that has been hidden and that God destined for our glory before time began. (1 Cor. 2:7)

> Now to him who is able to establish you in accordance with my gospel, the message I proclaim about Jesus Christ, in keeping with the revelation of the *mystery* hidden for long ages past. (Rom. 16:25)

> For he chose us in him before the creation of the world . . . he made known to us the *mystery* of his will according to his good pleasure, which he purposed in Christ, to be put into effect when the times reach their fulfillment—to bring unity to all things in heaven and on earth under Christ. (Eph. 1:4, 9-10)

For Paul and his fellow workers, the gospel announces God's decision to love the world from eternity in and through Jesus Christ, a mystery found in Israel's Scripture and now unveiled definitively in Jesus Christ. In accordance with Scripture, the death and resurrection of Jesus are good news, not only for Israel and the early church, but also for all people.

---

30. Acts 13:5, 14; 14:1; 17:1-2, 10; 18:4, 19.

31. In Galatians, these opponents are mentioned in virtually every chapter. See Gal. 1:6-9; 2:4-5; 3:1; 4:17; 5:10, 12; 6:12-13. Scholars disagree over who Paul's opponents are in his letters, but in this letter, anyway, on grounds internal to the letter it seems highly likely that they are Jewish Christians.

The Gospel Focuses on God's Action in Christ, which Frees Humanity from the Power of Sin and Death

> But now apart from the law the righteousness of God has been made known, to which the Law and the Prophets testify. This righteousness is given through faith in Jesus Christ to all who believe. There is no difference between Jew and Gentile, for all have sinned and fall short of the glory of God, and all are justified freely by his grace through the redemption that came by Christ Jesus. God presented Christ as a sacrifice of atonement, through the shedding of his blood—to be received by faith. (Rom. 3:21-25)

Across his letters, Paul uses a variety of concepts and images to describe God's saving action in Christ lying at the heart of the gospel. These include:

- "To save" and "salvation": "For God did not appoint us to suffer wrath but to receive salvation through our Lord Jesus Christ" (1 Thess. 5:9).
- "To reconcile" and "reconciliation": "All this is from God, who reconciled us to himself through Christ" (2 Cor. 5:18).
- "To redeem" and "redemption": "Christ redeemed us from the curse of the law by becoming a curse for us" (Gal. 3:13).
- "To conquer" and "triumph": "He disarmed the rulers and authorities and made a public example of them, triumphing over them in it [the cross]" (Col. 2:15).

With these wonderfully diverse images and concepts, Paul portrays God as acting in Christ on humanity's behalf and in its stead. God's action is necessary because humanity is caught in sin and death, so Christ takes our place.

Sin and death have a range of meanings in Paul's letters.[32] Sometimes, sin is described as particular acts by human beings: hence, sins (plural, as in Gal. 1:4; 1 Cor. 15:3). But it also is used in the singular to point to sin as a universal human condition which has human beings in its grip and even rules over them (as in Rom. 5:21; 6:12, 14). In a similar fashion, death sometimes describes the end of life, but it also is portrayed as the outcome of sin: "For the wages of sin is death, but the gift of God is eternal life in Christ Jesus our Lord" (Rom. 6:23). If sin and death are universal, God's action in Christ is

---

32. For an excellent overview of sin and death, see Dunn, *Theology of Paul*, 111-26.

equally universal. "All" are saved, reconciled, redeemed, and liberated in Christ Jesus. The universality of God's saving action in Christ is lifted up again and again in Paul's letters.[33] This lies at the heart of Paul's understanding of the gospel.

One of the most important and distinctive ways Paul portrays God's action on humanity's behalf is with the theme of *God's righteousness*.[34] The representative passage at the start of this section is an example. Here the universal scope of sin and salvation is evident: "*All* have sinned and fall short of the glory of God, and *all* are justified freely by his grace through the redemption that came by Christ" (Rom. 3:23-24). Righteousness and justification share the same Greek root (*dikaio-*), and justification (*dikaiōsis*) might be translated "made righteous," "right-wised," or "placed in a right relationship with God."

The theme of God's justification of the ungodly by grace through faith was prominent in the theologies of the Reformers of the sixteenth century. As Martin Luther puts it in his commentary on Galatians: "Nothing can take away sin except the grace of God. In actual living, however, it is not so easy to persuade oneself that by grace alone, in opposition to every other means, we obtain the forgiveness of our sins and peace with God."[35]

In recent decades, a number of biblical scholars have criticized Luther's interpretation of Paul as too individualistic and too focused on human guilt.[36] While there is much to learn from this discussion, it fails to account

33. See, for example, Rom. 5; 1 Cor. 15:22; 2 Cor. 5:14.

34. While this theme is treated most extensively in Romans and Galatians, it appears elsewhere in Paul's letters. "To justify" appears twenty-five times and "the bestowing of righteousness" twenty-one times. The frequency of these terms even surpasses "to save" (nineteen times) and "salvation" (fourteen times), "to reconcile" (five times) and "reconciliation" (four times), and "to redeem" (two times) and "redemption" (three times). See Arland Hultgren, *Paul's Gospel and Mission: The Outlook from His Letter to the Romans* (Philadelphia: Fortress, 1985), 82-83.

35. Martin Luther, *A Commentary on St. Paul's Letter to the Galatians*, trans. Theodore Graebner (Grand Rapids: Zondervan, 1949), 8.

36. Some critics contend that the Reformers were wrong to use the purported legalism of first-century Judaism as a foil for their gospel of grace. See, for example, E. P. Sanders, *Paul and Palestinian Judaism: A Comparison of Patterns of Religion* (Philadelphia: Fortress, 1977). Others believe the Reformers were far too individualistic in their interpretation of the theme of justification, relying too exclusively on the imagery of a law court in which the guilty party is pardoned on the basis of Christ's righteousness which is imputed to him or her as a free gift. Proponents of the "new perspective" on Paul argue that the theme of righteousness does not focus on the individual's standing before God but on group membership, dealing with the validity

for the complexity of Paul's discussion of righteousness and justification.[37] He develops these themes in two contexts in his letters.

The first context draws on the imagery of Jewish apocalyptic traditions to portray God's action in Christ as marking the turn of the ages in which God's righteousness is revealed and humanity is decisively set free from the evil powers of the world. Resonant with Old Testament usage, *righteousness indicates God's faithfulness in sending the Messiah to deliver humanity from sin and death and to reconcile it to God.* The emphasis is on God's saving action apart from humanity, a deed done, and the unveiling of a mystery. Not only has God acted in the stead of all in saving all, but this action looks ahead to the parousia when the cosmic lordship of Christ will be recognized by all.

Paul also uses the theme of God's righteousness in a second context in his letters. This focuses on the justification (making righteous) of human beings. Here the focus is on the reception and appropriation of God's saving action in Christ by Jews and gentiles, collectively and individually. In the representative passage at the beginning of this section, Paul writes: "This righteousness is given through faith in Jesus Christ to all who believe" and is "to be received by faith." Right after this passage in Romans 4, Paul holds up Abraham as the prototype of justification by faith, for it is Abraham's trust in God—faith alone—by which he is reckoned as righteous. Gentiles and Jews alike are "Abraham's children" solely by placing their trust in Christ through whom salvation is freely offered (Rom. 9:7-8).

Sometimes Paul draws on this understanding of justification to argue against those who believe that Gentiles must accept circumcision and dietary regulations to become members of the Christian community. No, Paul responds: "For we maintain that a person is justified by faith apart from the

---

of Jewish identity markers like circumcision and dietary regulations in the Christian community. Paul's discussion of justification by faith, not the law, is interpreted as directed at this issue. See James Dunn, *The New Perspective on Paul* (Grand Rapids: Eerdmans, 2007). Prior to the new perspective, some scholars had already begun to argue that it was European pietism and American evangelicalism that turned Luther's understanding of justification into an individualistic, guilt-oriented concept. These movements so emphasized *faith* as the means of receiving God's grace and the locus of salvation that the act of human trust became a kind of work. See Anders Nygren, *Commentary on Romans* (Philadelphia: Fortress, 1949), 68-71.

37. Throughout this section, I follow Arland Hultgren. See *Paul's Gospel and Mission,* cited above, and *Paul's Letter to the Romans: A Commentary* (Grand Rapids: Eerdmans, 2011). See especially appendix 1, "The 'Righteousness of God' in Paul" in Hultgren's commentary.

works of the law" (Rom. 3:28).[38] Jews and Gentiles alike are reconciled on the basis of God's action in Christ alone, which they receive in faith. In this second context, Paul sometimes portrays God's justification of individuals with the imagery of the law court. God is like a judge, and human beings stand before God as guilty sinners. But God is merciful and pronounces the sinner righteous on the basis of the righteousness of Christ. This is imputed to all who accept their pardon in faith.

It is very important not to confuse God's act of justifying human beings with human acceptance of this. There is a recurring tendency among Christians to turn faith into another kind of work, as if we were saved by our faith, not by what has been done for us on our behalf and in our place. Faith is evidence that "the gospel has exercised its power on the believer. It is not one's faith that gives the gospel its power; quite the contrary, it is the power of the gospel that makes it possible for one to believe."[39]

In short, for Paul the gospel is good news because it focuses on God's salvation of the world in Jesus Christ. It speaks of *God's* righteousness, the eternal, gracious, and faithful love of God for the world, shown in God's covenant relationship with Israel, but now fully revealed and enacted in saving humanity from sin and death in Christ Jesus. All human beings are asked to do is to trust what God has done on their behalf and in their stead. Surely this lies at the heart of the response we hope for in evangelism: to trust the saving grace of God in Jesus Christ.

The Gospel Portrays God as Acting to Free Humanity from Sin and Death through Christ's Death and Resurrection

He was delivered over to death for our sins and was raised to life for our justification. (Rom. 4:25)

Thus far we have described the gospel in general terms as God's salvation of the world in Jesus Christ. We now turn to the key events that Paul places at the heart of the gospel: the death and resurrection of Christ.[40] He was "delivered over to death." Here Paul portrays Christ's crucifixion as the result

---

38. Cf. Rom. 2:13; 3:20; Gal. 2:16.

39. Hultgren, *Paul's Gospel and Mission*, 39. He is drawing on Anders Nygren here.

40. Paul does not offer an extended narrative of Jesus's life as we find in the canonical Gospels, though there are good reasons to believe that he is familiar with traditions about Jesus. See Dunn, *Theology of Paul*, 183-95.

of God's action. It is God who hands over his Son. We find this emphasis on divine agency in the death of Christ elsewhere in Paul's letters.[41] Human actors and forces are complicit in Jesus's death, to be sure. The crowds, leaders, and occupying forces all play a role. But above all, Paul sees God's hand at work. As he puts it in 2 Corinthians 5:18: "All this is from God, who reconciled us to himself through Christ." The Greco-Roman world was quite familiar with heroic figures who would die on behalf of friends, family, or the state. It also was familiar with the need to offer sacrifices to assuage the anger of gods. But they found it strange and even repulsive that the Christian message of salvation portrayed God as the agent of reconciliation and the one who provided the means to accomplish this.[42]

It is noteworthy that Paul also uses the language of "handing over" to describe Christ's obedient and voluntary participation in the crucifixion. He is not a passive victim but a willing actor who "gave himself for our sins" (Gal. 1:4).[43] Many commentators believe this language comes from Isaiah 53 where it describes a suffering servant who is delivered over to death as a sin offering that brings peace and healing to the people.[44] The servant dies a vicarious death on behalf of the people, bearing their transgressions and iniquities. Since the idea of a crucified Messiah was not widely present in Israel's Scripture and traditions, it is not surprising that the early church would turn to Isaiah 53 to make sense of Jesus's death. Moreover, I believe it is likely that this is grounded in Jesus's own preaching and teaching.

Building on these early Christian traditions, Paul uses the imagery of cultic sacrifice to explain the saving significance of Jesus's death.[45] At points he portrays Christ in his death as a sin offering (Rom. 8:3), scapegoat (2 Cor. 5:21), paschal lamb (1 Cor. 5:7), and expiation (Rom. 3:25).[46] Various refer-

41. It is God who "presents Christ as a sacrifice of atonement" (Rom. 3:25), who sends "his own Son in the likeness of sinful flesh to be a sin offering" (Rom. 8:3), who "made him who had no sin to be sin for us" (2 Cor. 5:21), who "sent his Son . . . to redeem those under the law" (Gal. 4:4-5), and who "did not spare his own Son, but gave him up for us all" (Rom. 8:32). It is noteworthy that the language of "handing over" is also used to describe Christ's obedient participation in his crucifixion (Gal. 1:4; 2:20; Eph. 5:2, 25).

42. Hengel, *Atonement*, 31-32.

43. Cf. Gal. 2:20; Eph. 5:2, 25.

44. Hengel, *Atonement*, 35-36.

45. See Hengel, *Atonement*, for a helpful discussion of the genesis of the vicarious, substitutionary understanding of Christ's death.

46. The last of these is a translation of *hilastērion*, a reference to the lid of the ark, or mercy seat, where atonement was made on the Day of Atonement. See Hultgren,

ences to the "blood" of Christ also appear to have cultic settings in mind in which sacrifices were made.[47] Building on early Christian traditions, Paul appropriates this imagery to portray the death of Messiah Jesus as an atoning sacrifice that restores a guilty and estranged humanity to a right relationship with God. The one true sacrifice establishing a new covenant with God has taken place once and for all and is now open to the nations.[48]

The imagery of cultic sacrifice draws on the notion that sin is transferred to a clean and unblemished animal in order to remove it from the person offering the sacrifice. The purity of the animal is, in turn, transferred in reverse to the human. James Dunn describes this as the sacrificial chiasmus and Morna Hooker as an interchange:[49]

> By the sacrifice the sinner was made pure and lived free of that sin;
> By the sacrifice the pure animal was made impure and died for that sin.

There are a number of instances of this sacrificial chiasmus in Paul's letters. Only now, it is God who is offering the sacrifice on humanity's behalf and Christ who is the one sacrificed. Second Corinthians 5:21 is an example:[50]

> For our sake God made the sinless one into sin,
> So that in him we might become the righteousness of God.

Paul appears to have this theology of exchange in mind when he draws out the universal significance of Christ's death. As he puts it in 2 Corinthians 5:14: "For Christ's love compels us, because we are convinced that one died for all, and therefore all died." In Christ's death, all human beings are represented. He takes their place. We find Paul making this same point in his discussion of Christ and Adam (Rom. 5:12-21; 1 Cor. 15:21-22). The one represents and takes the place of the many. Indeed, more than representation is at stake.

Paul's Letter to the Romans, 151-53, and Dunn, *Theology of Paul*, 213-14, who notes the complexities of translating this term.

47. Dunn, *Theology of Paul*, 217, 218-22.

48. See Hengel's excellent discussion of this point, *Atonement*, 46-53.

49. This is Dunn's rendering in *Theology of Paul*, 222. See also Morna D. Hooker, *From Adam to Christ: Essays on Paul* (Cambridge: Cambridge University Press, 1990), 13-41.

50. Rom. 8:3; Gal. 4:4-5. Cf. Gal. 3:13.

Christ is a substitute for us; he takes our place and does what we cannot do because we are caught in sin and death. His death is both substitutionary and representative.

For Paul, Christ's death and resurrection are inextricably linked, as we see in the representative passage at the beginning of this section. They are two parts of the one work of salvation. The one crucified on behalf of all is the one vindicated by God who raises him from the dead. The resurrection also is closely linked by Paul to Christ's exaltation, the assumption of his lordship (for example, Rom. 14:9). In the hymn of Philippians 2:6-11, the confession of Christ's lordship is portrayed as the climax of creation's cosmic worship of God at the eschaton. For Christians, the confession of Christ as Lord was a part of their baptism (Rom. 10:9) and the beginning of their new life in Christ: "We were therefore buried with him through baptism into death in order that, just as Christ was raised from the dead through the glory of the Father, we too may live a new life" (Rom. 6:4).

The Gospel Proclaims the Identity of Jesus: Lord, Messiah, and Son of God

Paul, a bond-servant of Christ Jesus, called as an apostle, set apart for the *gospel* of God, which he promised beforehand through his prophets in the holy Scriptures, concerning his Son, who was born of a descendant of David according to the flesh, who was declared the Son of God with power by the resurrection from the dead, according to the Spirit of holiness, Jesus Christ our Lord. (Rom. 1:1-4)

The gospel, the message of salvation, tells us who Jesus is. Jesus is not just a good or heroic human being who did wonderful things on God's behalf. The gospel makes the claim that Jesus is God in human form who is acting to save the world. There are many good people and many heroes. There is only one savior. We see this in the representative passage cited above.

In this text, Jesus is described as a descendant of David and thus of the appropriate lineage of the promised messiah. The term Christ, or anointed one, became a virtual surname for Jesus in Paul's letters, giving rise to the practice of saying Jesus Christ instead of Jesus the Messiah. Jesus also is identified as the Son of God two times in this passage. Throughout his letters, Paul and his school portray Jesus as the preexistent Son of God, drawing on traditions that portray Wisdom as present and participating with God in the creation of the world (1 Cor. 8:6; cf. Col. 1:15-20).[51] They also portray the post-existence of Jesus. In the above passage, this is implied by stating that Jesus was raised from the dead "with power." This refers not only to the role of the Holy Spirit in raising Jesus from the dead, but also to Christ's role as one who shares in God's rule and final judgment, now seated at God's right hand in power (Rom. 8:34).[52]

Sharing in God's rule and judgment is only one example of the way Paul attributes to Jesus activities that belong exclusively to Yahweh in Israel's Scripture and traditions.[53] These include participation in God's creation, providential rule, salvation, and judgment. Jesus shares in the identity of the God of Israel. This is good news, for it means that God is present in Jesus, acting on humanity's behalf to save it from sin and death and to open up the possibility of new life in anticipation of the world's final transformation. God's mission to the world through Israel has been fulfilled in Jesus.[54] The one, true, and living God who chose Israel to make his name and ways known to the world has now made himself known through Jesus and effected the salvation of humanity. God's name can now be known in all the nations of the world.

Paul views his apostolic calling in terms of spreading the good news to the *ethnē*, which can be translated gentiles or nations. He describes his calling in terms of Jeremiah, who was a "prophet to the nations," and draws on passages from Isaiah that portray the nations as drawn to the light of Israel's God in the last day. The collection Paul was gathering for the church in Jerusalem likely was symbolic of the eschatological gathering of the nations.

The Attraction of Paul's Congregations

We cannot leave our discussion of Paul without some mention of the role of Paul's congregations in evangelism. I do not have in mind evangelism by individual Christians who belong to particular congregations. Rather, I am interested in some of the reasons people might have been attracted to

51. See Dunn, *The Theology of Paul*, 266-93, and Richard Bauckham, *God Crucified: Monotheism in the New Testament* (Carlisle: Paternoster, 1998).

52. Cf. Eph. 1:20; Col. 3:1.

53. Richard Bauckham, *Jesus and the God of Israel* (Grand Rapids: Eerdmans, 2008); Christopher Wright, *The Mission of God: Unlocking the Bible's Grand Narrative* (Downers Grove, IL: InterVarsity, 2006), 106-21.

54. For an excellent discussion of this point, see Wright, *The Mission of God*, part 2.

Paul's congregations during the first century AD. Paul's communities were distinctive in several ways.[55]

Social Composition

Analysis of the social composition of Paul's churches indicates that at least some of them were quite diverse. They included slaves, free persons, artisans, merchants, poor people, and people with enough wealth to own their own homes and slaves. While predominantly gentile, they also included Jewish Christians. Paul's churches were among the few associations in his society with this range of diversity. His letters constantly emphasized the oneness of the community in Christ and the belief that every Christian was gifted by the Spirit and had something to contribute to the common good of the community. He was not afraid to critique the wealthy members of his congregations or even the host of a church meeting if their actions threatened the community's affirmation of all participants as children of God in Christ and members of his body. The difference between this way of viewing one another and that of the surrounding culture would have been very evident to Christians. It also would have appealed to people who longed to find worth and dignity in a society that had rigid hierarchies of social status.

The Role of Women

The debate over the role of women in Jesus's ministry and the early church continues. I personally believe there are many indications that Jesus counted women among his disciples and followers.[56] Obviously, this was not the case for the Twelve, who had the symbolic function of representing the twelve tribes of Israel in Jesus's mission of renewing God's people. But I do not believe there is any legitimate way of moving from this fact to the exclusion of women from leadership in ministry, as found in Roman Catholicism and some forms of evangelicalism. None of the Twelve were present at Jesus's

55. I am drawing here on my book, *The Teaching Ministry of Congregations* (Louisville: Westminster John Knox, 2005), 18-20. See also Robert Banks, *Paul's Idea of Community: The Early House Churches in Their Cultural Setting* (Peabody, MA: Hendrickson, 1994). See Banks's fine summary of the role of women in Paul's mission, 153-55.

56. See Gerhard Lohfink, *Jesus and Community* (Philadelphia: Fortress, 1984), ch. 2 for a very helpful overview, as well as 96-98, 115-22.

crucifixion in the Synoptic Gospels (only the beloved disciple in John), but women from among his disciples were. They also were among the first to learn of Jesus's resurrection and the first to proclaim it. As for Paul, women seemed to play a variety of roles in his communities and even served as missionaries and emissaries delivering letters—a role that typically included answering questions and explaining the letter on Paul's behalf. The Spirit-led nature of Paul's communities, including the free-flowing nature of worship in which spiritual gifts open to all are exercised, lends plausibility to the idea that women experienced more freedom in the early church than in the surrounding culture. I agree with those scholars who believe 1 Corinthians 14:34-35 is an interpolation.[57] Paul presupposes that women speak as prophets and pray in worship in 1 Corinthians 11:5-16. Acts 21:8-9 portrays the four daughters of Philip the evangelist as speaking prophetically. It was not until the later writing of the pastoral epistles that the leadership of women began to be tamped down (1 Tim. 2:11-12).

Status Inconsistency of Leaders

Many of the leaders of Paul's churches appear to be people with high status inconsistency.[58] This means that they had resources, authority, agency, and expertise in some areas of life but were in subordinate roles in other areas. Contemporary research on persons with high status inconsistency reveals much stress as they move from one status to another. The church would have provided a welcome opportunity for the exercise of leadership, musical abilities, storytelling, and so forth to be recognized in the face of the status inconsistency of their everyday life. Also, with their identity rooted in Christ and one another, such people would likely have begun to see this identity as superseding the status shifts they experienced in everyday life. Who they really were was who they were in Jesus Christ.

It is little wonder that we find Paul's letters addressing issues of conflict again and again. His congregations were different than the kinds of associations and relationships that people experienced in everyday life. They were

---

57. See Richard Hays, *First Corinthians*, Interpretation: A Bible Commentary for Preaching and Teaching (Louisville: Westminster John Knox, 2011), 245-49; see also 181-92; Gordon D. Fee, *The First Epistle to the Corinthians*, New International Commentary on the New Testament (Grand Rapids: Eerdmans, 1987), 699-708.

58. See my discussion and sources in Osmer, *The Teaching Ministry of Congregations*, 19-20.

having to learn a new way of being together in community with few, if any, models to draw on. Paul realized how important the fellowship and "one-anothering" of his congregations were to his mission. He described them as called together by the gospel and knit into Christ and one another by the Spirit. He used various images to portray the fellowship and oneness of the people: God's loving family, God's temple, Christ's body, for example. He consistently worked to edify the community in love.

One of the important images that Paul used to help participants in his communities to understand what they were experiencing is new creation:[59]

Therefore, if anyone is in Christ, the new creation has come: The old has gone, the new is here! (2 Cor. 5:17)

Neither circumcision nor uncircumcision means anything; what counts is the new creation. (Gal. 6:15)

Although Paul is the only author in the New Testament to use this language, the eschatological framework it presupposes is shared throughout. While the present age is still inhabited by forces in opposition to God and Christians still struggle in their own lives with the power of sin and death, they are baptized into Christ. They have died with him and risen to new life. They partake already of the new creation. This must be reflected in how they live and relate to one another. Even amid the "not yet" of God's promised future, they are to give visible expression to the "already" of new creation that breaks down the boundaries by which people are separated. As Paul puts it so beautifully in what is likely part of the baptismal liturgy in his churches: "There is neither Jew nor Gentile, neither slave nor free, nor is there male and female, for you are all one in Christ Jesus" (Gal. 3:28; cf. Col. 3:11). The community in its very being is a witness to the gospel of reconciliation.

Reflection on the Case Studies in Conversation with Paul

As we look back at the cases with which we began this chapter in dialogue with Paul the Apostle, there are many things that stand out. The first case was "from scratch" evangelism in which two Christians stopped the man named Francisco at a mall, invited him to say a version of the sinner's prayer, and

59. Cf. Gal. 6:12–16; 2 Cor. 5:14–19; Eph. 2:11–22; 4:17–24; and Col. 3:1–11.

then watched him depart quickly to meet his friends. The class was critical of this form of evangelism. The context was interpersonal but the method was impersonal—"Repeat after me." There was no effort to invite Francisco to connect with a community of faith. Indeed, there are questions as to whether faith was involved at all. All of these things were important to Paul. He often worked as part of a team and mentored younger coworkers whom he gradually entrusted with more responsibility. That is what I think he might have done in this case. Paul's evangelism included preaching and teaching the gospel so people might understand what God had done on their behalf. He called them to a life-changing faith through the power of the Holy Spirit, taking shape in the context of a community of disciples. These are absent altogether in this case.

In short, Bob needs to think more deeply about salvation, the gospel, and their relationship to evangelism. Paul's gospel presupposes that people are caught in sin and death and that God has sent Christ to save them from these realities and reconcile them to God. Christ has done for them what they cannot do themselves. He has taken their place; they in turn are placed in a right relationship with God through him. In the case under discussion, there was no real effort to help Francisco understand this and to acknowledge with gratitude the love and grace of God involved. The sinner's prayer was used mechanically as a kind of magical mantra. This is a caricature of the way this prayer was commonly used in relational evangelism and revivalism. As a set formula, however, it lends itself to these kinds of abuses. Bob needs to understand the gospel more deeply so he can put it in his own words depending on whom he is talking to. He also needs to try to understand whom he is talking to.

Bob also needs to move beyond this highly individualistic approach to evangelism. It represents what Darrell Guder likes to call a form of "gospel reductionism," limiting the gospel by reducing it to taken-for-granted categories of a particular culture.[60] In this case American individualism overwhelms Paul's understanding that salvation involves participation in a community of people who are united to one another and to Christ by the Holy Spirit. The very existence of a community of Jews and gentiles from many nations is a sign that the reconciliation of the world has taken place and that the time is approaching when this is openly acknowledged by all. Congregations and their members bear witness to the new creation that already is

---

60. Darrell Guder, *The Continuing Conversion of the Church*, Gospel and Our Culture series (Grand Rapids: Eerdmans, 2000). His comments on gospel reductionism are scattered throughout the book, so see the index.

breaking into the old creation through the Holy Spirit. Evangelism is not just about an individual's personal decision. It is the invitation to community, a community that testifies to the reality of God's reconciliation of the world in Christ Jesus in its fellowship and its relationship to the world.

The second case we examined, "Tongues of Healing and Unity," told the story of the relationship between Ariana Diaz and Paula Arrowsmith. This started with Ariana's initial hospitality and moved to her support of Paula as she faced breast cancer, had a double mastectomy, and experienced depression following surgery. Ariana visited Paula regularly, prayed for her, shared her faith, and talked about her church. After her recovery, Paula asked to go with Ariana to her church, which was a large Pentecostal church with racial and ethnic diversity. Paula asked to come back the next week.

This case resonates with many dimensions of Paul's understanding of the gospel and evangelism. Ariana communicates the gospel in a face-to-face context. Her actions and attitudes bear witness to the undeserved love and grace of God in Jesus Christ. She rightly calls attention to the role of the Holy Spirit in her evangelism. This is certainly present in Paul's missionary activity, especially if you focus on Acts—where it is front and center—and not just on his letters, as I have done above.

There is no sense that Paula was Ariana's "conversion project." She did not befriend Paula to convert her. She simply loved her and served her. She shared her faith naturally as a part of her own identity. While Paul the great evangelist had a plan and a strategy that put in motion his calling to bring the gospel to the nations, there is no hint of this in Ariana's case. She was committed to showing hospitality to all people who move to her neighborhood. Beyond this, she appears to have been led by the Spirit. Her goal seems to have been to show God's love and to share her faith in God in this context. Her congregation embodied the sort of diversity found in some of Paul's communities and was a visible expression of the new creation.

These realities served as a point of entry for Paula to begin the journey of finding her way back to Christ, a process that Ariana does not force or control but leaves to the Spirit. Like Paul's coworkers and churches, Ariana reflects many aspects of his witness to the gospel.

For Further Reading

Cousar, Charles B., *The Letters of Paul.* Nashville: Abingdon, 1996. A clear, introductory overview of Paul's theology, themes, and rhetorical strategies.

Dunn, James D. G. *The Theology of Paul the Apostle*. Grand Rapids: Eerdmans, 1998. A magisterial book on all aspects of Paul's theology. Excellent bibliography.

Gathercole, Simon. *Defending Substitution: An Essay on Atonement in Paul*. Acadia Studies in Bible and Theology. Grand Rapids: Baker Academic, 2015. Excellent discussion of what is at stake in using substitution, not just representation, in describing the atonement.

Gaventa, Beverly Roberts. *When in Romans: An Invitation to Linger with the Gospel according to Paul*. Grand Rapids: Baker Academic, 2016. An exceptionally clear and insightful introduction to Paul's letter to the Romans, which also serves as an introduction to Paul's theology of the gospel.

Hengel, Martin, *The Atonement: The Origins of the Doctrine in the New Testament*. Eugene, OR: Wipf & Stock, 1981. Helpful overview of the background of the atonement in both Greco-Roman and Jewish culture. Primary focus on the early Christian community.

Hultgren, Arland. *Paul's Gospel and Mission: The Outlook from His Letter to the Romans*. Philadelphia: Fortress, 1985. Long before missional theology, Hultgren began to explore Paul's understanding of mission. An excellent resource.

———. *Paul's Letter to the Romans: A Commentary*. Grand Rapids: Eerdmans, 2011. Counters the so-called new perspective on Paul and provides a first-rate commentary on Romans.

Martyn, J. Louis. *Galatians: A New Translation with Introduction and Commentary*. The Anchor Bible, vol. 33A. New York: Doubleday, 1997. A once-in-a-generation commentary on Galatians. Takes very seriously the apocalyptic nature of Paul's theology and the ways this calls for rethinking how the church has typically portrayed him.

Watson, Francis. *Paul, Judaism, and the Gentiles: Beyond the New Perspective*. Grand Rapids: Eerdmans, 2007. An excellent introduction to the so-called new perspective on Paul and articulation of Watson's own position.

CHAPTER 2

Evangelism and the Gospel according to Mark

The New Testament begins with four stories of the life, death, and resurrection of Jesus. While Mark alone refers to his story as a Gospel (Mark 1:1), similar stories gradually came to be called Gospels in the church. They were introduced by the title, "The Gospel according to . . ." I follow those who believe these stories were fashioned out of traditions of eyewitness testimony handed down in early Christian communities.[1] Scholars generally recognize Mark as the first Gospel written, and Matthew and Luke as drawing on Mark in composing their narratives. Matthew and Luke also drew on a collection of Jesus's teachings and sayings commonly known as Q, as well as on special material each had at his disposal. In this chapter we focus on the Gospel of Mark, and in the next, the Gospel of John.

The Gospel as Narrated

As we have seen in the letters of Paul, the term "gospel" initially referred to the good news of God's salvation of the world in Jesus Christ. This message was shared with others via face-to-face preaching, teaching, and personal testimony. In a secondary way the term also was used to refer to acts of Christian witness that embodied this message and to letters Paul wrote to his communities, helping them deal with specific issues. With Mark, a new genre of gospel sharing comes into being. The gospel now takes the form of a written narrative. The purpose of Mark's story is the same as that of Paul's preaching, teaching, and personal testimony: to share the good news of God's salvation of the world in Jesus Christ. The gospel stories are a new genre of literature.

---

1. Richard Bauckham, *Jesus and the Eyewitnesses: The Gospels as Eyewitness Testimony* (Grand Rapids: Eerdmans, 2006).

Resembling Greco-Roman biographies, they tell the story of Jesus's life.[2] But unlike those biographies, gospel stories are told to persuade readers to follow Jesus as the Lord and Savior of the world and to guide and encourage Christian communities to engage in their mission. While the Gospels are similar to Greco-Roman biographies, they represent a new genre of literature.

As we explore what evangelism might mean today in conversation with Mark and John, it is important to take seriously the shift from letters to gospel stories as genres. Paul's letters were written to particular communities to help them bring the gospel to bear on specific issues. It is likely that the Gospels were written with a broader audience in mind. They were circulated among many congregations. Moreover, the Gospels take the form of a narrative. It is important to pay attention to the way each story is told: its structure, literary features, characters, and themes.

Each Gospel appeals to the imagination through the story itself, the ways it portrays Jesus as God's Messiah and Son and the response of other characters to him—the crowds, persons in need, the religious and political leaders, and, most of all, his disciples. The story of salvation unfolds through events that ultimately lead to Jerusalem, where Jesus is crucified and his disciples scatter—only to encounter him later as their resurrected Lord. It is no accident that the authors of the Gospels are often described as evangelists. In narrating the gospel, they are inviting people to faith, and they have much to teach us about how this might be done today. Lengthy books have been written about each Gospel. My purpose here is to describe some of the features of the stories told by Mark and John as they relate to our understanding of evangelism.

A Case of Evangelistic Practice: Too Late for Me

We begin with a case written by a student of mine, George, who served two tours in Iraq and now was studying to be a pastor. The case is written in a conversational style, and I stay close to George's original words. People who have experienced firsthand the dangers of active duty in a war zone will recognize the depths of suffering lying just beneath the surface. We will offer a few brief

2. Craig S. Keener, *The Gospel of John: A Commentary*, vol. 1 (Grand Rapids: Baker Academic, 2001), 3–52. For an alternate perspective, which views the Gospels as closer to Greco-Roman historical writing, see Luke Timothy Johnson, *The Gospel of Luke*, Sacra Pagina (Collegeville, MN: Liturgical Press,1991), Kindle edition, loc. 258–339.

comments after the case and then return to it at the end of the chapter. How might Mark's Gospel help us understand what evangelism involves in this kind of situation? How might the gospel be shared in situations of trauma and guilt? Mark's narrative of a crucified God is a story of God's participation in the pain and suffering of a world caught in sin and death. The ending of Mark's Gospel, especially, emphasizes what God has done on our behalf and in our stead in light of our "caughtness" in sin and evil. It offers good news to people suffering from trauma and guilt, as well as to others whose situations are quite different. Here is George's story as he told it:

My wife's church started partnering with an inner-city church on Wednesday nights to host pizza dinners and Bible studies for "the poor." I thought it was a good idea that her church was actually doing something instead of just talking about Jesus and social justice all the time to people who were well off. So my wife and I volunteered on Wednesday nights, after dropping our kids off at the Wednesday night children's church. The church just wanted us to sit with the people, have dinner with them, talk with them. They were encouraging us to share our faith stories if possible, but I was skeptical about that. I just wanted to help these people, and I didn't see how sharing my story could help. I started out serving the pizza, and when everyone was served, I would go and sit at a table and eat my own pizza. My wife would already be having conversations with people, but I'd just eat, and then help clean up once the guy started leading the Bible study.

As I attended the gatherings regularly, I noticed this really old guy who came every week to eat pizza. We didn't talk at first, but just kind of nodded to each other. Then, one evening, he hobbled over to my table and sat with me as I ate my pizza.

"United States Marine Corps, huh?" he said and nodded at the tattoo on my arm.

"Yeah," I said. "Fallujah, Iraq, 2006."

"You must have seen some sh-t," he said.

I nodded. "What about you?" I asked. "USMC?"

"Special Forces," he said. "The Pacific Front, 1943 to '45. They'd send us in first." He grinned.

I had heard about the Special Forces in the Pacific during my Marine training. Most of those sent in first never made it out alive. At first I thought he was joking, just bragging. But then he started sharing details of their missions—the scare tactics they used, how they remained invisible, would sneak into an enemy camp and then leave without anyone knowing they had been there until they woke up the next morning. I won't write the details here, but it became clear to me that he was telling the truth.

"So, where's the beer, huh?" he asked. "I thought this was pizza and beer night."

"No, just pop and water," I said. "This is a church thing."

"So are you born again?" he asked. "Did Jesus save you?"

I laughed. "Jesus never saved me," I said. "But he made me stronger." I drank some pop.

"What do you mean he never saved you? Then why the hell are you here?" he asked, laughing.

"I mean, I believe in Jesus," I said. "But I went through some sh-t and Jesus never saved me from that."

"You mean like Fallujah?"

"Yeah, and other sh-t," I said.

"Then why the hell do you believe? I never believed in Jesus, not after what I saw and did."

"I didn't, for a while," I said. "I mean, I grew up Christian. My family is all Christian—my wife and kids. So, I kind of believed in God, but I was angry at God. My brother is a preacher, and we talked a lot about it. And he helped me see that I had to work through my sh-t first so I wouldn't be so angry at God. So I went to a veterans' home, got help—saw a counselor, you know. I put it off for a long time, but my wife finally made me do it. And it actually helped. I'm not drinking anymore. I'm still married. And now I'm at this church thing."

We were silent for a while. I thought about what the church was always saying to the volunteers about how important it was to share our stories.

"Once, when I was in Iraq, I was on guard duty," I said. "It was the side of our compound where nothing ever happened—you know, no one ever attacked that side. So we'd go there and just rest. We were so stupid. We took off our gear, because it was hot. Then, all of a sudden, we were being shot at. So we started shooting back, you know. There were like fifteen guys shooting at us. After it was over, we turned and looked at the wall behind us, and it was just covered with bullet holes, like Swiss cheese. There was no way we could have survived that. No way." I drank some pop. "And I didn't even have a scratch on me. That helped me believe in Jesus. Even though I was angry for a long time, I believed."

The old man made a noise like, "Hm," and was silent for a moment.

"Yeah, I should be dead, too," he said finally. "I should be dead. It never made sense to me, why I got out and most of my friends died. Some of them were really good people. I'm not a good person. I beat my first wife, been a drunk most of my life. If there's a God, he wouldn't bother saving me. It's too late for me."

That very easily could have been me, I thought.

"I was a drunk, too, for a while," I said. "I got so angry sometimes I wanted to kill someone. The guys at work were scared of me. But the veterans' home helped me with that. I mean, my wife made me get into counseling. And it actually helped. You could go for free if you wanted. It's not far from here. I could drive you if you need a ride."

"Ah, I've been there. They wanted me to see a shrink, too, but I got no reason to. It's too late for me. I am what I am, son. Just a mean bastard. Could you get me another root beer? My knee ain't what it used to be."

I got up and got him another pop. He drank it and stared into space while I finished my pizza. Then the Bible study started. He had always left before the Bible study, but this time he stayed. I started gathering up plates, and the old man just stared at the guy leading the Bible study. He stayed the entire time, and then afterwards, he shook my hand and made a comment about my wife being pretty and that I was smart to listen to her.

"Look, if you change your mind, let me know," I told him. "Or if you want to talk to a pastor, I can help with that."

"Yeah, when I'm ready I'll let you know," he said. Then he left.

Reflection on Evangelistic Practice

When this case was discussed in precept, the other students were surprised that George had been a Marine and served in Fallujah—even though he had a small Semper Fi tattoo on the inside of his left forearm. He was just George to them—soft-spoken, serious, with a small circle of guy friends. He had been out of the Marines for over a decade and was now a second-year seminary student. He came to Princeton Theological Seminary because his brother had done so previously. As the case indicates, his brother played a very important role in his transition back to civilian life, keeping his family together, and regaining his faith.

During class discussion, several insights emerged. Several people mentioned that George seemed to be uniquely qualified to talk to the older man. As one person put it: "It seems like the Holy Spirit brought you two together. You'd served in Fallujah, and that meant something to him. You know what it's like to be in combat. You also may have been the only person in the room who understood what it meant to be in the Special Forces in the Pacific during

World War II." Another added, "When you shared your own problems coming back home, that seemed to allow him to talk about his problems."

Several times in his write-up of the case, George mentioned that he was skeptical about simply sharing his story with others as they ate pizza together. The leaders encouraged everyone to do this and, as George exchanged stories with the older man, he recalled this, perhaps appreciating the irony. Pretty much everyone in the precept agreed the sharing of their stories was the key dynamic in the conversation. One person wanted to know what happened, and I asked George to keep this to himself until the following week. I wanted us to focus on next steps. How should George proceed?

George was very clear that he would never evangelize this older man. To him, that meant trying to convert him. His experience in the military had been that conservative Christians used their faith as a kind of talisman that protected them and that guaranteed them eternal life if they were killed. It was like a security blanket, as George put it. They had their own group and their own language. He didn't fit in. Also, he said he was "too cynical" about what he was experiencing to identify with the evangelicals. The back-and-forth between the older man and George about being saved was viewed as important to everyone in the discussion. If the relationship were to move forward, this might be a way for George to share more of his own story and, in the process, talk about what he has come to believe.

Both men use salvation language in at least two ways: (1) as divine protection from harm; (2) as being born again, saved by a decision of faith and believing in Jesus. These two meanings show up in the first exchange: "So are you born again? Did Jesus save you?" George responds: "Jesus never saved me, but he made me stronger." The older man responds: "What do you mean he never saved you? Then why the hell are you here?" George answers: "I mean, I believe in Jesus, but I went through some sh-t and Jesus never saved me from that." Later, George shares an especially harrowing experience and comments, "There was no way we could have survived that. No way. . . . That helped me believe in Jesus. Even though I was angry for a long time, I believed." The older man responds back: "Yeah, I should be dead, too. . . . It never made sense to me why I got out and most of my friends died. Some of them were really good people. I'm not a good person. I beat my first wife, been a drunk most of my life. If there's a God, he wouldn't bother saving me. It's too late for me." Is it really too late for him? George does not seem to think so. In addition to sharing his story of receiving help at the VA hospital, he offers to drive the older man there. There are signs that the man might be listening. We will return briefly to this exchange after taking a closer look at the Gospel of Mark. What does Mark's gospel story of a crucified God teach us about sharing the good news with this veteran?

Later that week after the precept discussion, I ate lunch with George. It became clear that he was very knowledgeable about Post-Traumatic Stress Disorder, or PTSD, which he experienced himself. He felt pretty sure that the older man continued to suffer the lingering effects of this disorder since his time in the Pacific. He asked me whether he should have brought it up to the class. I said he probably should have done so. This got me thinking. Why is it that evangelism so rarely draws on the human sciences in accounts of this ministry? For that matter, why does this field rarely use the case study method? I share in the final chapters why I think this method is useful in courses on practical theology. But I rarely encounter stories in the form of case studies in books on evangelism. There always are plenty of illustrative stories but almost no cases offered for reflection. If any field should give close attention to the particularities of persons and communities, it is evangelism.

As to why evangelism does not draw more on the human sciences, part of the reason may be that many people writing on evangelism are conservative theologically and do not want the human sciences to replace theological and biblical perspectives. While I agree with their concern, I do not believe interdisciplinary work always ends up this way. Nobody was more worried about importing an "alien" framework at the expense of theology than Karl Barth. We will examine him in part II of this book, and then I will take up the questions of interdisciplinarity in the final chapter.

Mark: The Gospel of a Crucified God

Mark begins his story by writing: "The beginning of the good news about Jesus the Messiah, the Son of God" (Mark 1:1).[3] The story narrates the gospel, God's salvation of the world in Jesus Christ. Our purpose in exploring Mark's story is to deepen our understanding of evangelism. We cannot explore the

---

3. Though the author of Mark is unknown, throughout this chapter I will describe him as Mark, following the traditional ascription of authorship. On a separate note, I do not follow those scholars who believe Mark uses "Son of God" like the Psalms do, as an epithet for Israel's king. Rather, I think it is used to refer to Jesus as God's Son, that is, sharing in the identity of God. Many of the functions ascribed solely to God by Israel are now shared by Jesus. See Richard Bauckham, *God Crucified: Monotheism and Christology in the New Testament* (Carlisle: Paternoster, 1998).

narrative with the depth of a commentary. That would take an entire book. Rather, we will focus on two themes woven into the story: the theme of Jesus's identity and the theme of the characters' varied responses to Jesus, especially the disciples'.[4] These themes dovetail with our interest in exploring what the gospel is, its relationship to salvation, how we might invite others to respond, and the sort of response we might look for.

The theme of Jesus's identity is, perhaps, the most important way Mark depicts his understanding of the gospel. Jesus is the Messiah and Son of God. But unlike conventional expectations of these figures, Jesus must suffer and die. This is the "secret of the kingdom." Though readers know the identity of Jesus from the beginning, most of the characters in the story do not. Initially, only the unclean spirits recognize who Jesus is. Jesus tries to keep his identity a secret because he will not fulfill the expectations people hold about the Messiah. He will be a crucified Messiah. He will not be a political or religious leader who liberates Israel from oppression and restores it to glory.

At two key points, Jesus describes his mission as serving as a "ransom for many" (Mark 10:45) and as sealing a new covenant "for many" in his blood (Mark 14:24). These passages are best understood in the larger context of Mark's story. The narrative of Jesus's words and actions renders his identity. It also renders the identity of the one who sent him. Through Jesus, we come to know God as the Father of Jesus Christ. The story of Jesus's suffering and death reveals, not only who Jesus is, but also who God is.

The second theme deals with the characters' responses to Jesus: who they understand him to be, the faith they place in him, and the ways they, often, fail to grasp Jesus's identity and are disloyal to him. We pay special attention to the disciples and to Peter in particular. We will need to make sense of the negative portrait of the disciples as the story turns toward Jerusalem and the passion narrative. What is Mark trying to tell us by portraying the disciples so negatively? His depiction of Peter is especially puzzling. Peter is one of the most revered and respected leaders in the early Christian community. What is Mark communicating about the gospel through the theme of Peter and the disciples' failure?

We begin with a brief overview of the structure of Mark's story and then explore these themes together in parts of the Gospel, giving special attention to passages relevant to evangelism.

4. See Richard Hays, *The Moral Vision of the New Testament: Community, Cross, New Creation—A Contemporary Introduction to New Testament Ethics* (San Francisco: HarperCollins, 1996), 25-30.

Mark's narrative can be seen as falling into four basic parts:[5]

1. *Introduction—Mark 1:1-13:* A brief introduction that lets readers in on the secret of who Jesus is. In the end, this initial perspective does not provide readers with everything they need to know.
2. *The Galilean ministry—Mark 1:14-8:26:* Jesus's ministry in the area of Galilee, which focuses on his healing and teaching of the crowds and his disciples. Jesus's popularity is great in this part of the story, though he faces opposition from the beginning of his public ministry.
3. *Preparation for Jesus's suffering and death—Mark 8:27-10:52:* The story follows Jesus as he journeys from the area around Galilee to Jerusalem. Jesus is on his way to the cross. He attempts to prepare his disciples for what lies ahead. Three times he teaches his disciples about his death and resurrection. Three times his disciples fail to understand what this means. Jesus attempts to correct their misunderstandings about who he is and what it means to follow him on the way to the cross. Peter confesses that Jesus is the Messiah. But he does not really understand what this means. Nor do the rest of the disciples.
4. *The events in Jerusalem and the passion—Mark 11:1-16:8:* Jesus enters Jerusalem and his conflict with the religious leaders becomes more intense. In the end, Jesus goes to the cross alone. His frightened disciples have abandoned him. Only the women among his followers accompany him to the cross. Shortly before he dies, Jesus cries out: "My God, my God, why have you forsaken me?" Even God appears to have abandoned him. When Jesus dies, the Twelve are nowhere to be found. Even John the Baptist's disciples claimed John's body and buried him after he was killed by Herod (Mark 6:29). This is not true of Jesus's disciples. Mary Magdalene, Mary the mother of James, and Salome go to the tomb to anoint Jesus's body with spices. They encounter a man in a white robe who tells them that God has raised Jesus from the dead, and he has gone ahead to meet his disciples in Galilee, as he promised. They are to share this good news with the disciples and Peter. "Trembling and bewildered, the women went out and fled from the tomb. They said nothing to anyone, because they were afraid" (Mark 16:8). With these words, Mark's Gospel ends.

5. For different ways of viewing the structure of Mark's story, see Donald H. Juel, *A Master of Surprise: Mark Interpreted* (Minneapolis: Augsburg Fortress, 1994), 22-26, and Francis J. Mahoney, SDB, *The Gospel of Mark: A Commentary* (Peabody, MA: Hendrickson, 2002), 17-21.

Introduction—Mark 1:1-13

Mark begins by creating a link between his story and prior traditions of the gospel: "The beginning of the good news about Jesus the Messiah, the Son of God" (Mark 1:1). He then adds a quotation ascribed to Isaiah.[6] By citing Israel's Scripture, Mark indicates there is divine preparation for the story he is about to tell. John the Baptist, who is baptizing people in the Jordan River, is the promised forerunner of the Messiah who "prepares the way for the Lord" (Mark 1:2-3).[7] John tells the people that one is coming who is greater than him, for he will baptize them not with water but with the Holy Spirit.

Jesus comes to be baptized by John, "a baptism of repentance for the forgiveness of sin." As this takes place, Jesus sees the heavens "being torn open and the Spirit descending on him like a dove." A voice from heaven says, "You are my Son, whom I love; with you I am well pleased" (Mark 1:10-11). This draws on Psalm 2:7 and Isaiah 42:1. The former is part of a royal psalm in which God addresses his "anointed" as Son. By the first century, this psalm was regarded "as a prediction of the coming King from the line of David who would arise to save Israel."[8] The phrase "in you I am well pleased" relates Jesus to the mysterious servant of Second Isaiah: "Here is my servant, whom I uphold, my chosen one in whom I delight; I will put my Spirit on him and he will bring justice to the nations" (Isa. 42:1).

After Jesus's baptism, the Spirit sends him into the wilderness for forty days, where he is tempted by Satan. Mark adds few details about what takes place while Jesus is in the wilderness. The encounter with Satan signifies the cosmic dimensions of Jesus's mission. He does not merely face the opposition of human beings. He battles the forces of the evil one who holds human beings captive. Later, Jesus depicts his casting out of unclean spirits as plundering Satan's household (Mark 3:23-27; cf. 4:15; 8:33).

Mark packs a great deal into the opening of his story. He provides readers a preview of Jesus's identity and mission. Jesus is God's Son and Messiah, anointed with the Spirit. He identifies with the people by sharing their baptism for the forgiveness of sin. He resists the allure of the evil one. His story is foretold in Israel's Scripture. Yet there also is a note of tension in the introduction of Mark's story, captured nicely by Donald Juel:

6. This is actually a conflation of Malachi 3:1 and Isaiah 40:3.

7. Joel Marcus, *The Way of the Lord: Christological Exegesis of the Old Testament in the Gospel of Mark* (Louisville: Westminster John Knox, 1992), ch. 2.

8. Donald H. Juel, *Mark*, Augsburg Commentary on the New Testament (Minneapolis: Augsburg, 1990), 35.

The setting is all wrong. Jesus should be among the mighty, in the great city that served David as his citadel, not among sinners who have come to repent of their sins. . . . The promised deliverer has been confirmed and anointed for his appointed tasks. Yet he looks nothing like what was expected; he is in the wrong place, associating with the wrong people. Jesus' career begins with a tension between what is expected of God and what God actually provides. As the narrative progresses, the tension increases rather than decreases.[9]

Mark reminds us that evangelism cannot avoid the expectations people bring to conversations, relationships, and stories about Jesus. Some may have grown up in the church and dropped out during adolescence or young adulthood. Perhaps they remember Jesus as "meek and mild" or as a frightening figure used to keep them in line. Or maybe, they were not raised in the church and only know Jesus through popular culture or college courses antagonistic toward religion. Every person's expectations will be different, and good evangelism pays attention to them.

Mark's introduction reminds us that it is likely that our preconceptions of Jesus stand in tension with the gospel story he tells. He challenges our understanding of who Jesus is and who we are. He heals us, guides us, and offers meaning for our lives beyond anything we might expect. To receive these gifts, we must let go of our preconceptions of Jesus. Good evangelists know how to walk with people as they begin this process.

The Galilean Ministry—Mark 1:14-8:26

This section includes many stories of Jesus's healing, teaching, and preaching as he travels to villages throughout the area in and around Galilee. As Jesus moves from place to place, he proclaims "the good news of God" (Mark 1:14).[10] Mark summarizes Jesus's message: "The time has come. . . . The kingdom of God has come near. Repent and believe the good news" (Mark 1:15).[11] This frames the stories that follow. These stories will focus

9. Juel, *Mark*, 36.
10. The Gospel, thus, is not just Mark's story as a whole—the narrative about Jesus—but also what Jesus proclaims (and does). Helping readers understand the relationship between his Gospel and the gospel Jesus preached and taught is one of the purposes of Mark's story.
11. For an excellent discussion of this passage, see James Dunn, *Jesus' Call to Dis-*

on Jesus's relationship to the kingdom of God. This is one of the keys to understanding Jesus's identity.

Jesus's audience would have been familiar with the language of the kingdom of God. It is a frequent image of God in the Psalms and other parts of Israel's Scripture, where God is described as a king. The language of kingdom does not signify so much a place as the reign of God. During the period of Israel's exile and later, the idea of God's kingly reign was associated with the hope that God would save Israel from captivity and establish his rule over Israel anew in the sight of the nations. As Isaiah 52:10 puts it, when God returns to Zion to comfort and redeem his people, "The Lord will bare his holy arm in the sight of all the nations, and all the ends of the earth will see the salvation of our God." When this occurs, the nations will participate in God's salvation of Israel and will worship God.

The kingdom of God is a central theme in Jesus's preaching and teaching. He introduces his parables thirteen times in Mark with the expression, "The kingdom of God is like . . ."[12] During Jesus's Galilean ministry, he is accused by teachers from Jerusalem of casting out demons through the power of Satan. He responds by saying, "If a kingdom is divided against itself, the kingdom cannot stand." He casts out demons through the power of God's Spirit, not the power of Satan. Matthew later edits this story from Mark to make the point even clearer: "But if it is by the Spirit of God that I drive out demons, then the kingdom of God has come upon you" (Matt. 12:28).

In Mark, Jesus proclaims that "the time" has arrived and the kingdom has "come near." God's long-hoped-for reign, bringing salvation to Israel in the sight of the nations, has finally arrived in Jesus's words and deeds. Though the kingdom has come near (literally, "is at the door"), it is not yet present in its fullness. It remains a future reality. Later, Mark describes the future arrival of the kingdom with Jewish apocalyptic imagery in 13:1-37. Jesus is portrayed as saying that before the kingdom arrives in its fullness, "the gospel must first be preached to all the nations" and that his followers will suffer persecution on his account (Mark 13:10-11). The hour of the kingdom's coming is known only by God—not the angels or even God's Son (Mark 13:32). God's promised future, however, is breaking into the present through Jesus's ministry, and Jesus calls his hearers to respond: "Repent and believe the good news!"

---

cipleship (New York: Cambridge University Press, 1992). I am informed by Dunn in the following discussion.

12. Luke adds an additional eighteen references and Matthew thirty-six references, using the expression "the kingdom of Heaven."

The word translated "repent" (*metanoia*) means to change your mind or feel remorse and regret. Jesus, however, is calling for something more fundamental. The idea of repentance in Israel's Scripture is closely related to the prophets' call for people who have departed from God to turn around and return to him. Isaiah 55:7 puts it like this: "Let the wicked forsake their ways and the unrighteous their thoughts. Let them turn to the Lord, and he will have mercy on them, and to our God, for he will freely pardon." Similarly, Jeremiah (3:12, 14, 22) and Hosea (6:1) call Israel to return to God. Repentance is not about feeling guilty. It is about turning around and heading in a new direction, back to God.

This new direction is described in the second half of the sentence: "believe the good news." God's kingly rule has drawn near in Jesus's words and deeds. To believe involves acknowledging who Jesus is and trusting him. In the rest of Jesus's Galilean ministry, characters respond to Jesus in different ways. Some respond by placing their faith in him; others are amazed by his teaching and healings but do not really know what to make of him. Some believe and begin to follow him; others see him as a threat to the religious and the political order and begin to plot his death.

Mark's story makes it clear that turning from our former way of life and turning to a life of discipleship is not easy. He depicts this as a process of following Jesus. First steps are important in following Jesus, but they remain first steps. Jesus's disciples, in particular, show amazing trust in him at some points in the story. But these are followed by equally amazing acts of misunderstanding and disloyalty that reveal a failure to grasp who he is.

In dialogue with Mark's Gospel, we are encouraged to think of evangelism as inviting people to follow Jesus. This is a process of turning away from an old way of life and turning to a new life of discipleship. The emphasis is not just on the moment of calling, important as this is. It also is the process of following Jesus who lives in perfect obedience to his Father. Mark's story shows us that following Jesus is costly and difficult because it involves learning to follow a crucified Messiah who challenges our preconceptions. In the introduction, we initially portrayed evangelism in terms of calling: "communicating the gospel in ways that help particular individuals or groups hear God's call." We must now move beyond this to include supporting and guiding people as they begin to follow Jesus. Some of the parables of Jesus depict people who start strong and fade quickly. They need Jesus's continuing encouragement and teaching, as well as the support of other disciples. This is clear as Mark's story unfolds.

Immediately after Mark's summary of Jesus's message (Mark 1:14-15), he shares the story of Jesus calling Simon Peter and his brother Andrew while they are fishing. He says "Come, follow me and I will send you out to fish for people" (1:17). They leave "at once." Jesus then calls James and his brother John, and they too depart immediately. They leave their father in the boat with hired men and follow Jesus (1:20). Not long after this, Jesus calls Levi, a tax collector, telling him, "Follow me." Levi immediately leaves his booth and "follows him" (2:14). The disciples respond to Jesus's call. A first step is taken, and we should not underestimate what this involves.

Leaving families and livelihoods to follow Jesus is a radical step. It represents a breach of obligations to families, parents, and community. Later, Peter will say to Jesus, "We have left everything to follow you" (Mark 10:28). As the disciples take this first step it is clear that Jesus wants them to share in his ministry, to "fish for people" as he puts it. Later, he appoints twelve of his followers to share in his preaching and healing ministry (3:13–19), and not long after he sends them out two by two. Mark tersely summarizes their ministry by saying that they preached repentance, cast out unclean spirits, and healed the sick (6:7–13). These are precisely the things Jesus does in this part of Mark's story.

The calling of the disciples thus initiates the first step of following Jesus. It is an invitation to become part of the community Jesus is gathering around him. When Jesus's mother and brothers come to take him away, he looks at those around him and says, "Here are my mother and my brothers! Whoever does God's will is my brother and sister and mother" (Mark 3:32–34). Jesus is gathering a new family around him to share in his ministry. The invitation to join this family is a very important part of evangelism. As I have said and will say again, we must move beyond our highly individualistic views of evangelism. Inviting people to acknowledge that God has come near in Jesus to bring us salvation always includes an invitation to follow him as part of a community of disciples.

We learn three other things about evangelism from this part of Mark's story. First, words and deeds are both central to the way Jesus communicates the good news of God's kingly rule. Stories of healing are just as prominent in Jesus's Galilean ministry as stories of Jesus's teaching. They are manifestations of God's power, his kingly rule through Jesus. They elicit amazement from the crowds. Even when Jesus tells those he has healed not to share what they have experienced, they often cannot contain themselves. After he heals a leper, for example, and tells him not to share what has happened with anyone, the leper "began to talk freely and share the news" (Mark 1:45). Large crowds begin to come to Jesus, bringing those afflicted by diseases, infirmities, and unclean spirits. Jesus tries to escape to "lonely places" (1:45), but the crowds seek him out. They are so large that he must teach them from a boat on a lake. Clearly, healing and deeds of compassion strike a chord with the crowds, and they continue to do so today. We saw this in the case of Ariana Diaz who prayed that Paula Arrowsmith's depression would lift. Ariana believed it was important in renewing Paula's faith. The importance of words and deeds also helps us to move beyond the dichotomy between ministries of social justice and compassion, on the one hand, and evangelism, on the other. This is a false and unbiblical dichotomy. Deeds are just as important as words in the way Jesus shares the gospel of God. They are part of the way he embodies the kingdom drawing near.

Second, Jesus crosses religious boundaries to bring the healing power of God's kingdom to those in need. He heals a leper, who is ritually unclean (Mark 1:40-42); he forgives and heals a paralyzed man, drawing the charge of blasphemy from the Pharisees (2:3-12); he heals a man with a shriveled hand on the Sabbath, violating the law according to the Pharisees (3:1-6); he acknowledges the faith of a woman bleeding for many years who has the audacity to touch his cloak and who is ritually unclean (5:25-34); and he heals the daughter of a Syrophoenician woman, an outsider to Israel, because of her faith (7:24-30). Those in desperate need seek Jesus out. They trust him to provide help, and he responds by healing their afflictions.

The love and compassion of God's kingly rule are not confined to those who are "deserving" according to the standards of the teachers of the law who are trying to protect Israel's holiness. When criticized by the Pharisees for eating with "tax collectors and sinners," Jesus responds: "It is not the healthy who need a doctor, but the sick. I have not come to call the righteous, but sinners" (Mark 2:17). Every character in Mark's Gospel is sick and a sinner in need of a doctor. The boundaries set up by religious leaders to separate the holy from the unclean are broken down in Jesus's ministry. The religious leaders are worse off than the sinners they condemn. They do not recognize that God's kingly rule is breaking in through Jesus's ministry.

We would do well to acknowledge the ways we too draw boundaries between good people and sinners that keep us from reaching out to those in need. Observing such boundaries, whether consciously or not, aligns us with the religious leaders in Mark's story who begin to plot to kill Jesus because of his indiscriminate sharing of God's love with those considered unworthy.[13]

---

13. The involvement of the Herodians in plotting to kill Jesus (Mark 3:6; 12:13) is indicative of the threat he must have represented to the political establishment. Obviously, Pontius Pilate later passes the sentence of death.

Today, as then, it is the needy, marginalized, and excluded who often are most open to placing their faith in God's Son.

This leads to a third issue raised by his healings. Why does Jesus consistently forbid the unclean spirits who recognize his identity from sharing who he is with others? Why does he repeatedly tell people he has healed to remain silent about what he has done? This is an important dimension of the "messianic secret" in Mark's story. We, the readers, know who Jesus is from the very first sentence of Mark's Gospel. He is God's Messiah and Son. But Jesus does not want this secret to be widely shared. We have noted one reason already. Jesus will not fulfill popular expectations associated with the Messiah. We now can add another reason.

Jesus's healing ministry is one of the ways he turns common understandings of power upside down. God's kingly rule as manifested in his healings is offered to those who are ritually unclean, marginalized, or vulnerable. This brings Jesus into conflict with the powerful in the religious and political establishment of his day. Later, Jesus will explain to his disciples that the great among them are those who serve (Mark 9:33-37; 10:37-45). By serving, he means following his way of embodying the kingdom, working on behalf of those who are most needy, and helping one another. He is concerned that his healings might be misconstrued as the powerful deeds of a wonder-worker or charismatic leader who gathers power to himself. There were other charismatic leaders during Jesus's time who attracted followings built on displays of powerful preaching and dramatic healings. They are found in our age as well. Evangelism on the pattern of Jesus is not based on this kind of power. God's power manifested in and through Jesus is the power of the cross. It is the power of love and forgiveness, reconciliation and redemption. It reaches out to those in need, even to the point of dying in their place. This is the power of the gospel we share. It stands at the heart of evangelism.

In addition to healing, Mark also portrays Jesus as teaching during his Galilean ministry. Jesus typically teaches in parables, a form of speech in which Jesus uses things his audience is familiar with to help them understand the kingdom of God.[14] Parables draw on common situations in everyday life to depict God's kingly rule in Jesus's ministry. We see this in three parables

14. After studying the parables in Matthew and Luke, as well as in Mark, Arland Hultgren offers a more comprehensive definition: "A parable is a figure of speech in which a comparison is made between God's kingdom, actions, or expectations and something in this world, real or imagined." See *The Parables of Jesus: A Commentary* (Grand Rapids: Eerdmans, 2000), 3.

often associated with evangelism: the parables of the sower, the growing seed, and the mustard seed.

The parable of the sower (Mark 4:3–8) draws on the image of a farmer who scatters seeds on various kinds of terrain. His planting appears lavish and even careless, for he does not take account of the potential hazards of the field he is planting. Some seeds fall on the path and are eaten by birds. Others fall amid rocks and are scorched by the sun as soon as they begin to grow. Others fall among thorns and are choked off, so they do not bear grain. Finally, some seeds fall on good soil and produce a bountiful harvest, multiplying a hundred times. In private, the disciples ask Jesus to explain what the parable means. This serves as an opportunity for Jesus to share why he teaches in parables and to explain the parable he has just shared.

Many commentators view the parable of the sower as authentic to Jesus and the explanation as later Christian exposition in allegorical form that applies it to the church. Whether this is the case or not, Mark's narrative weaves the parable and explanation together in ways that are instructive. The parable appears to address people who are skeptical of Jesus's claim that God's kingly rule is at work in his ministry among such unpromising circles. His work will bear fruit in spite of how careless or extravagant he might appear in spreading his message among all kinds of people. Indeed, the yield will far surpass what might be expected.

In his explanation, Jesus clarifies how this might apply to the situation of the disciples when they begin to share the gospel (here called "the word") in the future. The seed of the word will fall on different kinds of soil, which represent people who respond to the word in different ways. Some of these responses are discouraging, but the disciples must trust that their work, like that of Jesus, will yield a great crop. It will far surpass what might be expected.

Like the disciples, we too are called to share in Jesus's ministry of proclaiming the word, the gospel of God. Too many churches and Christians neglect this ministry. From the very first, Jesus tells his followers that he will teach them to "fish for people." If we were to take this seriously, we too might grow discouraged with the way people respond. We would do well to remember Jesus's explanation to his disciples. We should not expect every evangelistic initiative to be successful. But we can trust that God will use our work to yield a great crop. We must also remember that Jesus seemed to be careless and even extravagant in sharing the gospel with all kinds of people. Perhaps we restrict our work to "those like us," failing to plant seeds on "good soil" open to God's word.

Jesus offers two additional parables that add to our understanding of evangelism. These are offered to the crowd (Mark 4:33-34). Perhaps Jesus explained them in private to the disciples, though Mark does not record what he says. In one parable Jesus draws again on the imagery of planting seeds to describe the kingdom of God (4:26-29). Here he emphasizes the importance of patience and trust in God. Once the farmer has planted the seeds, he has little control over the natural process. Growth will come in its own time. It cannot be forced. But it will come, and when the grain is ripe the farmer will reap the harvest. In Jesus's ministry, God's kingly rule is at work, and he trusts that God will bring the harvest in his own good time. Like the disciples who share in Jesus's ministry, we too are encouraged to remain patient and trust God in evangelism. The results cannot be forced! God is working in unseen ways. In the end only God can bring to fruition the seeds we plant. We must trust this and refrain from manipulating or pressuring others.

The final parable Jesus offers in this section draws on the imagery of the mustard seed (Mark 4:30-32). It is the smallest of seeds but becomes the greatest of shrubs. Like a tree, it provides shade for birds. The inbreaking of God's kingdom in Jesus's ministry seems small and insignificant. But just wait, he implies, something great will follow. Is Jesus hinting here at the spread of his movement or the later growth of the church? Is this a church growth parable? This is unlikely. In this parable of the kingdom, he is comparing the small beginnings of God's reign in his ministry to the fulness of God's kingdom in all its glory at the consummation. The two are related, like a small seed and a great shrub. If you want to understand the nature of God's kingly rule, then look at what Jesus is doing. This is a key task of evangelism: helping people grasp the Christian claim that when we look at Jesus we see what God is like, or even better we see one who shares in the identity of God.[15] The challenge this poses becomes clear as we focus on the disciples' struggle to grasp the secret of the kingdom— that Jesus will suffer and die on a cross.

Mark introduces this theme in the midst of Jesus's teaching of the parables we have just examined. Jesus tells the disciples why he teaches in parables. Following the parable of the sower Jesus draws the disciples aside, and they begin to ask him about the parables. He responds: "The secret of the kingdom of God has been given to you. But to those on the outside everything is in parables so that 'they may be ever seeing but never perceiving, and

---

15. As noted above, I follow here Bauckham, *God Crucified*, who argues this high Christology is found across the New Testament and not confined to the Gospel according to John.

ever hearing but never understanding; otherwise they might turn and be forgiven'" (Mark 4:11-12; Isa. 6:9-10).

Jesus appears to be creating a sharp distinction between "insiders" and "outsiders." He explains this with Isaiah 6:9-10. On one side are those who see but don't perceive and hear but don't understand. On the other side are those who grasp what Jesus is teaching them about the kingdom. Those on the "inside," his disciples, will be taught the secret of the kingdom, that he must suffer and die as God's crucified Messiah and Son. Those on the "outside," the crowds and religious leaders, will not grasp this secret and thus will fail to understand what God is doing through him. They will not repent and believe. Indeed, the Isaiah passage almost seems to imply that Jesus teaches in parables to prevent outsiders from understanding.

Evangelism often relies heavily on the distinction between insiders and outsiders. Those who are saved, go to church, and live according to the conventional standards of Christian morality have no need to hear the gospel anew. They are insiders. Evangelism is for outsiders who need the message that insiders have to offer them. Is this what Jesus is saying here? It is true that Jesus calls some to be his disciples and not others. It also is true that he draws his disciples aside to teach them the secret of the kingdom. As Mark's story moves along, however, the clear distinction between insiders and outsiders breaks down. Those who have been given the secret of the kingdom are like "outsiders" who see but don't perceive and hear but don't understand.

Already during the Galilean ministry this begins to take place. It foreshadows what is to come. In one story Jesus sleeps while they cross a lake and a storm begins to swamp the boat. The disciples wake Jesus up and say, "Teacher, don't you care if we drown?" After calming the winds, Jesus replies, "Why are you so afraid? Do you still have no faith?" (Mark 4:36-41). Later, after Jesus feeds five thousand people, the disciples begin to cross the lake. They see Jesus walking on the water and are terrified. Jesus calms their fears and joins them in the boat. The narrator comments that "they were completely amazed, for they had not understood about the loaves; their hearts were hardened" (6:47-52). Not long after, Jesus feeds another large crowd. He is challenged by the Pharisees to offer a sign and warns his disciples to beware of the yeast of the Pharisees. The disciples think he is upset because they have forgotten to bring bread for their journey. Jesus responds: "Why are you talking about having no bread? Do you still not see or understand? Are your hearts hardened? Do you have eyes but fail to see, and ears but fail to hear?" (8:17-18). The language echoes Isaiah 6:9-10, which Jesus used to explain why he teaches in parables. Only now it is the disciples who are outsiders.

A pattern is emerging in Mark's story. Jesus calls the disciples and describes those who follow him as his new family. He uses parables to teach the crowd that the kingdom is breaking in through his ministry. He explains the parables to the disciples so they will understand the secret of the kingdom. But they fail to understand. All is not lost. Jesus follows his explanation of the parable of the sower by saying: "Do you bring a lamp to put it under a bowl or a bed? Instead, don't you put it on its stand? For whatever is hidden is meant to be disclosed, and whatever is concealed is meant to be brought out into the open" (Mark 4:21-22). "Insiders" and "outsiders" alike await the disclosure of the secret of the kingdom of God. Mark's Gospel challenges us to rethink evangelism as directed exclusively to outsiders. Those who are "insiders" need to hear the gospel anew. Otherwise, they will never learn what it means to follow Jesus on his way to the cross.

Preparation for His Suffering and Death—Mark 8:27-10:52

The third part of Mark's story describes Jesus on his way to Jerusalem. Six times in this part, Mark uses the term "way," recalling the passage from Isaiah with which Mark introduced his gospel story: "Prepare the way of the Lord, make straight paths for him" (Mark 1:3).[16] As Jesus turns toward Jerusalem, he is on the way to fulfilling his mission. His disciples follow him on the way. Three times on the journey, Jesus teaches the disciples that he will be killed in Jerusalem and will be raised from the dead.[17] Each time, the disciples do or say something that indicates they do not understand what Jesus is telling them. Each time, Jesus follows with teaching that focuses on the nature of true discipleship.

Richard Hays outlines this pattern:[18]

Passion Prediction	Misunderstanding	Corrective Teaching
8:31	8:32-33	8:34-9:1
9:31	9:33-34	9:35-37 (35-50?)
10:32-34	10:35-41	10:42-45

16. Mark 8:27; 9:33-34; 10:17, 32, 46, 52.

17. While I refer to the passages as "passion predictions," this is not quite accurate. They refer to Jesus's resurrection from the dead as well.

18. Hays, Moral Vision, 81.

The first instance of this pattern begins with the story of Peter's confession at Caesarea Philippi (Mark 8:27-38). Jesus asks his disciples: "Who do people say I am?" They reply that some believe he is John the Baptist, Elijah, or one of the prophets. Jesus then asks the question in a more pointed way: "But what about you? Who do you say I am?" Peter responds, "You are the Messiah." Jesus "warns" them not to tell anyone about him. He then teaches them that he must suffer many things. He will be rejected by the religious leaders and "must be killed and after three days rise again."[19]

Peter pulls him aside and rebukes him. Jesus in turn rebukes Peter, saying: "Get behind me, Satan. You do not have in mind the concerns of God, but merely human concerns." Jesus is the Messiah, as Peter has confessed. But he is not the sort of Messiah Peter has in mind. Peter is oblivious to the secret of the kingdom that Jesus is trying to teach his disciples: He will be a crucified Messiah. Jesus invites the crowd to join the disciples and teaches them that his followers must "take up their cross and follow me," adding that "whoever loses their life for me and for the gospel will save it" (Mark 8:34-38). At the beginning of Mark's story, Jesus invites people to repent and believe in response to the inbreaking of God's kingdom in his ministry. We are now beginning to realize the radicalism of this claim on those who follow his way. They are to give up (crucify) old ways of life and follow the way of Jesus. We gain further insight into the way of Jesus as Mark's story unfolds.

After Jesus teaches the disciples a second time that he will be delivered into the hands of men who will kill him and that he will rise after three days, the disciples once more fail to grasp his teaching: "But they did not understand what he meant and were afraid to ask him about it" (Mark 9:31-32). As they continue on their way, they begin to argue about who is the greatest. When Jesus asks them what they were talking about, they refuse to tell him. Jesus calls the Twelve to him and says, "Anyone who wants to be first must be the very last, and the servant of all" (9:35). He takes a child in his arms and says, "Whoever welcomes one of these little children in my name welcomes me, and whoever welcomes me does not welcome me but the one who sent me" (9:37).

Jesus is traveling the way to the cross; the disciples are arguing about rank, position, and status. They do not grasp what it means to follow in his way.

---

19. Note the elements of divine necessity implied by "must" and the clear reference to the resurrection. Both also are present in the second and third passion predictions (Mark 9:30-32; 10:32-34), where the language of "delivered over" signals divine involvement. These elements are important to our interpretation of the way Mark ends his Gospel.

Children had no status in the ancient world. Jesus's parabolic action of drawing a child to him represents the kind of leadership and hospitality he expects his followers to embody. They are to serve and welcome those with no status, not argue about "human concerns." When they follow his way, they welcome not only him but also the one who sent him. God is present among those with no status. Disciples must welcome them just as Jesus heals those outside the boundaries of religious purity and eats with tax collectors and sinners.

The third passion prediction follows a similar pattern. As they continue "on their way up to Jerusalem with Jesus leading the way" (Mark 10:32), Jesus speaks of his death and resurrection a third time, adding more detail about his suffering than the first two predictions. Perhaps he is trying to shock the disciples into grasping what he is saying. Shortly afterward, James and John, the sons of Zebedee, ask Jesus if he will place them on his right and left hands when he comes in his glory. The other disciples are indignant, and once more Jesus tries to teach them the nature of true discipleship. It is not about positions of power and authority like the gentiles who lord it over their subordinates. He continues, "Instead, whoever wants to become great among you must be your servant, and whoever wants to be first must be slave of all. For even the Son of Man did not come to be served, but to serve, and to give his life as a ransom for many" (10:43–45).

Once again Jesus teaches his followers that discipleship turns conventional standards of status and power upside down. The term translated "slave" literally means "one who waits on tables." Leaders are to wait on others. They are to serve as Jesus serves, not to worry about their status and authority. They are to serve God's kingly rule that reaches out to those in need—those in the grip of evil, those excluded from religion and society, those devastated by terrible afflictions.

A new element appears in this third passion prediction. Jesus tells his disciples that he will give his life as "a ransom for many" (Mark 10:45). We explore this later in the context of Jesus's final meal with his disciples, where he portrays his death as sealing a new covenant for many in his blood (14:24). For now, we focus on the disciples' response to Jesus. Earlier in the story, they responded to Jesus's call. They left their families and livelihoods to follow him. They now recognize his identity as the Messiah. But three times in this part of the story the disciples fail to grasp what it means to follow a Messiah who will suffer and die.

Two things very important for evangelism emerge from this part of Mark's story. The Twelve are not the only people who have difficulty understanding why Jesus had to die and what this has to do with salvation. Any pastor who is serious about equipping his or her congregation to share the gospel with others needs to teach and preach on this again and again. The keys are God's love and the reality of human sin. Mark uses the imagery of ransom and new covenant to explain this, which adds to the images and concepts that the apostle Paul employs. The second note sounded in this part of the story is the cruciform shape of discipleship. The disciples are stuck in categories of power, status, and authority that directly oppose those Jesus is trying to teach his disciples. Those who live under his kingly rule begin to live in a different way than the surrounding world. While learning what it means to follow Jesus to the cross is never completed, I believe the elementary catechesis provided new Christians and even people who are joining a particular congregation for the first time, should include teaching on this theme as part of Discipleship 101. If you do not get the meaning of the cross in at least an elementary way, then you are going to have difficulty understanding the gospel.

The Events in Jerusalem and the Passion—Mark 11:1–16:8

The fourth part brings us to the climax of Mark's story, which culminates in the passion of Jesus and the announcement of the good news that Jesus has risen and gone ahead of his disciples to Galilee. We focus on three themes that are central to Mark's portrait of Jesus's identity in this part of his story and the characters' responses: (1) Jesus's death as being "according to Scripture," (2) the Passover meal and trial of Jesus, and (3) the failure and disloyalty of the disciples in the events leading up to Jesus's crucifixion, starkly portrayed in the lack of closure in the ending of Mark's story. Each theme has important implications for the way we think about evangelism.

According to Scripture

At three points in this part of the story, Jesus describes events as unfolding according to Scripture: Mark 14:21, 27, and 49. We found this theme in Paul too, but in Mark it plays a different role.

Jesus enters Jerusalem riding on a donkey (Mark 11:1–10). The scene is filled with imagery from Israel's royal traditions. The crowd cries out with words from Psalm 118:26: "Blessed is he who comes in the name of the Lord." The scene alludes to Zechariah 9:9 (cited in Matt. 21:5), which draws on the role of a donkey in the ritual installation of kings in Israel (described in 1 Kings 1). Mark continues to draw on royal imagery throughout this part of the story. In spite of all appearances, the events of Jesus's suffering and death embody the kingly rule of God. But this will be evident only to those who interpret these events in light of Israel's Scripture.

Jesus briefly visits the temple and then goes to Bethany to spend the night. He returns to the temple courts the next day and disrupts the business of the money changers and those selling animals for ritual sacrifice (Mark 11:15-17). Jesus explains his parabolic action by drawing from Isaiah 56:7-8 and Jeremiah 7:4-11: "Is it not written: 'My house will be called a house of prayer for all the nations'? But you have made it 'a den of robbers.'" The first part depicts gentiles as included in God's salvation if they keep justice, do righteousness, and honor the sabbath. The second part comes from Jeremiah's famous denunciation of the temple and his prediction of its destruction: "Do not trust in deceptive words and say: 'This is the temple of the Lord, the temple of the Lord, the temple of the Lord.' . . . Has this house, which bears my Name, become a den of robbers to you?" (Jer. 7:4, 11). Jesus is not merely condemning the corruption of the merchants but alluding to the destruction of the temple. The chief priests and teachers of the law begin to look for a way to kill him.

The next day they challenge his authority, and Jesus deftly turns their attack away. He then teaches the parable of the tenants, in which an absentee owner of a vineyard sends a succession of servants to collect the fruit (Mark 12:1-11). Each is beaten and sent away, until at last the owner sends the son "whom he loved," which recalls the way God refers to Jesus at his baptism and transfiguration. The tenants kill him. What will the owner now do? He will come and kill them, giving the vineyard to others. Jesus concludes with Psalm 118:22-23: "The stone the builders rejected has become the cornerstone; the Lord has done this, and it is marvelous in our eyes."

The imagery of the vineyard is used widely in Israel's Scripture to refer to God's people. Likely, the parable's references to a hedge, winepress, and tower allude to Isaiah 5, which concludes with a threat that God will tear up his vineyard because it has yielded only wild grapes. The verses from Psalm 118 were used in the early Christian community to interpret Israel's rejection of Jesus as providing the cornerstone for the new people of God composed of Jews and gentiles.

Once again, the chief priests, teachers of the law, and elders look for a way to arrest Jesus. But they fear the crowds and leave the scene. They send others to "catch him in his words" as Jesus continues to teach (Mark 12:13-44). He draws on Scripture and even poses his own question by citing Psalm 110:1:

How can David refer to his own son as his lord? Christian readers will know this can only be the case if the Messiah from the line of David is raised from the dead and exalted to the right hand of God. Only then can he be David's son and Lord.

As they are leaving the temple, a disciple comments on the magnificence of the buildings. Jesus responds by saying: "Do you see these great buildings? Not one stone here will be left on another; every one will be thrown down" (Mark 13:2). When they return to the Mount of Olives, his inner circle of disciples (Peter, James, John, and Andrew) ask him in private when these events will happen. What will be the signs?

Jesus prepares them for what is to come so they later can prepare his community of followers. He warns them of messianic pretenders. He tells them his followers will be persecuted and brought before political authorities where they will serve as his witnesses, for the "gospel must first be preached to all nations" (Mark 13:9–10). They are not to worry about what they will say, for the Holy Spirit will provide them with words. It will be a time of terrible suffering, but they are not to lose hope, for these events are the "birth pangs" of the new creation. In the midst of this tribulation they "will see the Son of Man coming in clouds with great power and glory" (13:26).

The image comes from Daniel 7, which Mark draws on two other times (Mark 8:38–9:1; 14:62).[20] In the early Christian community, this figure was interpreted as referring to the risen and exalted Lord Jesus, who would return at the consummation to establish God's kingly rule in its fullness. As Jesus now speaks of the trials and tribulations awaiting his followers and of his own suffering and death, he offers hope. His disciples should be confident that his suffering and death are not the end of the story. They too will face suffering and death in the future, but they must not lose faith, for spreading the gospel to all nations is their mission. He will return in glory. Until then, they are to be watchful, for no one knows the hour of his return.

We will continue to point out ways Mark draws on Israel's Scripture to portray the events leading to Jesus's death. Let's pause to reflect on what this helps us learn about evangelism. Two things stand out. First, Mark is signaling to his readers that events are unfolding according to God's design. Jesus is isolated and appears to be powerless. But all of this is according to Scripture. Through the suffering and death of Jesus, God is saving the world. Second, Jesus places the disciples' mission in the context of his mission. Just as he is moving toward suffering and death, they are as well. Just as he is brought

---

20. For background and discussion, see Marcus, *The Way of the Lord*, 164–71.

before the authorities, they will be too in order to serve as his witnesses. The Holy Spirit will accompany them and give them the words to say. Just as he has already begun to open God's salvation to the gentiles, they will take the gospel to all nations. And they will succeed, for when the Son of Man comes, "he will send his angels and gather his elect from the four winds, from the ends of the earth to the ends of the heavens" (Mark 13:27). Just as Jesus's suffering and death are part of God's design, so is the affliction they will face. This is inevitable. Jesus's mission evokes opposition at every point. Bearing witness to the gospel will do the same. If this is not the case for us today, then the question is: Why not?

The Passover Meal and Trial of Jesus

Mark begins the final part of his narrative by noting that the Passover is about to begin (Mark 14:1). This is the festival that celebrates God's deliverance of Israel from slavery in Egypt. It begins with the Passover meal that recalls the story in which the Israelite slaves were told to mark the doors of their homes with the blood of a sacrificed lamb so their firstborn sons would be saved when God brought a final plague upon Egypt. Mark not only is placing the ensuing events in the context of the Passover festival, he also is reminding his readers that Jesus is the new Passover Lamb who delivers all people.

While still in Bethany, Jesus is anointed with expensive perfume by a woman (Mark 14:3–9). Some of the disciples grow angry at such a wasteful act. Jesus intervenes and tells them her act of generosity is preparing his body beforehand for burial and will be remembered "wherever the gospel is preached throughout the world," a reference once more to their mission. After Jesus is anointed, Judas goes to the chief priests to betray him, setting in motion the events leading to his arrest.

The following day Jesus sends some of his disciples to prepare for the Passover meal. That evening as they are celebrating the meal, he takes bread and breaks it, saying, "This is my body" (Mark 14:22). He then gives thanks over the cup and gives it to them, saying, "This is my blood of the covenant, which is poured out for many" (14:23–24). The language here resonates with several very important passages in Israel's Scripture, especially Exodus 24:8, where Moses seals God's covenant with Israel following its deliverance from Egypt.[21] Earlier, in his third passion prediction, Jesus

---

21. The use of "my covenant" also links his words to Zech. 9:11, part of a block of

told his followers that he would give his life as "a ransom for many" (Mark 10:45). The language of "for many" in both passages creates a link with Isaiah 52:13–53:12, which portrays God's servant as suffering vicariously on behalf of the people and as one who "bore the sin of many and made intercession for the transgressors." The symbolic resonances of the words and setting are rich. Jesus is the servant and Lamb of God whose suffering on behalf of "the many" brings deliverance as did the original Passover and God's covenant with Israel.

After the Passover meal Jesus returns to the Mount of Olives. Drawing on Zechariah 13:7, he tells the disciples that they will all "fall away . . . for it is written, 'I will strike the shepherd, and the sheep will be scattered'" (Mark 14:27). He then tells them for the fifth time that he will rise from the dead and go to Galilee where he will meet them. When Peter insists that he will remain faithful, Jesus tells him that he will disown him three times before the night is over. Once more, the disciples' shortcomings come to the fore. But now they are portrayed as part of events unfolding according to Scripture in which the shepherd is struck down.

Jesus takes his inner circle of disciples with him to the garden of Gethsemane (Mark 14:32-42). He instructs his disciples to watch and pray, recalling 13:35-36. While Jesus has predicted his suffering and death at earlier points in the story, now for the first time he expresses personal anguish and fear: "My soul is overwhelmed with sorrow to the point of death." The language alludes to psalms of the righteous sufferer in Israel's Scripture—psalms that originally were individual laments.[22] These psalms express the situation of suffering, abandonment, and violated innocence, but they also include profound trust in the ultimate victory of God over the source of evil.[23] Here, Jesus calls on God in the most intimate of ways, *Abba*, an Aramaic term reserved for one's own father. He asks his Father to take from him the cup, an image of God's judgment and wrath poured out on a sinful people in Israel's Scripture.[24] The prayer concludes with an expression of trust in God and acceptance of the role he has been given to play as God's Son. Three times Jesus returns to the disciples and finds them asleep. An element of divine necessity seems to pervade their response. Their eyes literally "were weighed down"

---

material Mark has drawn on throughout the passion narrative, as we see in the next passage.

22. See Pss. 30:8-10; 40:11-13; 42:5-6, 11; 43:5; 55:4-8; 61:1-3; 116:3-4. See Marcus, *Way of the Lord*, 172-86.

23. Mahoney, *Mark*, 291.

24. See, for example, Isa. 51:17, 22; Jer. 25:13-16; 49:12; 51:7.

(a passive form comparable to their "hearts were hardened"). After the third time, Jesus says, "Enough. The hour has come." His betrayer has arrived. He is arrested and taken before the Sanhedrin.

Mark alludes extensively to the psalms of the righteous sufferer and the servant songs of Deutero-Isaiah as he describes the events taking place in Jerusalem. Marcus reckons that there are eleven allusions from the former and fifteen from the latter in Mark. This is especially the case in the trials of Jesus before the Sanhedrin and Pilate, his treatment by the soldiers, his crucifixion, and his death. Mark 15, for example, uses language from Psalm 22 five times. Mark is continuing to remind his readers that these events are unfolding according to God's design.

The story of Jesus before the Sanhedrin is especially rich with irony (Mark 14:53–72). Jesus is taken to the high priest, and the rest of the Sanhedrin gathers. Peter alone follows him to the courtyard of the high priest. The Sanhedrin has difficulty presenting a coherent case against Jesus, and he remains silent, likely an allusion to Isaiah 53:7. Finally, the chief priest asks Jesus: "Are you the Messiah, the Son of the Blessed One?"[25] This is the first time a human refers to Jesus as the "Son of God." Previously only God, at Jesus's baptism and transfiguration, and the demons refer to him in this way. Jesus breaks his silence and responds, "I am. . . . And you will see the Son of Man sitting at the right hand of the Mighty One and coming on the clouds of heaven." At last, Jesus affirms his identity as the Messiah, as the agent of God's kingly rule who will deliver God's people. The messianic secret is finally out in the open. Yet Jesus's helplessness is never more apparent. The court sentences him to death. The guards mock and beat him. He looks nothing like a Messiah. The only countervailing note is Jesus's response to the high priest that he will be exalted to God's right hand and return in glory, when he will judge the very leaders (and all people) who are now judging him.

The story now returns to Peter. While he is standing in the courtyard, a servant asks him if he is a follower of Jesus. Three times he denies this is the case. A rooster crows a second time, and Peter recalls Jesus's prediction of his denials. He breaks down and weeps. Jesus has shared the truth of his identity, and it will cost him his life. Peter has lied about his identity in order to save his life. This is the last time Peter appears in Mark's story.

---

25. "Blessed One" is a reverential way of referring to God without using God's name. We see this in Matthew's use of "kingdom of heaven" instead of "kingdom of God" throughout his Gospel.

The next morning Jesus is brought before Pilate. The charge once more focuses on whether Jesus claims to be the Messiah, the "King of the Jews," as Pilate puts it. Jesus responds, "You have said so" (Mark 15:1–15), but then is silent in the face of the charges brought against him by the religious leaders. The soldiers and bystanders ridicule Jesus as the helpless, suffering King of the Jews. He is dressed in a purple robe and crown of thorns by his guards, who fall on their knees and pretend to pay homage. After he is brought to Golgotha and crucified, some of the religious leaders mock him: "He saved others but he can't save himself. Let this Messiah, the king of Israel, come down now from the cross that we may see and believe" (Mark 15:31–32).

Their ridicule of Jesus's royal status as God's Messiah is deeply ironic. The soldiers and leaders are testifying to his identity though they do not understand the deeper meaning of what they are saying. In his suffering and death, Jesus embodies God's kingly rule just as surely as he has throughout the story—even more so. For here, God's love for those who are helpless and in need is realized through his death on their behalf and in their stead, which delivers them from the power of evil.

All of this is by God's design, which is signaled by the many allusions to Psalm 22 throughout Mark's account of Jesus's crucifixion and death:[26]

Mark		Psalm 22
15:24	division of garments	22:18
15:29	mockery, head shaking	22:7
15:30–31	"Save yourself!"	22:8
15:32	reviling	22:6
15:34	cry of dereliction	22:1

Psalm 22 is an individual lament, one of the psalms of the righteous sufferer. It brings together the themes of innocent suffering (providing the language for Jesus's cry of forsakenness on the cross), the kingship of Israel's God who will vindicate the sufferer, and the universal dominion of God over the nations, who will turn and worship him. Mark's many allusions to this psalm carry forward the most important theme of his Gospel: Jesus will be a suffering Messiah, contrary to common expectations. Through his suffering and death God will deliver God's people. If the psalm as a whole is implied in these references, then Jesus's vindication by God will serve as testimony to his dominion over the earth and lead the nations to turn to the Lord and bow

26. Marcus, *Way of the Lord*, 175.

down before him (Ps. 22:27–28). Perhaps the beginning of this acknowledgement is found in the confession of the centurion standing at the foot of the cross when Jesus dies: "Surely this man was the Son of God!" (Mark 15:39).

Of his followers, only the women who accompanied him to Jerusalem remain. They watch Jesus's crucifixion from a distance, see where Joseph of Arimathea has his body buried, and go to the tomb following the Sabbath to anoint him with spices. They find the tomb empty and a young man dressed in white who tells them that Jesus has risen. They are to tell Peter and the disciples that Jesus is going ahead of them to Galilee, just as he told them. "Trembling and bewildered, the women went out and fled from the tomb. They said nothing to anyone, because they were afraid" (Mark 16:8).

The ending is abrupt and feels incomplete. There is no sense of closure. Yet, this is where the oldest manuscripts of Mark end. Most scholars agree that Mark 16:9–20 was added later. Was Mark's original ending lost? Why does he end without accounts of the resurrected Jesus's encounter with his disciples? Why does the story end on such a down note?

There is no question that Mark affirms the resurrection of Jesus. Jesus repeatedly predicts his death and resurrection in Mark's story. The angel at the end of the story shares the Easter message with the women: "You are looking for Jesus the Nazarene, who was crucified. He has risen!" Mark and his Christian readers take this for granted. Otherwise there would be no reason to tell the story. God vindicated the crucified Jesus by raising him from the dead.

Mark and Evangelism

Why then does Mark end the story as he does? I think there are three reasons, and they are important to our understanding of Mark's contribution to evangelism. They have something to teach us about how George, in the case study near the beginning of this chapter, might share the gospel with the older veteran who says, "It's too late for me. I am what I am, son. Just a mean bastard."

1. *The gospel is the story of God's love for the world in Jesus Christ, a love willing to suffer and die on behalf of the world.* This is where evangelism must start: with God's love and how it has connected with the person who is sharing their faith.

Mark begins his narrative by writing: "The beginning of the good news about Jesus the Messiah, the Son of God" (Mark 1:1). He ends the story with an account of the empty tomb, an angel, and women fleeing in terror. Clearly

Mark hopes to keep the readers' attention on the suffering and death of Jesus, which dominate the final part of his narrative of the gospel. He refers to Jesus's death as a ransom and blood of the covenant. He draws on psalms of the righteous sufferer and Deutero-Isaiah to portray Jesus as the innocent sufferer who bears the sins of many and will be vindicated by God. While Jesus must suffer and die because of the sin of the world, Mark's account of the gospel is primarily about God's love for the world. It tells the story of how far God is willing to go to save the world.

Mark does not offer confessions of faith or theological traditions, as Paul sometimes does. He offers a story of God's love, which creates many possible connecting points for Christians and non-Christians alike. The center of this story is God sending his Son Jesus to save the world—first, by freeing, healing, and welcoming those who are afflicted, vulnerable, or marginalized and, second, by suffering on behalf of God's people that they might be forgiven and brought into a new relationship with God, which is open to people from all nations. It is Mark's narrative as a whole, thus, that renders the gospel and helps us to imagine how the gospel might be shared today.

In the case study above, George sharing his story gave the older man the freedom to share his. It also was the story of George's anger at God when he returned home and the back-and-forth of the two men about being saved that moved the conversation in the direction of the gospel. Indeed, it is highly likely that this is how the gospel will be shared in this relationship. George's own stories of healing, forgiveness, call to ministry, and reconciliation with God will be the best way to communicate the gospel. George can speak with authenticity to this former soldier—profanity and all. The starting point is the story of God's love for the world in Jesus Christ that he has experienced himself. He needs to share this in his own words and in ways that are true to his own story.

2. *Mark's narrative of the gospel includes the disciples as well as Jesus.* Mark's story is not just about Jesus. It also is about the disciples he calls to follow him. As we have pointed out, evangelism involves more than calling others to Jesus. It also involves calling them to follow him. It is calling them to discipleship among a community of disciples who are seeking to follow in Jesus's way. Ultimately, they are to take up their cross and follow him. They are to serve as he serves. They are to embody the reversal of values found in God's kingly rule as manifested in the deeds and words of Jesus: "But many who are first will be last, and the last first" (Mark 10:31). Jesus calls the disciples to sacrificial love. But Mark's Gospel is clear that moving toward mature discipleship is a journey. That is not where George needs to begin when sharing

his faith with the older veteran. He needs to begin by building a relationship with this man, walking and talking with him.

In surprising ways, Mark's story emphasizes the failure of the disciples. They fail to understand why Jesus must suffer and die, and consequently they fail to remain loyal to him as he moves to the cross. This is something George should remember as he builds a relationship. He should avoid the mistake of thinking that he should just share success stories in evangelism. These exist in Mark, but the dominant picture he paints is one of failure. Peter represents an exaggerated version of the disciples' positive and negative characteristics.[27] He surpasses them in both understanding and misunderstanding, in both loyalty and faithlessness. He recognizes that Jesus is the Messiah but is rebuked for rejecting Jesus's declaration that he must suffer and die. He claims that he will never abandon Jesus and, alone, follows him to the courtyard of the high priest. But there he denies him three times.

While the story oscillates between positive and negative descriptions of Peter and the disciples, the negative dominates. The failure of the women at the very end of the gospel narrative is a final example of this pattern. They alone follow Jesus "at a distance" to the cross and then go the tomb. But they fail to carry out the task they are given by the angel. If the Gospel includes stories of failure by the disciples, then it certainly allows room for a person who thinks it is too late for him, who says he is nothing but a mean bastard! I wonder how Peter felt after denying Jesus three times. Too often evangelism is all about success stories and happy talk; Jesus is going to solve all your problems. That is not the story told by Mark, who tells of the struggles and failures of the disciples. George needs to be honest about learning to follow in Jesus's way and discovering the forgiveness he offers. It is never too late.

3. *While the disciples are included in Mark's story, Jesus is the main character. His words and deeds render his identity, as well as the identity of the one who sent him.* Not only at the end of his story, but throughout, Mark is drawing a bright red line between Jesus and the disciples. Jesus alone is the Messiah and Son of God who is the savior of the world. He is their Lord; they are his servants. The disciples, like all the other characters depicted in the story, are the ones who need to be ransomed and reunited with God in a new covenant. God effects this through Jesus's suffering and death while the disciples are nowhere to be found.

Ultimately, it is not enough to talk about our own experience in evangelism. We have to point beyond ourselves to Jesus, who points us to his Father.

---

27. Throughout this section, I draw on Bauckham, *Jesus and the Eyewitnesses*, ch. 7.

Evangelism must include ways of helping people learn the story of Jesus. The weekly gathering for pizza that George attends includes Bible study after supper. This is one way of learning about Jesus, but there are many others: watching teaching clips online; checking out videos from the church library, reading something together and talking about it over the phone, and so on. Any church that is serious about evangelism needs to develop a pool of resources and methods for people to learn about Jesus—for new Christians or seekers or people who once were Christians. Such a church needs to make sure the congregation knows about these resources through preaching, the church newsletter, and other means.

Knowing about Jesus, however, is not the same thing as knowing Jesus. The best way for this to take place is to help people learn to pray. This is basically talking to Jesus in plain language. Learning to do this by oneself and with others is a starting point. It also includes learning to listen for God in worship and preaching and, eventually, while serving God by helping others. It can take place through journals, retreats, and camps. We will talk about these kinds of things in the last part of the book. Knowledge of Jesus and relationship with Jesus go hand in hand. Sharing our own faith experiences with others can take us only so far. In the end, Mark teaches us that it is not about us. We are too much like the disciples. It is about him, about the one who lived and died and was raised from the dead that we might know the love of God. He is the Savior; we are not. Perhaps this is the first and last thing to say about evangelism in dialogue with Mark.

For Further Reading

Bauckham, Richard. *God Crucified: Monotheism and Christology in the New Testament*. Carlisle: Paternoster Press, 1998. A persuasive argument for the recognition of Jesus's divinity in the Gospels.

———. *Jesus and the Eyewitnesses: The Gospels as Eyewitness Testimony*. Grand Rapids: Eerdmans, 2006. Extremely helpful discussion of the oral nature of Jewish culture at the time of Jesus and the collection of eyewitness testimony in the Gospels.

Hengel, Martin. *The Four Gospels and the One Gospel of Jesus Christ: An Investigation of the Collection and Origin of the Canonical Gospels*. Harrisburg, PA: Trinity Press International, 2000. A classic that focuses on the atonement in the New Testament.

Hultgren, Arland J. *The Parables of Jesus: A Commentary*. Grand Rapids: Eerdmans, 2000. Identifies, classifies, and interprets the parables by comparing them in different Gospels and explaining their meaning. Wonderful resource for students and preachers.

Juel, Donald H. *A Master of Surprise: Mark Interpreted*. Minneapolis: Augsburg Fortress, 1994. Opens up fresh perspectives on Mark. Very helpful for Bible studies and preaching preparation.

———. *Mark*. Augsburg Commentary on the New Testament. Minneapolis: Augsburg, 1990. In nontechnical language, treats the most important interpretive issues in Mark.

Marcus, Joel. *The Way of the Lord: Christological Exegesis of the Old Testament in the Gospel of Mark*. Louisville: Westminster John Knox, 1992. Groundbreaking when it first appeared, it remains one of the best books available on the apocalyptic nature of Jesus and early Christianity against the background of Hebrew Scripture and intertestamental Jewish apocalyptic literature.

Moloney, Francis J., SDB. *The Gospel of Mark: A Commentary*. Peabody, MA: Hendrickson, 2002. One of the best available commentaries on Mark. Treats scholarly issues in depth and opens up new lines of interpretation. Discussion of Mark's ending is superb.

Watson, Francis. *The Fourfold Gospel: A Theological Reading of the New Testament Portraits of Jesus*. Grand Rapids: Baker Academic, 2016. Explores the history and theological significance of the canonical tradition of the four Gospels.

CHAPTER 3

Evangelism and the Gospel of John

W e turn now to the Gospel of John. As we shall see, John tells his gospel
story very differently than Mark. He adds many new insights to our
exploration of evangelism in dialogue with Scripture. We begin once more
with a case study from one of my classes on evangelism. We then engage
John and bring this Gospel into dialogue with the case over the course of
the chapter.

Washed Clean: A Case of Evangelistic Practice

Sponsored by a national organization, James and Ivy were working in a beautiful national park in the southern part of the United States. James had literally walked from his high school graduation ceremony to a packed car in the
parking lot and driven off with Ivy and a friend to reach their summer place-
ment. It was a two-day drive, and they had to leave immediately to get there
on time. Over the course of the summer, they worked for a concessionaire in
the park. James was assigned to the laundry room and Ivy the restaurant as
a hostess. Their hours were long, but their "real work" that summer was "to
befriend their coworkers, host Bible studies, and lead church services in the
campgrounds on Sunday mornings." James and Ivy thought of their ministry
that summer primarily as "relational evangelism."

Their sponsoring organization had placed young people in this park many
times. So almost immediately the summer staff began to refer to them as "the
Christians." James considered this an opportunity and embraced it: "This is
great! Everyone was already expecting us to talk about our faith. So we did."
But James soon realized that something more was needed. Since most of the
summer staff grew up in the Bible Belt, they had heard Christians share their
testimonies all their lives. They were perfectly nice in response but had built
up resistance to this kind of evangelism. One older man told James, "I think

God is OK with my vices. He forgives me. I just keep doing them." So James decided to modify his approach in three ways.

First, he worked at becoming a really good listener. He drew out the stories of his coworkers and tried to build relationships of trust. He grew more patient and waited for opportunities to emerge naturally in relationships. He shared his own story of faith in the context of others' sharing bits and pieces of their life stories. Second, he decided that he needed to be "an exceptionally hard worker." The workload everyone carried was enormous. For example, Ivy opened the restaurant every morning at 6:45 and worked until 11:30 every night getting it ready for the next day—with a long break in the middle of the day. James was in the laundry room all day, while his coworkers were taking ten to twelve smoke breaks. In spite of this, James shared, "I wanted to show that I cared about them while working without complaining—doing things with a smile. This attracted people to talk with me. Even my boss prayed with me." He didn't flinch when his coworkers began to tease him: "You know why those sheets are soiled, don't you? Been going at it all night long." He took precautions to protect his health but kept working harder than anyone else. Third, he made an effort to do small acts of kindness for others. Everyone was very tired at the end of each day. James and Ivy would do small things for others, especially the older workers.

Among the many relationships James formed that summer, one stands out. Meredith was a fifty-five-year-old woman who worked alongside James in the laundry room. She stayed in one of the staff cabins in the park during the summers. The rest of the year she lived with her daughter and granddaughter in a trailer. She had long dark hair and a voice raspy from smoking. She had a deep Southern accent. Meredith and James worked together folding sheets out of the dryer, so they had a lot of time to talk. James learned that Meredith lived in poverty—just one accident or lost paycheck away from homelessness. But she liked James and appreciated how friendly he was and how hard he worked. She lived in a staff cabin next to his, and often when he stepped on the back deck, she would call out: "Hey Baby. Come on over." They would talk, and James recalled "telling her about my life and faith, and how I came to be part of 'the Christians' on the mountain." Their relationship grew and "it became commonplace for us to talk and pray together in the laundry room. I learned that Meredith knew about Christianity but had not gone to church for many years and never made any sort of a commitment to Christ."

Several weeks before the end of the summer, Meredith and James were chatting as usual while folding sheets. Their conversation became serious:

Meredith: I've been wanting to tell you something about my childhood. I played a lot by myself as a child without adults around. I could pretty much go anywhere in our neighborhood during the day, but when it began to get dark I was supposed to come home. One time I was feeling rebellious and decided to stay out a little later. It wasn't too long after the sun had begun to set that I was approached by a car with four men in it. They were in their forties. They asked for directions and when I came close, they grabbed me and drove down the road. [Tears in her eyes] Four grown men raped me. I was just nine. [She begins to sob.]

James: I am so sorry. Those men were evil.

Meredith: I didn't tell an adult at the time because I was afraid that I'd get in trouble for staying out late. I was afraid they'd tell me: "That's what you get for breaking curfew."

James: No, Meredith. You didn't deserve that. You were a child, and no one deserves that. [They grew quiet, and James thought about the ways this terrible incident might have affected Meredith's whole life. She was living in poverty, working a low-paying seasonal job, and struggling with drug abuse. He didn't really know what he should say, so he did what came naturally to him.] Can we pray together?

Meredith: [Nods and continues to weep.]

James: God, I don't know why this world is so broken. Meredith has been hurt, and she's been hurting for a long time. Lord, I know that nothing can take this away from her until you come again, but I pray that you would show her the love she deserves. Even now, Lord, heal her. Let her know that you care about her through my care for her. Let Meredith know that you have pursued her throughout her whole life. Lord, speak through me now to her heart so that she knows it is you who loves her. [Just as he finished, their supervisor came into the room.]

Supervisor: Everything OK in here?

Meredith: Yeah. [She dries her eyes. They begin to fold sheets again.]

The next day Meredith was noticeably happier. She shared things with James that she wanted to pray about—her family and finances—and then said, "I'd like you to baptize me. I've never been baptized." As an eighteen-year-old right out of high school, James did not know what to do. The guidelines of the organization placing him in the park were clear that workers should not offer the sacraments. But Meredith was insistent. She didn't have a home church, she said, and the closest church to the state park was forty miles away. Plus, she didn't have a car.

James called his pastor back home and shared Meredith's story. After a long conversation, the pastor gave him permission to baptize her, pointing to the story of the Ethiopian eunuch's baptism by Philip in Acts 8:26–40, which includes this passage:

> As they traveled along the road, they came to some water and the eunuch said, "Look, here is water. What can stand in the way of my being baptized?" And he gave orders to stop the chariot. Then both Philip and the eunuch went down into the water and Philip baptized him. When they came up out of the water, the Spirit of the Lord suddenly took Philip away, and the eunuch did not see him again, but went on his way rejoicing.

That evening, James shared with Meredith what his pastor had told him and added that the baptism would have to be private because of the rules of the organization he was working for.

So late one afternoon, James, Ivy, and one of their friends, along with Meredith, her daughter, granddaughter, and her daughter's boyfriend, walked up a trail into the woods. They came to an open space where the Vanderbilts once had a hunting lodge. All that was left were the foundation and a watershed that still flowed with fresh water. Wildflowers surrounded them, and the sun beamed down. The group sang "Down by the River," and James led them in a simple baptismal service, using the cold water from the shed to baptize Meredith. They walked down the path together. Two weeks later James and Ivy were back in their car on the long trip to college.

This case raises important questions about the relationship between the individual and community in evangelism. James and Ivy (who participated in class discussion of the case) were glad that "God had used them" to help Meredith begin a relationship with Christ but were aware that this was not enough. As an individual, she needed a church. Ivy put it like this: "Meredith needs support and follow-up. She needs some sort of counseling to help her deal with the rape. She needs to learn how to begin living as a Christian. She needs a faith community that will help her cope with her poverty and future crises." James wondered how all of that might have been accomplished. His remaining time at the park was very short. He had no local knowledge of congregations near the trailer where Meredith would live when the summer ended—over thirty miles away from the park. What was he to do? He stressed to Meredith the importance of finding a home church when the summer was over. I know that part of the world very well and share James's perplexity. There are a lot of fundamentalist churches in the area that preach a gospel of judgment and legalism far removed from what we find in the New Testament. James would need to know the lay of the land in order to help Meredith find a church home.

Should James have baptized Meredith? This was a second issue raised by the members of the precept, and they were not of one mind. Some believed strongly that James should *not* have baptized Meredith. He was not ordained, and, more importantly, the appropriate context for baptism is a congregation. Baptism signifies incorporation into the death and resurrection of Christ and becoming part of Christ's body, a concrete community of disciples. Others argued just as strongly that James's pastor raised exactly the right question when he pointed him to the story of the Ethiopian eunuch, who asks Philip: "What can stand in the way of my being baptized?" After Philip baptized the eunuch, he was immediately taken away by the Holy Spirit—just as James would be taken out of Meredith's life in only two short weeks. Meredith had shared with him a terrible experience of evil—perhaps her first time telling another person the story of her rape as a nine-year-old. She seemed to express a deep longing to be washed clean. As one precept member put it, "Who are we to let the niceties of denominational polity stand in the way of the Holy Spirit?"

Both of these issues highlight the relationship between the individual and the community in evangelism. James supported Meredith as she confessed the pain of her past and took a first step in her relationship with Christ. She was surrounded by loving witnesses at her baptism. But she needs a congregation for healing, learning, and support as a Christian. Connecting new Christians to communities of disciples is a key part of evangelism.

One of the goals of this chapter is to explore the relationship between the individual and community in evangelism. We will reflect on the case as we move along rather than waiting until the end of the chapter, for the relationships between individual Christians and faith communities appear throughout. In many ways, John's Gospel gives more explicit attention to the individual's relationship to Jesus than any other. Jesus is the vine to which every individual Christian must remain attached if he or she is to bear fruit (John 15:5-8). At the same time, John offers some of the most memorable images in the New Testament of the individual's relationship to the Christian community. The image of the vine opens out to one of community: "As the Father has loved me, so have I loved you. Now remain in my love. . . . My command is this: Love each other as I have loved you" (15:9, 12).

As our dialogue with John proceeds, three themes will emerge as important to our thinking about evangelism. The first is the in-one-another theme, and we will start with that. In John's Prologue, two additional themes appear.

One is Jesus's mission as the revelation of the glory of God in human flesh. The other is the mission of the disciples as witnesses. While John uses the term "witness" (*martyreō*) and not "evangelize" (*euangelizō*), we will use these terms interchangeably in our discussion of John. In a later chapter, we will explore the relationship between evangelism and witness more extensively.

The In-One-Another Theme in John

One of the most important motifs in John's narrative is the in-one-another theme.[1] It goes beyond simple interaction and reciprocity to mutual indwelling and interpenetration in which the identity and being of human beings are shaped and even constituted. The theme is used to describe a variety of relationships: Jesus and his Father, Jesus and the Holy Spirit, Jesus and individual Christians, Jesus and the Christian community, Christians and other Christians, the Holy Spirit and Christians. Paul develops a similar theme in his letters: "in Christ" (*en Christō*), which appears seventy-four times in the Pauline corpus (excluding the pastorals). Paul also uses the phrase "in the Lord" (*en Kyriō*), or occasionally "in the Lord Jesus," an additional forty-seven times.[2] John and Paul use their themes as ways of portraying the participation of individual Christians and Christian communities in Christ. But they go well beyond this.

Paul's use of "in Christ" falls into three broad categories.[3] First, it is used to refer to the objective act of reconciliation that has already taken place in Christ: "But they are justified freely by his grace through the redemption that is in Christ Jesus" (Rom. 3:24 NET). Second, "in Christ" is used to refer to those who have appropriated subjectively the objective salvation taking place in Christ: "Therefore, if anyone is in Christ, the new creation has come: The old has gone, the new is here!" (2 Cor. 5:17). In some verses, both objective and subjective uses appear: "I have been crucified with Christ and I no longer live, but Christ lives in me. The life I now live in the body, I live by faith in the Son of God, who loved me and gave himself for me" (Gal. 2:20). Third, Paul uses this phrase to describe his relationship to others—"In Christ Jesus

---

1. Richard Bauckham, *Gospel of Glory: Major Themes in Johannine Theology* (Grand Rapids: Baker Academic, 2015), especially chs. 1–2.

2. James D. G. Dunn, *The Theology of Paul the Apostle* (Grand Rapids: Eerdmans, 1998), 396. These numbers do not include verses that use pronouns: "in him," "in whom."

3. Dunn, *Theology of Paul*, 397–98.

I became your father through the gospel" (1 Cor. 4:15); "Greet Priscilla and Aquila, my co-workers in Christ Jesus" (Rom. 16:3).

John uses the in-one-another theme in equally rich ways. While he does not offer a fully developed doctrine of the Trinity, the mutual indwelling of the persons of the Trinity is portrayed in ways that gave rise to this doctrine. Many times the *oneness* of God is described as a unity of relationships. Moreover, those who follow Jesus are drawn into the Trinitarian life of God. This is the source of their glorification of God and their witness to God's love for the world in Jesus Christ. Here are some examples of the in-one-another theme that appear throughout the Gospel:

> *Prologue:* "The Word was with God, and the Word was God" (1:1); "No one has ever seen God, but the one and only Son, who is himself God and is in closest relationship with the Father, has made him known" (1:18).
>
> *Jesus as the Good Shepherd:* "As the Father knows me and I know the Father" (10:15); "I and the Father are one" (10:30); "Understand that the Father is in me, and I in the Father" (10:38).
>
> *Jesus to Philip and the disciples:* "Don't you believe that I am in the Father, and that the Father is in me? The words I say to you I do not speak on my own authority. Rather, it is the Father, living in me, who is doing his work. Believe me when I say that I am in the Father and the Father is in me" (14:10–11).
>
> *Jesus as the vine:* "Remain in me, as I also remain in you. No branch can bear fruit by itself; it must remain in the vine. Neither can you bear fruit unless you remain in me" (15:4–5); "As the Father has loved me, so have I loved you. Now remain in my love" (15:9).
>
> *The final prayer of Jesus for his disciples:* "My prayer is not for them alone. I pray also for those who will believe in me through their message, that all of them may be one, Father, just as you are in me and I am in you. May they also be in us so that the world may believe that you have sent me" (17:20–21).
>
> *The Holy Spirit:* "And I will ask the Father, and he will give you another advocate to help you and be with you forever—the Spirit of truth. The world cannot accept him, because it neither sees him nor knows him. But you know him, for he lives with you and will be in you" (14:16–17).

The "in Christ" theme in Paul and the in-one-another theme in John are directly relevant to the case we shared at the beginning of the chapter.

They portray participation in Christ in terms of relationality and mutual indwelling. Entering the Christian life is not simply a matter of choice by an individual. It is a matter of being drawn into a network of relationships. A relational and Trinitarian framework opens up some key images of entering the Christian life found in John.[4]

Jesus tells Nicodemus, for example, "Very truly I tell you, no one can see the kingdom of God unless they are born again" (John 3:3). The word translated "again" (*anōthen*) can also mean "from above." John uses above-below imagery throughout his Gospel, so it is likely the word has a double meaning. Nicodemus misunderstands what Jesus is saying, so Jesus refers to being born by the Spirit, which cannot be brought under human control: "The wind blows wherever it pleases. You hear its sound, but you cannot tell where it comes from or where it is going. So it is with everyone born of the Spirit" (3:8). The Spirit plays the role of a mother here. She is the one giving birth, not the one about to be born. Earlier, John described those who receive Jesus as given "the right to become children of God—children born not of natural descent, nor of human decision or a husband's will, but born of God" (1:12-13).

Clearly, becoming a follower of Jesus is not merely a human act based on human will. It is being born anew within a network of relationships in which a person receives a new identity as part of a new family. This is a far cry from deciding or choosing to give one's life to Jesus. Indeed, it is almost the opposite of evangelism as conversionism, which places so much emphasis on the individual. We introduce the other two themes noted above as we move further into John's story.

Background

John tells his story of the gospel in ways that are different than the stories of Mark, Matthew, and Luke, commonly known as the Synoptic Gospels.[5] In John, for example, Jesus does not cast out demons or eat with tax collectors

---

4. My understanding and discussion of the imagery of being born again or born from above is informed by Joy L. Arroyo, "Spiritual Transformation and Church Involvement in Matrescence: How the Transition to Motherhood May Lead to Spiritual Change and the Church's Role in This Transformation." Submitted in partial fulfillment of the doctoral program at Princeton Theological Seminary, December 15, 2017, ch. 3.

5. See Marianne Meye Thompson, *John: A Commentary* (Louisville: Westminster John Knox, 2015), on whom I rely here.

and sinners. There are no stories of his temptation in the wilderness, the transfiguration, or the institution of the Lord's Supper. The story unfolds primarily in and around Jerusalem, not Galilee. The way Jesus teaches is different. In the Synoptics, Jesus teaches in parables. In John, he offers long discourses. These often include sayings that start "I am" and are followed by images that describe his identity and mission: I am the bread of life; the light of the world; the gate; the Good Shepherd; and the way, the truth, and the life. As Jesus develops these images, his teaching often evokes conflict with the religious leaders. Unlike in Mark, his divine identity and origin are not kept a secret. As Jesus puts it himself: "I have spoken openly to the world. . . . I have said nothing in secret" (John 18:20).

Even the language and imagery in John are different than in the Synoptics. Perhaps most importantly, language of the kingdom of God, dominating Mark, is used only twice (John 3:3, 5). Far more common are terms like "eternal life" and "glory." Imagery of above and below—not present and future as in Mark—dominates John's Gospel. Jesus comes from above to reveal God and offer eternal life; he is "lifted up" on the cross, raised from the dead, and exalted to the glory he shared with his Father before his incarnation. Moreover, Mark uses "Father" only four times to refer to God. In John, this occurs around 130 times! It is an essential part of John's depiction of Jesus's deity, the Father's sending of the Son, and the mutual love between the Father and Son that is the source of Jesus's relation to his disciples.

A final background issue is the author of this Gospel. I follow those interpreters who believe the author of John was a disciple of Jesus living in Jerusalem but not one of the Twelve.[6] He is portrayed in the story as the one Jesus loved (John 13:23; 19:26; 20:2; 21:7, 20). He is portrayed as the only male disciple who is present at Jesus's crucifixion (19:26).[7] Near the end of the Gospel, Jesus reinstates Peter, and then Peter asks him about the disciple who is following them, "the disciple whom Jesus loved." This

---

6. For extensive discussion of this perspective, which notes the wide range of scholars who argue along these lines, see Richard Bauckham, *The Testimony of the Beloved Disciple: Narrative, History and Theology in the Gospel of John* (Grand Rapids: Baker Academic, 2007), introduction and chs. 2–3. Francis J. Moloney makes a convincing case for the literary unity of John's story, though he acknowledges that the material it contains reflects different stages of telling and a final compilation. See his *Gospel of John*, Sacra Pagina (Collegeville, MN: Liturgical, 1998), Kindle edition, loc. 742–70.

7. Also mentioned are Jesus's mother Mary, her sister Mary wife of Clopas, and Mary Magdalene in John 19:25.

is "the one who had leaned back against Jesus at the supper and had said, 'Lord, who is going to betray you?'" (21:20). The Gospel then states: "This is the disciple who testifies to these things and who wrote them down. We know that his testimony is true" (21:24). Likely, this was added to speak for those closely related to the author who could testify to his special relationship to Jesus.

Drawing on his own memories and those of this circle, it is likely that John took a long time to write his distinctive narrative of Jesus. Two times John states that his Gospel is intentionally "incomplete." It does not include everything that Jesus said and did:

> Jesus performed many other signs in the presence of his disciples, which are not recorded in this book. But these are written that you may believe that Jesus is the Messiah, the Son of God, and that by believing you may have life in his name. (20:30–31)

> Jesus did many other things as well. If every one of them were written down, I suppose that even the whole world would not have room for the books that would be written. (21:24)

Marianne Meye Thompson helps us understand what these passages tell us about John's Gospel: "It is a carefully crafted account of a select number of words and deeds from Jesus' life that presents a particular understanding of Jesus, who he was and what his ministry accomplished. . . . [Its purpose is] to present Jesus as the embodied Word, the Son of God, through whom God's glory is manifested and God is revealed, and through whom God gives life to the world."[8]

As we begin to move into the story itself, it may be helpful to have an overview of the way I understand the structure of John:

1. The Prologue of the Gospel—John 1:1–18: An introduction to the divine status and mission of the Word of God. Readers are provided guidance in how to read the Gospel.
2. The Book of Signs—John 1:19–12:50: Jesus's public ministry in which he reveals his Father through miraculous "signs" and accompanying

---

8. Thompson, *John*, 8. Richard Bauckham argues that John assumes traditions and stories about Jesus found in the Synoptics. By being selective, he is able to focus on the "symbolic" meaning of the stories he does include. See *Gospel of Glory*, loc. 195–201.

discourses, leading some to acknowledge him as God's Son and Messiah and others to reject him. The religious leaders begin to plot his death. Throughout this part, Jesus alludes many times to his death.

3. The Book of Glory—John 13:1–20:31: Jesus focuses on the disciples as his "hour" grows near. The Gospel then reaches its climax: the events in which Jesus glorifies his Father through the humiliation of his crucifixion and in turn is glorified by his Father in his resurrection from the dead. During the forty days Jesus remains with his disciples, he breathes the Holy Spirit on them and commissions them for the mission of bearing witness to God's love of the world, which he has revealed and embodied.

4. The resurrected Lord and the new community—John 21:1–25: Through three symbolic actions Jesus prepares the post-resurrection community to carry out its mission as his witness. He guides his disciples in accomplishing a great catch of fish. He shares a fellowship meal with them on the shore. He reinstates Peter as a leader of the community.

As we have done with Mark, we will point to some of the implications for our thinking about evangelism as we move through John's story. As noted above, John uses the language of witness, not that of announcing the gospel, in his story, so we will need to think about the relationship between witness as John understands it and the way evangelism is understood today. The entire story is one in which Jesus reveals God to the world—light in the midst of darkness. Certainly, there is no theme more central to evangelism and witness than this one.

The Prologue as Introduction: The Mission of Jesus as the Glorification of God

One of the distinctive ways John portrays the mission of Jesus is with the theme of glory. While glory and related terms appear elsewhere in the New Testament, John, employs this language extensively, using "glory" and "to glorify" forty-two times. Only 2 Corinthians uses "glory" with such frequency. The theme of glory is important in John's Gospel.

The Greek term translated "glory" in English is *doxa*. Originally it meant opinion or judgment. The word took on new meaning when the Hebrew Bible was translated into the Greek Septuagint during the third and second centuries BC. *Doxa* was used to translate terms like *kavod* that refer to God's majesty, splendor, power, and beauty.[9] Related Greek words, like *endoxazomai*, were used to translate Hebrew terms meaning to honor, reverence, or praise God for his works of creation, salvation, and judgment. Psalm 96 is a beautiful example.

The Prologue of John draws especially on glory as depicted in the stories of the Exodus. God manifests his glory in ways that are visible but indirect. To encounter God's glory directly would destroy a human being. It must be mediated by earthly means. In the Exodus stories, for example, it is mediated by natural phenomena, like clouds, thunder and lightning, or fire. When Moses leads Israel to Mount Sinai to enter into a covenant with God, a cloud covers the mountain and "the glory of the Lord" settles on it (Exod. 24:15-16). At one point, Moses has the audacity to ask God: "Now show me your glory" (33:18). The Lord responds: "I will cause all my goodness to pass in front of you, and I will proclaim my name, the LORD, in your presence. . . . But you cannot see my face, for no one may see me and live" (33:19-20). Moses gets a passing glimpse of God's glory, his back(side?) (33:23), but more importantly he hears a description of God's character:

> Then the LORD came down in the cloud and stood there with him and proclaimed his name, the LORD. And he passed in front of Moses, proclaiming, "The LORD, the LORD, the compassionate and gracious God, slow to anger, abounding in love and faithfulness, maintaining love to thousands, and forgiving wickedness, rebellion and sin. (34:5-7)

When Moses descended from the mountain, his face was so radiant that the people were afraid to come near him. He put a veil over his face (Exod. 34:30, 33). John alludes in his Prologue to the story of God passing Moses to reveal his glory, as we shall see.

John also alludes to Exodus stories in which Moses receives detailed instructions from God about the construction of the tabernacle. This is the "tent of meeting" which served as the center of Israel's worship and the symbol of God's presence with Israel until the temple was built. After the construction of the tabernacle, the cloud surrounding Sinai covers the taber-

9. *Doxa* was also used to translate words like *hadar* and *hod*. Such terms can also refer to human beings, as well as God. In such cases, they often refer to markers of human glory, like power, wealth, fame, and splendid deeds. Such things may enhance the reputation or status of persons and elicit honor and praise.

nacle, and the glory of the Lord fills it (Exod. 40:34). Other stories in Israel's Scripture draw on this account. During the dedication of Solomon's Temple, for example, a cloud covers it and "the glory of the LORD filled his temple" (1 Kings 8:10-13). Likewise, when the temple was about to be destroyed by the Babylonians, the prophet Ezekiel sees the glory of God leaving Jerusalem (Ezek. 11:22-23). He later shares a vision of the restored temple and the glory of the Lord filling the building once more (Ezek. 44:4). These stories about the revelation of God's glory in Exodus and the prophets will prove important to John.

The Prologue of John's Gospel offers readers guidance in how to interpret the story that follows. He begins by placing the story in the cosmological context of creation.[10] The opening words of the Prologue are a literal translation of the first words of Genesis: "*In the beginning* was the Word, and the Word was with God, and the Word was God. He was with God in the beginning. Through him all things were made; without him nothing was made that has been made" (John 1:1-3). The Word is depicted as participating with God in creation. Moreover, a distinction and a relationship are posited in God: the Word was "with" God and "was" God.

The Prologue goes on to identify the Word as God's Son, who stands in the closest relationship with his Father (John 1:14, 18). The oneness of God thus is a *relational unity*. The Father is in the Son, and the Son in the Father (10:30). They are one in their mutual love. This is the source of the in-one-another theme. Jesus and his Father are in one another. Jesus and his followers are in one another. The disciples are in one another. In chapter 17, Jesus prays that believers may be one as he and the Father are one (vv. 11, 21-23). He includes those who will later believe through his disciples' message (cf. 11:52).

In verse 14 of the Prologue, John uses the term "glory" for the first time: "The Word became flesh and made his dwelling among us. We have seen his *glory*, the *glory* of the one and only Son, who came from the Father, full of grace and truth" (John 1:14). "Made his dwelling" literally means "pitched his tent." It is an allusion to the tabernacle. As we have seen, this is the "tent of meeting" that served as the dwelling place of God's presence and glory while Israel wandered in the wilderness and after it settled in the promised

10. Many scholars see the Prologue as an early Christian hymn of praise to the Word, interrupted with statements about John the Baptist. See Raymond E. Brown, SS, *The Gospel according to John*, vol. 1, *I-XII*, The Anchor Bible Series, vol. 29 (Garden City, NY: Doubleday, 2003), 18-21. Others believe it is written by the author of John since so many themes are further developed in the Gospel.

land. It is likely that John also has in mind the story of God's glory coming upon Solomon's Temple at its dedication, as well as Ezekiel's visions of its departure and promised return. John is telling his readers that the incarnation of the Son is the return of God's glory, its visible manifestation in human flesh (v. 14).

In verse 14, John also describes Jesus as full of "grace and truth" (repeated in v. 17). This is an allusion to the Exodus story in which God reveals his glory as he passes by Moses (Exod. 34:6) and offers a verbal identity-description portraying him as "abounding in love and faithfulness." "Grace and truth" is a translation of the Hebrew words *hesed* and *'emet*, meaning steadfast love and faithfulness. Throughout Israel's Scripture, these words are used to express the heart of God's covenant love.[11] Truth, here, means God's faithfulness to his word and promises, God's truth as trustworthiness.

Why does John allude to this story of God passing by Moses as he introduces the theme of glory for the first time? Richard Bauckham offers the following reason: "The glory is the radiance of the character of God, the grace and truth about which Moses heard, but which the disciples of Jesus have seen in his human person and life."[12] Jesus manifests God's glory visibly in human flesh. He both fulfills and surpasses Moses.

John says this directly in the final verses of the Prologue: "Out of his fullness we have all received grace in place of grace already given. For the law was given through Moses; grace and truth came through Jesus Christ. No one has ever seen God, but the one and only Son, who is himself God and is in closest relationship with the Father, has made him known" (John 1:16–18). What Moses only heard, Jesus has seen, and he alone is in a position to manifest God's glory visibly in human flesh.

We come here to the basic premise of John's Gospel. Jesus is the incarnation of God, God's only begotten Son and Word. He alone reveals God's glory in human flesh. In short, God's self-revelation is given through Jesus Christ in a unique and unsurpassable way. Just as Jesus glorifies his Father and his Father glorifies him, the disciples are called to glorify Jesus. If Jesus is the light coming into the darkness of the world, his followers are called to reflect his light in their own lives and as a community. This is a basic image of evangelism and witness in John's story of the gospel.

11. For other pairings of these words, see Pss. 25:10; 61:7; 86:1; Prov. 20:28.
12. Bauckham, *Gospel of Glory*, loc. 52.

The Book of Signs: John 1:19–12:50

The Theme of Witness

The theme of witness is important throughout John's story and is introduced in the Prologue and when Jesus calls his first disciples. The Prologue has the meter and rhythm of an early Christian hymn or a poem. Yet John interrupts the flow at two points to insert comments about John the Baptist (John 1:6–8, 15). In both cases, he introduces the Baptist as a "witness" who "testifies" to Jesus, using language derived from *martys, martyria,* and *martyreō.* This language reappears across the Gospel to describe those who witness to Jesus: his Father, the Holy Spirit, Israel's Scripture, John the Baptist, and his disciples.

John the Baptist embodies three of the most important qualities of a witness. They appear early in John's Gospel in order to help readers identify the key elements of a witness in the rest of the story. First, John's mission is to testify to One who is greater than himself (John 1:8, 15, 26–27, 35). As he puts it later: "He must become greater; I must become less" (3:30). Witnesses do not point to themselves, though they share things they know on the basis of firsthand experience. Like John the Baptist, they prepare the way for another. Second, John bears witness to the identity and mission of Jesus, calling him "the Lamb of God, who takes away the sin of the world" (1:29, 35); recognizing him as the chosen One on whom the Spirit has descended (1:32–34). Witnesses point beyond themselves to Christ and what he does on their behalf and in their stead. Third, the Baptist leads other people to Jesus. In this case, it is two of John's disciples, Andrew, Peter's brother, and another who remains unnamed (1:35). After John identifies Jesus as the Lamb of God a second time, they "followed Jesus."

When John's disciples find Jesus and ask him where he is staying, he responds by saying: "Come and you will see." They spend the rest of the day with him. After departing, Andrew immediately finds his brother Simon and shares with him that they have found the Messiah. He brings Simon to Jesus, who gives him a new name, Peter, which anticipates his role as the rock of the early church. Before departing to Galilee the next day, Jesus finds Philip and tells him, "Follow me" (John 1:43). Philip immediately finds Nathaniel and tells him they have found the one of whom the Scriptures speak, Jesus of Nazareth. When Nathaniel asks if anything good can come out of Nazareth, Philip repeats Jesus's words, "Come and see" (v. 46). Jesus tells Nathaniel things about himself that are seemingly impossible for Jesus to know. Nathaniel responds by confessing that Jesus is the Son of God and king of Israel.

The stories of Jesus's call of his first disciples add to our understanding of witness. The phrase "come and see" is initially used by Jesus and then is repeated by Philip. Thompson points out the importance of this phrase: "When Jesus invites these disciples to 'come and see,' he is inviting them not only to follow him and to see what he will do, but also, to discern in his acts just who he is, and thus to believe and follow on the path of discipleship."[13] Everyone can *see* with their eyes what Jesus is doing; only the disciples and other believers have *insight* into what this means.

Later, a Samaritan woman who encounters Jesus by a village well tells others, "Come and see" (John 4:29 NRSV). When we think about this phrase in relation to evangelism and witness, it is frightening if we are honest. The Samaritan woman did not exactly lead an exemplary life. Nor is the church in the United States always the paragon of discipleship. Yet this what we are called to do in evangelism and witness: to invite others to "come and see" what God is doing in our lives and our congregations as a way of pointing beyond ourselves to God's Son. They will know we are Christians by our love, the popular song goes. But let's be honest, our love is a pale reflection of God's love as revealed in Jesus Christ. Like John the Baptist, our lives can only serve as a visible but very fragile witness to the one who alone is the Lamb of God, the Passover lamb, handed over for sacrifice so his blood could mark the doors and free us from bondage of the evil one.

Also, like the Baptist, the first disciples and the Samaritan woman invite others to Jesus. They have received good news and want to share it with others. The narrator comments at the end of the story about the Samaritan woman: "Many of the Samaritans from that town believed in him because of the woman's testimony" (John 4:39). In evangelism and witness, we too invite others to come and see.

Finally, it is important to note the link between seeing and glory. The Prologue introduces this motif: "We have *seen his glory*, the glory of the one and only Son, who came from the Father, full of grace and truth" (John 1:14; emphasis added). Many people encounter Jesus, but only a few see God's glory revealed in his signs and in his humiliating death on the cross. Yet these are the ways Jesus reveals the glory of God's love in his words and work. This is what we are inviting people to in evangelism: recognition that the glory of God is revealed in the love of God in Jesus Christ.

In the remainder of this chapter, we will follow the interrelated themes of glory, in-one-another, and witness as they are developed in John's narra-

13. Thompson, *John*, 50.

tive. Building on the outline of the Gospel offered above, we examine (1) the signs of Jesus during his public ministry; (2) Jesus's farewell discourse and his passion, death, resurrection, and ascension; and (3) his formation of the post-resurrection community of disciples who are to serve as his witnesses. In each part of John's gospel story, we learn something important about evangelism and witness.

Signs: Actions and Interpretation

Stories of the miraculous deeds of Jesus are treated differently in John than in the other Gospels. In the Synoptics, Jesus's healings, exorcisms, and miraculous feedings are called "mighty deeds" (*dynameis*, Mark 6:2, 5, 14), "marvels" (*thaumasia*, Matt. 21:15), and "remarkable things" (*paradoxa*, Luke 5:26).[14] Usually in the Synoptics, they are presented in brief, self-contained stories with little interpretation beyond pithy sayings. They are viewed as actions in which the kingdom of God is breaking in through Jesus's ministry in anticipation of God's final transformation of the world.

In contrast, John refers to Jesus's miraculous deeds as "signs" (*sēmeia*).[15] Each sign is followed by a lengthy discourse in which Jesus invites those who have seen his miraculous action to move beyond the deed itself and gain insight into its meaning. Three miraculous deeds are explicitly identified as signs (John 2:11; 4:54; 6:14), and other deeds are followed by summaries using the language of signs (2:23-25; 11:47; 12:37). I follow those scholars who believe there are seven signs in John.[16]

1. turning water into wine (2:1-11)
2. healing an official's son (4:46-54)
3. healing a lame man on the Sabbath (5:2-9)
4. feeding the five thousand (6:1-26)
5. healing a blind man on the Sabbath (9:1-12)
6. raising Lazarus from death (11:1-45)
7. the resurrection of Jesus (20:1-29).

14. See Thompson's helpful discussion of signs in Excursus 1 of *John*, 65-68.

15. This is perhaps a further link to the Exodus stories. When Moses and Aaron gather the elders of Israel to share the news that the Lord will free them from bondage, Aaron performs "signs before the people, and they believed" (Exod. 4:30-31).

16. See Bauckham, *Gospel of Glory*, loc. 56-57. See Thompson, *John*, for a different perspective.

The signs of Jesus accomplish three things in John's story: They reveal the glory of God; they raise questions about who Jesus is; and they call for a response from the characters. John states directly that the first and sixth signs reveal God's glory. After Jesus changes water into wine at the wedding in Cana, the narrator comments: "What Jesus did here in Cana of Galilee was the first of the signs through which he revealed his glory; and his disciples believed in him" (John 2:11). Similarly, when Jesus receives word from Mary and Martha that their brother Lazarus is very sick, Jesus comments: "This sickness will not end in death. No, it is for God's glory so that God's Son may be *glorified* through it" (11:4; cf. v. 40).

In these passages, Jesus's revelation of God's glory and his own glorification through the signs are mutually implicated. Jesus reveals the glory of his Father. In turn, he is glorified by his Father: "If I glorify myself, my glory means nothing. My Father, whom you claim as your God, is the one who glorifies me" (John 8:54). Throughout the Gospel, John describes the reciprocity between the Father and Son. This is the source of Jesus's words, authority, and work. At the end of his signs ministry, Philip asks Jesus to show the Father to the inner circle of disciples, and he responds: "Don't you know me, Philip, even after I have been among you such a long time? Anyone who has seen me has seen the Father. How can you say, 'Show us the Father'? Don't you believe that I am in the Father, and that the Father is in me? The words I say to you I do not speak on my own authority. Rather, it is the Father, living in me, who is doing his work. Believe me when I say that I am in the Father and the Father is in me" (14:9-11). This sort of intimate but differentiated reciprocity informs every aspect of Jesus's identity and mission, including his signs. Through them he glorifies his Father and his Father glorifies him.

The signs also raise questions about who Jesus is. Each sign is followed by a lengthy discourse that tells the characters (and readers) something about Jesus's identity, which is related to the miraculous deed he has just performed. For example, after the feeding of the five thousand (John 6:1-13, 25-59), Jesus speaks of himself as the bread of life who provides sustenance surpassing all earthly hunger (vv. 35, 48) and grants eternal life at the resurrection of the dead (vv. 40, 44, 54). He is critical of the crowd that seeks him out the next day because they had their fill of bread. They failed to understand what the sign revealed (vv. 26-27).[17] He implores

17. Misunderstanding by the characters in the story is a literary technique that allows Jesus to explain himself more thoroughly. More fundamentally, it signals the world's inability to see the truth. See Brown, *The Gospel of John*, vol. 1, cxxxvi.

them to look for the deeper meaning of the sign, which will lead them to realize that God is working through him.[18] At the level of the story, the characters are invited to discern what the sign reveals about his identity and to believe in him.

This also is true for readers of John's Gospel who are Christians. They might ponder the meaning of this sign along several lines: (1) the relationship between the Lord's Supper and Jesus's description of himself as the bread of life and as flesh and blood they must eat if they are to have eternal life (John 6:32–33, 48–51, 53–58); (2) the ways Israel's Scripture is being fulfilled and surpassed in him (in vv. 45, 49–51, 58 they are being "taught by God," recalling Isaiah 54:13, and Jesus is the new manna from heaven, recalling God's feeding of Israel in the wilderness); (3) the promise of eternal life on the last day, which they enter even now through their relationship with Jesus (vv. 27, 39–40, 47); (4) Jesus gives his flesh for the life of the world (v. 33); and (5) the paradox of Christians being drawn to Jesus by his Father and the need for individuals to make their own response (vv. 36–40, 44–45, 65, 70). Clearly, the discourses following Jesus's signs are designed to elicit responses that move deeper and deeper into the mystery of Jesus's identity as the revealer of God's glory through his embodiment of God's love.

Even more important for our purposes is the interplay between action and interpretation. Each sign begins with a miraculous action on Jesus's part. It is followed by a discourse that interprets what this action reveals about Jesus's identity and mission. It commonly introduces includes symbolic meanings that invite readers to go deeper and deeper into the mystery of God's self-revelation.

With appropriate cautions, this can be a helpful way of thinking about evangelism and witness. Actions and attitudes often are the starting point. In the case study beginning this chapter, James went out of his way to work especially hard doing his job, taking some of the load off others. He also tried to do small acts of kindness for others.[19] One church plant with which I am familiar cancels worship once a month and sends teams and families

---

18. As Thompson notes, Jesus is sometimes critical of those who believe in him only because of the signs, understood solely as miraculous deeds or displays of power. They fail to understand who he is and the work he has been given to do by his Father. Such faith is not ruled out altogether but is inadequate and must move toward a fuller understanding of discipleship. *John*, 67.

19. Sometimes, this approach is called servant evangelism. Steve Sjogren has quite a bit about this online. See also his *Conspiracy of Kindness: A Unique Approach to Sharing the Love of Jesus* (Bloomington, MN: Bethany House, 2003).

out to peoples' homes volunteering to rake leaves, shovel snow, or do other jobs. It has made them known in their neighborhood and created a mission orientation in the church. They act to help someone out and do not try to sell the church in any way. They simply leave a pamphlet at the front door sharing who they are and why they serve in the Spirit of Jesus.

In John, actions are followed by interpretation through discourses in which Jesus reveals who he is. Is this necessary in every case for evangelism to take place? Is it enough just to be kind to people or to act on their behalf? In the case study, James and Ivy's actions created a relational context in which they were evaluated by others. They were known as "the Christians" as soon as they arrived because the national Christian organization that sponsored them placed high school graduates in this state park every summer. James says that initially people did not really listen to him share "his testimony." These were Southerners; they had heard it all before. It was only as he worked exceptionally hard and helped people out that he was taken seriously. He was pretty sure that some people were taking advantage of him, taking more smoke breaks than usual, for example. Others were friendly but basically indifferent to what he had to say about Christ. Meredith responded to his kindness and willingness to listen by revealing something deeply personal from her past. In John's story, we also see a variety of responses to Jesus's signs.

Belief

The most important response to Jesus is to believe. As John puts it: "Jesus performed many other signs in the presence of his disciples, which are not recorded in this book. But these are written that you may believe that Jesus is the Messiah, the Son of God, and that by believing you may have life in his name" (John 20:30–31). John describes belief in two closely related ways: to believe *that* (*pisteuein hoti*), and to believe *in* (*pisteuein eis*, as in John 2:23; 3:18; 4:39).[20] The former involves the recognition and confession of who Jesus is. He is the Messiah and Son of God. Those who believe acknowledge this to be true, not only for themselves, but also for the entire world. The latter—to believe in—has the connotations of *believing into* Jesus. This is forming a relationship in which Jesus and believers are in one another. Each retains their

20. George Allen Turner, "Soteriology in the Gospel of John," *Journal of the Evangelical Theological Society* 19, no. 3 (1976): 272.

identity. After all, Jesus remains their master, teacher, and savior; and they are his disciples, students, and recipients of eternal life and salvation. Yet their relationship is one of mutual love and friendship. This is what it means to *believe into* Jesus.

It is important to keep in mind both the confessional and relational dimensions of belief, for this helps us understand its connection to eternal life. As Jesus puts it: "Very truly I tell you, the one who believes has eternal life" (John 6:47). John uses "life" and "eternal life" with the same kind of frequency as the Synoptics use language of the kingdom of God.[21] The Synoptics speak of eternal life as beginning in the age to come (Mark 10:29-30; 9:43, 45, 47). In John, a person who believes "will not be judged but has crossed over from death to life" (John 5:24). He or she is born again, from above, becoming a child of God through the Holy Spirit (3:3-8).[22] While eternal life continues after death, John accentuates those qualities of life that flow from a person's *present relationship* with God's Son and through him with his Father.[23]

Jesus speaks of eternal life as life abundant, life to the full (John 10:10). The signs in John help us understand what this means. If you look again at the seven signs identified above, you will see that eternal life is the provision of abundance: serving the best wine last; healing of an official's son, a lame man, and a blind man; feeding those in need (a large crowd of people who have followed Jesus to a desolate place); and overcoming death in the raising of Lazarus.[24] Each sign is a visible expression of God's glory and bestows an aspect of life lived to the full. Such life begins in the present among those who

21. The Greek is helpful to catch the nuances of John's distinctive vocabulary of eternal life. *Zōē* (life) is used nineteen times, *zōē aiōnios* (eternal life) eighteen times, *zaō* (to live) seventeen times, and *zaō eis ton aiōna* (to live forever) or a comparable term five times. All of these terms refer to eternal life. John also uses terms that refer to mortal life. *Psychē* (soul or life) appears in contexts of losing or giving up one's life. Its meaning overlaps *sarx* (flesh) since both refer to mortal life, life that ends in death. Jesus lays down his *psychē* for his friends (John 15:13). He gives up his *sarx* (flesh) for the life (*zōē*) of the world (6:51-58). Life (*zōē*) and eternal life (*zōē aiōnios*) are the life Jesus gives to those who know him and believe in him. It is different than mortal life (*psychē* or *sarx*). See Thompson, *John*, 87-90.

22. The Spirit's role becomes more prominent in the third part of John, examined more fully below.

23. John writes of the resurrection of the dead in which those who believe in Jesus are raised to life and those who do not are raised to judgment (John 5:28-29; 6:40, 44, 54; 11:24). Those who believe live because Jesus lives.

24. See Bauckham's very helpful discussion of the relation between the signs and eternal life. *Gospel of Glory*, loc. 71-72.

believe and continues into life everlasting through a relationship with Jesus and, through him, with his Father. These relationships are made possible through the mediating presence of the Holy Spirit.

Returning to the case study above, we do not know how Meredith's story unfolded. There were indications that some healing occurred and that her baptism allowed her to feel "washed clean." But again we are back to the importance of a congregation where this might continue through the support of spiritual friendships and other kinds of relationships. Life abundant, as John describes it, involves a relation that begins in the present and continues into eternal life. It is a relationship that is supported by a Christian community that is concerned about Meredith's spiritual and psychological well-being.

Signs-Faith

In addition to those who respond to Jesus's signs with belief, John also depicts characters who respond with "signs-faith."[25] They are captivated by the miraculous nature of the signs and follow Jesus to see more and receive more. They do not really understand that the signs point beyond themselves to Jesus's identity as God's Son, revealing his Father's glory. They do not really believe in Jesus. We see this if we return to Jesus's feeding of the five thousand. When the crowd seeks him out the next day, Jesus tells them: "Very truly I tell you, you are looking for me, not because you saw the signs I performed but because you ate the loaves and had your fill. Do not work for food that spoils, but for food that endures to eternal life, which the Son of Man will give you" (John 6:26-27; cf. 2:23-25).

At the end of this discourse, many of Jesus's followers begin to grumble because he has told them, "I am bread that came down from heaven" (John 6:41-42). Their grumbling grows louder when Jesus tells them they must eat his flesh and drink his blood (vv. 53-58). The narrator tells us how they finally respond: "From this time many of his disciples turned back and no longer followed him" (v. 66). Simply seeing the signs and responding positively is not enough. Signs-faith must lead to believing in Jesus and following him. Without a congregation, this may be where Meredith ends up through no fault of her own. And I really cannot blame James and Ivy either.

25. Craig S. Keener, *The Gospel of John: A Commentary*, vol. 1 (Grand Rapids: Baker Academic, 2003), 276-79.

They had just graduated from high school. They were not familiar with this part of the world. I wonder if their sponsoring agency might provide some guidance for this kind of situation. This is worth pondering. What might they have done?

Hostility and Rejection

The Prologue sounds the first note of rejection by telling readers that "his own did not receive him" (John 1:11). It is in the context of hostility that John often speaks of "the Jews" in highly negative ways. In Appendix 1, I discuss this more thoroughly and trace some of the horrific history of antisemitism by Christians based on John. It is important to realize that the narrative context of John likely reflects a history of animosity between John's community and the Jewish community from which it had been expelled. We should reject all interpretations that seek to justify anti-Jewish actions or attitudes on the basis of this Gospel.

Keep this in mind as we explore the hostility and rejection Jesus encounters from the Jewish leaders in response to his signs and discourses. These leaders have many reasons. They know his earthly parents and dismiss any notion that he comes from God (John 6:42). They accuse him of being demon-possessed and raving mad (7:20). More than once the crowd is ready to stone him because he claims to be equal to God (8:59; 10:31). The Pharisees resent the way he is reinterpreting Israel's faith and violating their understanding of the law (9:40). Along with the chief priests, they also fear that Jesus will be viewed by the Roman authorities as one more messianic pretender who will stir up trouble among the people (11:45–53). As the leaders decide what to do, the high priest Caiaphas offers this deeply ironic depiction of the situation: It is better "that one man die for the people than that the whole nation perish" (11:50). He speaks the truth, though not in the way he means. The leaders reject Jesus and begin to plot his death.

John accounts for this unwillingness to believe in Jesus by quoting Isaiah 6:10 (John 12:40; cf. Mark 4:11–12 and Matt. 13:15):

> He has blinded their eyes
> and hardened their hearts,
> so they can neither see with their eyes,
> nor understand with their hearts,
> nor turn—and I would heal them.

In John, the responses of belief and unbelief are a matter of God's action. The Father gives Jesus his own (John 6:44; 10:29; 17:2, 24). Jesus chooses his disciples and those to whom he grants eternal life (5:21; 6:70; 13:18; 15:16, 19). The Holy Spirit gives birth to the children of God (3:5-8) and blows where it will. In the quotation from Isaiah, the negative side of God's action is portrayed: Eyes are blinded and hearts are hardened. But John holds in tension God's action in belief and unbelief and the human capacity to respond to Jesus positively or negatively (3:35-36; 4:39, 42; 5:40). The capacity to respond with belief is not inherent to human beings. John depicts humankind as living in darkness. It emerges as the light draws near and their true situation is illumined for the first time. Will they move toward the source of this light or respond with hostility and rejection?

To return to the case, James learned at some point during the summer that a few of his fellow workers were slipping off during breaks to "have a smoke" and were smoking marijuana. He and Ivy never witnessed this, but they heard little comments from other workers. As Christians with a strong sense of morality they needed to figure out what to do. After praying about it, they decided to keep their sights focused on their ministry through the relationships they had begun to build. They were pretty sure they would have experienced a backlash if they had shared what was going on with the higher-ups.

Christians face these kinds of choices all the time. Remaining true to their faith and moral convictions places them at odds with those around them. Locker talk about girls and gay people and racial slurs still go on all the time in high school, at work, and among friends. Those who speak up often become the next target for bullying. I think that James and Ivy did the right thing in this case. Meredith is the evidence of that. But still, credible witnesses have to expect hostility and opposition when they stand for the gospel. Jesus did, and so must we. Most young Christians do not think of these kinds of actions as evangelism or witness. But surely they are in John's view.

Faith That Remains Hidden

John also portrays characters who respond to Jesus with sympathy and may even be hidden disciples. These are Jewish leaders who keep their faith secret because they are afraid of the disapproval of their peers (John 12:42; 19:38). John explicitly identifies Joseph of Arimathea as a hidden disciple (19:38). It is possible that Nicodemus is one as well. He acknowledges that Jesus's signs come from God. But he comes to Jesus in the secrecy of night and struggles to understand what Jesus means when he says people must be born from above (3:1–21), though the failure to understand is found among other disciples. Later, during the Festival of Booths, Nicodemus argues with his fellow Pharisees and the chief priest who send temple guards to have Jesus arrested. He tries to convince them that Jesus should be given a fair trial (7:50–52). After Jesus is executed Nicodemus goes with Joseph of Arimathea to prepare him for burial, bringing around seventy-five pounds of myrrh and aloes—an extravagant amount fit for a king (19:39–42).

In the end, we do not know if Nicodemus was a hidden disciple among the leaders, but we *do* know that John evaluates this sort of response as inadequate. While Jesus seeks the glory (the praise) of the one who sent him and not that of human beings (John 5:41; 7:18; 8:54), this is not true of leaders who believe but remain hidden: "Yet at the same time many even among the leaders believed in him. But because of the Pharisees they would not openly acknowledge their faith for fear they would be put out of the synagogue; for they loved human praise more than praise from God" (12:42–43).

This sort of response is related to our reflections on hostility and rejection immediately above. The leaders remain hidden because they have a lot to lose. They are criticized by John. He is thinking of the situation of his own community in which people were being cast out of the synagogue for their faith and leaders were remaining hidden. Broadly considered, this is a form of sloth. Pride, falsehood, and sloth are the most widespread forms of sin. Secret leaders were failing to do and be all they could on behalf of God. They stayed in the safety of "the crowd."

This is a major obstacle to sharing the gospel with others in actions and words. It is safer staying among the crowd than speaking up or even taking the small risk of reaching out and sharing one's faith with another person. In James and Ivy's case, I think their decision to remain quiet about a few staff members smoking marijuana was the right one, as I've noted. Remember, Joseph of Arimathea and Nicodemus, who may have been hidden leaders, were in a position to ask for Jesus's body and bury him. There are no hard and fast rules about remaining hidden or speaking up. But it should be an issue on the table in evangelism and witness. Sloth is a powerful force, dragging us down into the safety of the crowd. We need to resist this when it is wise to do so.

Response of Witness

The men and women who are Jesus's closest disciples represent a fourth response to Jesus's signs. As we have seen, they are invited by Jesus to "come and see," and they respond with belief. But John describes a new response that emerges among these disciples after they see the seventh sign: Jesus's resurrection from the dead. They become active witnesses to the love of God revealed in Jesus Christ and the salvation he offers. Up to that point Jesus is the primary witness to his identity as the Son of God, a title that refers to his unique filial relationship to his Father and their mutual indwelling and oneness. After his resurrection, it is the disciples who bear witness to him, empowered by his continuing presence and bestowal of the Holy Spirit. John foreshadows the transformation of the disciples' understanding of Jesus and their role in bearing witness to him throughout his Gospel. While washing his disciples' feet, for example, he tells a resistant Peter, "You do not realize now what I am doing, but later you will understand" (John 13:7). Jesus or the narrator make similar comments throughout the story (13:19; 14:30-31; 16:4). The cross and resurrection transform the disciples' understanding of who Jesus is and their share in his mission.

This response of witness is important not only at the level of the story but also for the Christian readers of John's Gospel. As we have seen in our discussion of the signs, Jesus's miraculous deeds and accompanying discourses are designed to evoke multiple levels of interpretation by readers. Those readers who believe are like the disciples; they are following Jesus already. But their understanding of his identity and their share in his mission must remain open to transformation. It is little wonder that many patristic authors called John the spiritual Gospel, for it invites engagement through extended reflection, prayer, and discussion among Christian friends.

What Evangelism Can Learn from the Book of Signs

1. Action, service, and kindness often precede interpretation linking these acts to Jesus. Belief involves believing *that* Jesus is God's Son and Messiah and believing *into* Jesus, forming a relationship by beginning to follow him.
2. Signs-faith is a form of attraction to Jesus that is based entirely on what people receive. It is a starting point at best and must give way to

learning a new way of life as part of a community of disciples following Jesus to the cross.

3. Jesus's witness evoked hostility and rejection. John portrays the world as living in darkness, captive to the evil one, "the prince of the world" and the "father of lies" (John 8:44; 12:31; 14:30; 16:11). Christians should not seek out hostility; indeed, they should seek the way of reconciliation and peace. But hostility will find them just as surely as it found Jesus. They must not give in to the sin of sloth, remaining in the safety of the crowd, but rather must stand out and up as witnesses to Jesus. This calls for discernment.

The Book of Glory: John 13:1–20:31

As we explore evangelism in the Book of Glory, a few words of background may be helpful. Unlike the Book of Signs, in which each sign is followed by a discourse interpreting its meaning, this book *begins* by interpreting the meaning of the climactic events that are to follow. Interpretation precedes action. It addresses the disciples, a much smaller group than the crowds who witnessed Jesus's earlier signs and discourses. John uses a common literary device to frame Jesus's final comments to his disciples: the farewell speech of Greco-Roman historical biographies and the "last testaments" of leaders in the Old Testament.[26] Such discourses frequently offer comfort to those who will be left behind and instruction pertinent to the challenges they will face. This is precisely what we find in the Farewell Discourse.

The Death of Jesus as the Glorification of God

The pattern of Jesus's mission in John has been compared to the arc of a pendulum.[27] I imagine this as a pendulum swinging downward from a high point on the left until it reaches the lowest point in the middle. It then swings upward to a high point on the right. In John, the Son of God has come down from heaven (John 3:13) to reveal God's glory in his person, signs, and words.

---

26. Keener, *The Gospel of John*, vol. 2, 896–98; Raymond E. Brown, SS, *The Gospel according to John*, vol. 2, *XIII–XXI*, The Anchor Bible Series, vol. 29A (Garden City, NY: Doubleday, 2003), 581–86; Thompson, *John*, 295–98.

27. Brown, *Gospel of John*, vol. 2, 541–42.

Near the end of the Book of Signs, a low point is reached: "Even after Jesus had performed so many signs in their presence, they still would not believe in him" (John 12:37). As the Prologue anticipates, he is rejected by "his own" (1:11), who prefer darkness to light. The Book of Glory traces the upward swing of the pendulum back to God. Jesus is "lifted up" on the cross, a phrase John uses three times to describe his death (3:14; 8:28; 12:32-33).[28] The upward movement continues in his resurrection and is completed in his ascension to the Father (20:17). The entire movement of the pendulum—the incarnation, ministry, death, resurrection, and ascension of Jesus—reveals the glory of God and accomplishes the salvation of the world.

Yet within this comprehensive pattern, the cross and resurrection are the climax of John's story.[29] The story moves relentlessly toward Jesus's "hour" (John 2:4; 7:6, 8, 30; 8:20; 12:23, 27; 13:1; 17:1). This hour arrives with the onset of the events leading to his crucifixion.[30] Among the Gospels, John alone describes the humiliation of Jesus's crucifixion as part of his exaltation. The more common pattern in the early Christian tradition is humiliation followed by exaltation, suffering followed by glory.[31] But for John, Jesus's shameful and dehumanizing death is part of his glorification of God. In his death he is revealing God's glory.

John's understanding of this is shaped by two parts of Isaiah, which he interprets together (cf. John 12:41).[32] In Isaiah 6, the prophet shares a vision of the

28. Jesus alludes to his death and resurrection many times, though typically quite cryptically (for example, John 2:17, 19-21; 3:14-16; 6:51, 62; 7:33-36; 8:21-22, 28; 12:7-8, 24-25, 33-34) . He speaks directly of these events only once to make it clear that his death is voluntary (10:11-18).

29. Until recent decades, many modern interpreters of John have viewed the theme of glory and the use of imagery of above and below to portray Jesus's mission as exclusively one of revelation. Jesus's death was portrayed as having no salvific significance in itself. Rudolf Bultmann and Ernst Käsemann were particularly important in establishing this paradigm. A helpful overview of the movement to new lines of interpretation is found in John Dennis, "Jesus' Death in John's Gospel: A Survey of Research from Bultmann to the Present with Special Reference to the Johannine Hyper-Texts," *Currents in Biblical Research* 4, no. 3 (2006): 331-63. For a broader perspective on this shift, see Bauckham, *Testimony of the Beloved Disciple*, ch. 1. I follow the more recent lines of interpretation.

30. I take Jesus's words from the cross, "It is finished" to mean that the "work" he was to given by his Father which led him to become flesh (John 1:14) was completed. Obviously, his resurrection and ascension led to new ways of relating to his followers, both on earth and in heaven.

31. Bauckham, *Gospel of Glory*, loc. 54. See for example Phil. 2:6-11.

32. Bauckham, *Gospel of Glory*, loc. 54. There are verbal connections between these

Lord seated on his throne, "high and lifted up," and "the whole earth is full of his glory!" (Isa. 6:1, 3). In Deutero-Isaiah 52–53, the author shares the prophecy of a servant whose appearance is "disfigured" and "marred beyond human likeness" but will be "raised and lifted up and highly exalted" (Isa. 52:13–14). In his suffering this servant bears the transgressions of the people, "an offering for sin" bringing healing and peace (Isa. 53:5, 10). In John's telling of the gospel story, Jesus's suffering and death as he is "lifted up" on the cross is the beginning of his exaltation and the climax of his revelation of God's glory. It is part of the upward swing of the pendulum back to the glory he shared with his Father prior to the creation of the world and his incarnation in human flesh (John 1:14; 17:5).

Now that his hour has arrived, Jesus will "finish" the work that his Father has given him to do (John 17:4), his death on the cross. Prior to the Book of Glory, there are at least fourteen allusions to Jesus's death.[33] John offers two complementary lines of interpretation of the saving significance of the cross. One focuses on the universal significance of Jesus's death. The other focuses on the significance of his death for those who believe in him. He lays down his life for his friends, those who are closest to him.

The line of interpretation most explicitly universalistic draws on imagery of the atonement. Near the beginning of the narrative, John the Baptist speaks of Jesus as "the Lamb of God, who takes away the sin of the world!" (John 1:29, 36; cf. 1 John 2:1–2). This draws on the early church's traditional imagery of Jesus's death as a vicarious sacrifice on behalf of humanity. By placing this interpretation of Jesus's death so early in his story, John is signaling to readers its importance in understanding the narrative that follows.[34]

The note of universalism is echoed in John 3:16–17: "For God so loved the *world* that he *gave* his *one and only Son*, that whoever believes in him shall not perish but have eternal life. For God did not send his Son into the world to condemn the world, but to *save the world through him*." As God's "one and only Son," Jesus stands in unique, filial relationship with his Father. He was with God and was God before creation (1:1). He shares his Father's love for the world. His Father "gave" his one and only Son to save the world. The language of God "giving up" his Son to save the world is found elsewhere

---

passages, and it was common for interpreters to link such passages together during this period.

33. John 2:17, 19–21; 3:14–16; 6:51, 62; 7:33–36; 8:21–22, 28; 10:11, 15; 11:49–53; 12:7–8, 24–25, 33–34.

34. This is contrary to Rudolf Bultmann, Ernst Käsemann, Mark L. Appold, and others who view John's statements as merely a "residual" of preexistent Christian tradition that has no real importance in the story he tells.

in the early Christian tradition.[35] So too is the language of Jesus of "giving up" (6:51) and "laying down" his life for others (10:11, 15; cf. 6:51; 10:11, 15; 11:50–52; 15:13, and 1 John 3:16).[36]

The basic message here is that Jesus's death on the cross has universal scope. He is the Savior of the world (John 4:42) who dies *for* the world, on behalf of and in the place of all people. All people are invited to respond to this good news by believing in Jesus through the Holy Spirit. This response includes acknowledging his identity as God's Son, beginning a relationship with him, and joining a community of his followers.

Alongside this line of interpretation John also portrays the significance of Jesus's death as dying out of love for his friends. Here, the universal scope of Jesus's death for the world is given concrete expression in particular events and relationships in John's story. It is perhaps the most important way John portrays the humanity of Jesus. He does not simply love everyone in general. He loves the people he is closest to in particular. They are Jesus's "own" (John 10:3–4, 14; 13:2) and his "friends" (15:13–15; cf. 11:11). He tells his disciples: "Greater love has no one than this: to lay down one's life for one's friends. You are my friends" (15:13–14). Bauckham summarizes the significance of this line of interpretation: "By representing Jesus as giving his life for the circle of his disciples, those specific people whom he knew and loved as friends, John gives concrete narrative form to the love of God for the world that Jesus lives out in his actual path to death."[37]

Both interpretations of Jesus's death are important for evangelism. Jesus is sent on his mission to accomplish two basic things: to reveal God and to die for the sins of the world. God loves all people and gives himself to atone for their sins. Evangelism thus must approach every person as someone Jesus loves and for whom he has died. He has not just died for people like us: not just the people of our tribe, not just the people of our racial or ethnic background, not just the people of our nation. He has died for all people. This is expressed concretely in Jesus's love for his friends. He dies for those he is closest to, but he is also constantly offering his friendship to people beyond his inner circle: to a Samaritan woman and her village, to a lame man by the pool of Bethesda, to a Jewish leader who comes to him under the cover of

35. See Gal. 1:4 and 1 Tim. 2:5–6. Closely related is *paradidōmi*, handing over for others, as in Rom. 4:25; 8:32; and Eph. 5:2.

36. Surrendering imagery is found in Gal. 1:4; Eph. 5:2; and 1 Tim. 2:5–6. Use of the preposition "for" (*hyper*) us is seen in 1 Thess. 5:9–10; 1 Cor. 15:3; and 2 Cor. 5:14–15. Similar language in early tradition portrays Jesus as dying "for" (*hyper*) others.

37. Bauckham, *Gospel of Glory*, loc. 64.

night. He invites them to become a part of the circle of his friends. He wants them to understand that he lays down his life for them too.

The theme of Jesus's death on behalf of his friends first emerges in Jesus's discourse on the good shepherd (John 10). The shepherd "lays down his life for the sheep" who know his voice and trust him (vv. 11, 14-15). The mutual knowing of Jesus and his disciples is compared to the mutual knowing of Jesus and his Father. The love of Jesus for his disciples, which extends to his willingness to lay down his life on their behalf, partakes of the self-giving love uniting the Father and Son (cf. 17:24).

The story of Jesus raising Lazarus carries this theme forward in significant ways. It is a key event that leads to his death. Just a short time before this story, Jesus barely escapes from Jerusalem without being stoned (John 10:39-40). In choosing to return to the home of friends in Bethany—only two miles outside of Jerusalem—Jesus is placing himself in danger.[38] The disciples are clear about this and offer many reasons why Jesus should not go (11:8-16). Nonetheless, he makes up his mind to travel to Bethany. Since Jesus is placing himself in grave danger, Thomas tells the other disciples: "Let us also go, that we may die with him" (11:16).

When Jesus is just outside the village, Martha comes out to meet him. After a brief conversation, Jesus asks her to send Mary. She is accompanied by women who have gathered to comfort her. The description of their encounter in John 11:32-37 portrays a very human Jesus who loves his friends:

> When Mary reached the place where Jesus was and saw him, she fell at his feet and said, "Lord, if you had been here, my brother would not have died."
>
> When Jesus saw her weeping, and the Jews who had come along with her also weeping, he was deeply moved in spirit and troubled. "Where have you laid him?" he asked.
>
> "Come and see, Lord," they replied.
>
> Jesus wept.
>
> Then the Jews said, "See how he loved him!" But some of them said, "Could not he who opened the eyes of the blind man have kept this man from dying?"

Mary, like her sister, appears to rebuke Jesus indirectly for not coming sooner. When he experiences the pain this has caused her, Jesus becomes

---

38. Jesus refers to Lazarus as his friend in John 11:11.

very emotional, and some of the women accompanying Mary rightly interpret Jesus's grief as an expression of love. After he frees Lazarus from death,
so many people respond by believing in Jesus that the news is taken to the
Pharisees. A meeting of the Sanhedrin is convened. The chain of events leading to Jesus's death begins to gather momentum. Jesus lays down his life for
his friends by returning to Bethany and provoking the religious leaders: "So
from that day on they plotted to take his life" (John 11:53).

There are other events in the narrative that give concrete expression to
Jesus's love for his friends. Even as he is dying on the cross, for example, he
tells his mother and best friend to live together as family (John 19:25-27).
Later, when Mary Magdalene stands by the empty tomb weeping and fails to
recognize Jesus, he calms her by speaking her name in a familiar way (20:11-
18). Such stories give expression to Jesus's love for those who are closest to
him. He lays down his life for his friends as well as for all people. This theme
is especially prominent in the first part of the Book of Glory as Jesus gathers
with his disciples for their last meal together

The first verse sets the tone: "Jesus knew that the hour had come for him
to leave this world and go to the Father. Having loved his own who were in the
world, he loved them to the end" (John 13:1). Jesus's love for his friends comes
to expression in two striking ways in this part of John: Jesus's washing of his
disciples' feet and the comfort and guidance he offers them in the Farewell
Discourse. In both, he is preparing his friends for his impending death.

The Footwashing

We usually view the footwashing as an example of humble service that Jesus
offers his disciples who will serve as leaders of the church.[39] There is no
question that this is true, as John 13:15 makes clear. But more importantly,
the footwashing is a symbolic action in which Jesus interprets the meaning
of his death for his closest circle of followers. In John, there is no account of
his "institution" of the Lord's Supper. Instead, as the meal progresses, Jesus
rises and washes his disciples' feet. This is an act of hospitality. Typically, the
host would provide water and each guest would wash his or her own feet. If
the host was wealthy, this might be performed by a servant or slave. It would
be highly unusual for the honored guest to perform this service for others.

39. For detailed exegesis of this passage, see Brown, *Gospel of John*, vol. 2, 563-72,
whom I follow here.

Peter realizes that Jesus is breaking normal social conventions by performing this menial task. He objects. Jesus responds: "You do not realize now what I am doing, but later you will understand" (John 13:7; cf. v. 19). This refers to understanding that emerges after Jesus's death and resurrection (cf. 2:22; 12:16; 14:29; 20:9). Jesus continues: "Unless I wash you, you won't belong to me" (13:8 NLT). The emphasis at this point is on *Jesus's* action, not the disciples'. The latter would be the case if he were simply referring to their imitation of his example. But Jesus says, unless *he* washes them, they will have no part in him.[40]

The footwashing points ahead to the humiliating death that Jesus will suffer on the cross. It will cleanse them of the stain of sin and unite them to him and one another in a new way. By adopting the posture of a servant, Jesus is likely reminding the disciples of the Suffering Servant of Isaiah 52–53, who bore the sin of many in his death and was "raised and lifted up and highly exalted" (Isa. 52:13–14). Soon Jesus will be "lifted up" on the cross, glorifying his Father and being glorified by him. By washing his disciples' feet, he acts as the servant of friends he loves and will die for.

In the passage immediately following (John 13:12–17), Jesus exhorts the disciples to "do as I have done for you" (v. 15), introducing a prominent topic in the Farewell Discourse. They are to love one another as he has loved them. They are to serve one another as he has just served them. In doing so, they keep his commands and glorify him just as he glorifies his Father. This gives expression in a powerful way to the role of community in evangelism. In the love among Christians, others will see and, perhaps, experience for the first time the self-giving love of God embodied in a concrete community of human beings. Jesus loves the people who surround him and bids his followers to do the same: "As I have loved you, so you must love one another. By this everyone will know that you are my disciples, if you love one another" (vv. 34–35). This is central to evangelism.

The passage also reminds us of the importance of helping those who respond to the good news of God's love to begin learning this new way of life. American culture today is very me-centered and pleasure-centered. The example of Jesus's footwashing may seem alien and even foolish. Evangelism

40. This line of interpretation is strengthened by the use of "wash" in John 13:8, which is commonly associated with baptism in the New Testament and the cleansing of sin by being washed. The language of "washing," as Brown notes, is likely a secondary reference to baptism. See his *Gospel of John*, vol. 2, 566–67. See Acts 22:16; Titus 3:5. This language also appears in 1 Cor. 6:11; Eph. 5:26; and Heb. 10:22. Keener also is very helpful. See *The Gospel of John*, vol. 2, 901–14.

thus must invite people who are new to Christianity into relational contexts that will help them learn what self-giving love looks like in their everyday lives. Without this, the evangelist is like a gardener who plants flowers but fails to provide the nutrients and water they will need to grow.

The Farewell Discourse

The footwashing is followed by Jesus's last discourse. As we have mentioned, it is similar in form to a farewell speech or last testament. This literary genre often depicts a dying father instructing his children, warning them of dangers they will face and offering advice and comfort. Here Jesus addresses his disciples as "little children"—the only time this occurs in John—and tells them he will be with them only a little while longer (John 13:33; cf. 1:12 ESV). The events leading to his death are beginning to unfold at a rapid pace. Soon those who have followed him throughout his ministry will no longer be able to do so (v. 36). This is the final opportunity Jesus has to prepare his disciple-friends for what lies ahead.

Jesus offers various forms of comfort, advice, and instruction in this lengthy and rich part of John's narrative. Much of what Jesus shares may be grouped together under two headings: Jesus's presence in absence and the hallmarks of faithful discipleship after he has departed.[41]

Presence in Absence

Even though Jesus is soon to depart and return to his Father, he promises his friends that he will not abandon them (John 14:18). He will reveal himself to them (14:21); he will dwell with them (14:18) and in them (14:20; 15:4-5). The in-one-another theme intensifies in this part of the story. Though they will mourn, this will turn to joy when they see him again after he is raised from the dead (16:20-24). The resurrection is the presupposition of the many promises Jesus makes to his disciples that he will continue to be with them (14:19; 16:16; 20:18, 25, 29). As Jesus tells them: "Because I live, you also will live" (14:19).

After his resurrection, their relationship will continue, though in a different form. It is this relationship that gives them eternal life, life to the full. Jesus also promises that he will be with them when they face death (John

41. Thompson, *John*, 295-96. I rely on Thompson throughout this section.

14:1–4). He has gone to prepare a place for the disciples and promises them, "I will come back and take you to be with me" (14:3; cf. 14:18, 28). He also refers in passing to his future "return" (21:23).

Jesus also promises the disciples that both he and his Father will send them the Paraclete (John 14:16, 26; 15:26; 16:7), also identified in the Farewell Discourse as the Holy Spirit (14:26; cf. 7:39) and the Spirit of truth (14:17; 15:26; 16:13). In relation to the disciples, the Paraclete will remind them of Jesus's words, guide them into all truth, comfort them, and tell them what is yet to come (14:26; 16:13, 14), In mediating Jesus's presence, the Spirit glorifies Jesus (16:14), just as Jesus has glorified his Father.

In relation to the world, the Paraclete bears witness to Jesus in the face of the world's hostility and empowers the disciples to bear witness as well (John 15:26–27). Sometimes, the Greek term *paraklētos* is translated "advocate" (as in John 14:16), which brings to mind the image of an attorney in a court of law. Jesus will soon be put on trial. In the future the disciples will be asked to defend their faith not only before legal authorities but also in the face of skeptical questions from friends, families, neighbors, and people holding ideologies hostile to Christianity. The advocate, Jesus says, will testify on his behalf and prove the world wrong in its understanding of sin, justice, and judgment (16:8–11). In some ways the Spirit is more like a prosecuting attorney than a defense attorney.[42] Yet the Paraclete's primary role is not that of an attorney but a *witness* who testifies about Jesus and inspires the disciples to testify as well (15:26–27). Those disciples who have followed Jesus "from the beginning" can provide eyewitness testimony (15:27). Those who become disciples in the future will rely on the apostles' witness in their testimony, as well as on their own knowledge and experience.

The image of the Paraclete as a prosecuting attorney and a witness who empowers the disciples to testify is very important to evangelism. But we must be cautious about how we think about these images, especially the former. It sometimes has led to the worse forms of evangelism: cross-examining non-Christians, attempting to prove them wrong or putting them on trial. These approaches will not prove effective nor do they really capture what John has in mind. The Paraclete is not just an advocate in the legal sense but is also a consoler, teacher, guide, and helper. The Spirit's role as an advocate and witness is very close to what is depicted in Acts 5:32, where Peter appears before the Sanhedrin and states: "We are witnesses of these things, and so

---

42. Brown, *Gospel of John*, vol. 2, 1136. John's picture is different than that of Matt. 10:20 and Acts 6:10, where the Spirit defends the disciples when they are put on trial.

is the Holy Spirit." The Paraclete helps disciples find ways to illuminate the situations of others with the light that shines into the darkness. The Spirit will give them the words to say, so they should not be afraid.

The prominence of the Holy Spirit in the Farewell Discourse includes some of the richest "Trinitarian" passages in the New Testament (such as John 14:26; 15:26; 16:12-15). Here, the in-one-another theme is depicted not only as a relationship between Jesus and his followers but also as a relationship that includes the Father and Spirit. The Father will continue to be with the disciples (14:23; 17:11, 15, 26), as will the Spirit who comes after Jesus departs. Indeed, the Father and Son will *both* make their home with those who faithfully embody Jesus's way (14:23), and the Spirit will live with them and be in them (14:17).

This should give us pause when we hear evangelism described as leading people to a personal relationship with Jesus Christ. As we have shown extensively, Jesus *does* form relationships with individuals and such relationships *are* personal. The Son and the believer are in one another, a friendship of mutual love and care. But John also describes the Father and Spirit as coming to and dwelling with believers. As such, evangelism is better described as inviting people into a relationship with a loving God, the God revealed in Jesus Christ. This God lives in the eternal and mutual love shared by the Father, Son, and Holy Spirit. The Son is sent into the world to make this love known and to invite people to participate in it. So are his disciples.

The Hallmarks of Discipleship after Jesus Has Departed

In his Farewell Discourse, Jesus also offers his final words about how the disciples should live and relate to one another after he has departed. He tells the disciples to continue to believe (John 14:1, 10-11, 29; 16:30-31), to abide in him (15:1-11), and to love one another as he has loved them (13:1, 34; 14:15; 15:12-13, 17). Most importantly of all, he tells them their mission is to bear witness to the saving love of God he has revealed to the world (15:1-8, 16; 15:18-16:2; 16:8-11, 33), which is directly relevant to the comments about evangelism above. The disciples' love for one another is a form of this witness (13:34-35). The continued presence of the Father, Son, and Holy Spirit among the disciples is not for their benefit alone. It also is to strengthen and guide them as they share the gospel with the world. Jesus prays to his Father, "As you sent me into the world, I have sent them into the world" (17:18). He also prays for those who will believe through the disciples' message (17:20-26) and that all of his followers will be one as he and the Father are one, for "then the world will know that you sent me and have loved them even as you have loved me" (17:23). Once again, the witness of the congregation as a community is lifted up. The individual and the community go hand in hand.

The Passion Narrative

John's passion narrative is structured around three parts of relatively equal length: the arrest of Jesus and his encounter with the high priests Annas and Caiaphas (John 18:1-27), the trial of Jesus before Pilate (18:28-19:16), and the crucifixion of Jesus and his burial (19:17-42). In this account of Jesus's passion, John portrays Jesus's suffering and death as the culminating act of his revelation of God's glory and salvation of the world.

Jesus and the High Priests (18:1-27)

Following Jesus's final prayer of intercession for he disciples, he leads them to a garden across the Kidron Valley, where he frequently met with his disciples. Familiar with Jesus's actions, Judas leads soldiers and officials connected with the chief priests and Pharisees to the garden. The scene is an extraordinary portrayal of Jesus's willing acceptance of his way to the cross.[43] He asks the soldiers: "Who do you want?" They respond: "Jesus of Nazareth." He replies: "I am he." This is a form of the divine name the Father has given his Son: I Am (cf. John 13:19; 17:11). It appears in many different ways throughout John's story.[44] When Jesus says "I am he," those who have come to arrest him "drew back and fell to the ground" (18:6). Yet Jesus hands himself over, asking only that his disciples go free. He uses the power of the divine name to protect not himself but his friends. When Peter cuts off the ear of the high priest's servant, Jesus tells him: "Put your sword away! Shall I not drink the cup the Father has given me?" (18:11). He is not a hapless victim; he goes willingly to complete the work his Father has given him to carry out.

The soldiers take Jesus to Annas and then Caiaphas. The narrator reminds readers that Caiaphas was the one who advised the Jewish leaders "that it

43. It appears to embody in narrative form Jesus's statement that he gives up his life of his own accord in John 10:17-18.
44. For an excellent discussion of "I Am" in John, including its background in the Old Testament, see Brown, *Gospel of John*, vol. 2, 533-38.

would be good if one man died for the people" (John 18:14; cf. 11:47–50). Peter and "another disciple," who was known to the high priest, follow the soldiers to the home of Annas. At first Peter must wait by the door of the courtyard, but the other disciple returns and gains his admittance. In response to a query of the maidservant, Peter denies that he is one of Jesus's disciples for the first time. Jesus is now inside the home of Annas, and Peter outside. The action shifts inside to the interrogation by Annas. He asks Jesus about "his disciples and his teaching" (18:19). Jesus responds that he has always spoken openly in the synagogues or the temple, and he asks Annas why he does not call on those who heard him to share what he said. Even after being slapped for rudeness toward the high priest, Jesus persists: "If I said something wrong, testify as to what is wrong. But if I spoke the truth, why did you strike me?" (18:23).

While Jesus is bound and taken to Caiaphas, the scene shifts back outside where Peter waits. Jesus has just asked the high priest why he has not called those who heard him to give testimony. Peter, who heard Jesus speak from the very beginning of his ministry, now denies for a second and third time that he is one of Jesus's disciples. Jesus proceeds to his trial alone. Peter has taken a step away from him. The future of the disciples' witness appears at risk. Nonetheless, the scene ends on a hopeful note. When the rooster crows, readers are reminded that events are unfolding as Jesus predicted.

The Trial of Jesus before Pilate (18:28–19:16)

This scene takes place at the praetorium, Pilate's headquarters. Once again, it shifts back and forth between conversation taking place inside and outside. The Jewish authorities remain outside, for it is the Day of Preparation and they do not want to become unclean. Thompson summarizes the action as follows:[45]

> Outside: The Jews bring their accusation against Jesus.
> Inside: Pilate enters the praetorium to ask Jesus whether he is the King of the Jews.
> Outside: Pilate declares Jesus' innocence and offers to release him.
> [Pilate has Jesus flogged.]
> Outside: Pilate again declares Jesus' innocence and presents him,

45. Thompson, John, 371.

dressed in a purple robe and with a crown of thorns, with the words, "See the man!"

Inside: Pilate enters the praetorium to ask Jesus about his origins.

Outside: Pilate again brings Jesus out to the Jews, this time presenting him with the acclamation, "See your king!"

[*Pilate hands Jesus over to be crucified.*]

On one level, the back-and-forth action depicts a struggle between the Roman governor and high priests to determine what will happen to Jesus. At this level the trial of Jesus is about the manipulation and compromises of power politics. The action on the outside is where the real power lies. But is this really true? Each time Pilate steps inside, Jesus challenges the presuppositions of Pilate's questions. The key theme is kingship. Pilate introduces this in response to the Jewish authorities' call for his death, a call that implies that Jesus is a messianic pretender who threatens the peace of Rome. Pilate asks Jesus if he claims to be the king of the Jews, and Jesus replies by asking him whether this is his question or one suggested by others. When Pilate persists, Jesus responds: "My kingdom is not of this world. If it were, my servants would fight to prevent my arrest by the Jewish leaders. But now my kingdom is from another place" (John 18:36). Pilate tries to turn Jesus's word to his advantage: "So you are a king, then." Jesus responds: "You say that I am a king. In fact, the reason I was born and came into the world is to testify to the truth. Everyone on the side of truth listens to me" (18:37). Pilate replies cynically, "What is truth?"

After this brief exchange, Pilate begins referring to Jesus as "your king" in his conversations with the Jewish authorities and presents him to them with a crown of thorns and purple robe after Jesus is flogged. In his final exchange with Jesus, Pilate asks. "Don't you realize I have power either to free you or to crucify you?" Jesus responds, "You would have no power over me if it were not given to you from above" (John 19:10–11).

The conversation between Jesus and Pilate during the trial is the only extended discussion of kingship in John's story. But it is consistent with the themes and imagery used throughout: the contrast between above and below to depict Jesus's origin, ministry, and destination; Jesus's coming into the world to testify to the truth; his Father's sovereignty over all things, including his trial and impending death, and Pilate's role in these events. As Thompson points out, the real question is not whether Jesus is the king of the Jews but the nature of his kingdom. In contrast to those who seek his death, "Jesus' kingdom is characterized, not by taking life, but by giving life; not by fighting

to avoid death at the hands of others, but by dying for others; not by dominating power, but by bearing witness to the truth."[46]

The Crucifixion of Jesus and His Burial (19:17-42)

Pilate finally sits in the judgment seat and hands Jesus over to be crucified.
This takes place on the Day of Preparation when the lambs are slaughtered
for Passover. More than in any other part in his story, John points out directly
that specific events during the crucifixion are the fulfillment of Scripture
(John 19:24, 28, 36, 37). They are unfolding according to God's will. When
Jesus dies he says, "It is finished" (19:30). He was sent into the world for a
reason. This has now been accomplished through his death on the cross.

The Resurrection

The resurrection is God's vindication of Jesus's mission, which has culmi-
nated in his death on the cross. As Jesus promised, he will continue to be
with his followers in new ways, give them the Holy Spirit, and send them
in mission. Together, the resurrection and ascension complete the upward
swing of the pendulum. Jesus is returning to the glory he shared with the
Father before his incarnation. It is now time for the community of disciples
to glorify the Father by witnessing to the saving love of his Son through the
mediating presence of the Holy Spirit.

The resurrection appearances take place in two locations, which structure
this part of John's story: at the tomb (John 20:1-18) and where the disciples
are gathered (20:19-29). Following Jesus's death, Joseph of Arimathea asks
Pilate for his body. With the help of Nicodemus, he takes it to a tomb nearby.
Together, they wrap it with linen strips along with spices, and they presumably roll a stone over the opening.

At the Tomb

Very early the next day, Mary Magdalene goes to the tomb and finds the
stone removed from the entrance. She runs to tell Peter and the disciple Je-

46. Thompson, *John*, 372.

sus loved: "They have taken the Lord out of the tomb, and we don't know where they have put him!" They run to the tomb. The disciple Jesus loved arrives first. He looks inside and sees the strips of linen, but does not enter. Peter arrives and immediately enters the tomb. He is followed by the disciple Jesus loved, who now "saw and believed." The narrator comments: "They still did not understand from Scripture that Jesus had to rise from the dead" (John 20:9).

After the disciples depart, Mary Magdalene remains and is weeping. She looks into the tomb and encounters two angels who ask her why she is weeping. She responds, "They have taken my Lord away, and I don't know where they have put him" (John 20:13). Turning around, she encounters Jesus but does not recognize him. Thinking he is the gardener, she asks him where he has placed the body. Jesus responds, "Mary" and she recognizes him, calling out "Rabboni!" Jesus tells her: "Do not hold on to me, for I have not yet ascended to the Father. Go instead to my brothers and tell them, 'I am ascending to my Father and your Father, to my God and your God'" (20:17).

John alone includes the story of Peter and the disciple Jesus loved running to the empty tomb in response to Mary Magdalene's report. Here, as elsewhere in John, when these two disciples appear together, the disciple Jesus loved appears to surpass Peter in some way.[47] He arrives first and upon entering the tomb he "believes" when they find it empty. He understands that the empty tomb and burial cloths signify that Jesus lives, as he promised he would (John 14:19), and that he is returning to his Father (13:1, 33, 36–38; 14:3; 16:28; 17:11, 13; 20:17). His body is not missing; he has risen from the dead. The beloved disciple believes in the resurrection apart from seeing the risen Lord, as will all new disciples in the future, with the exception of Paul.

Mary is the first to encounter the risen Lord. Along with Jesus's mother and her sister, Mary had gone to the cross with Jesus and witnessed his death. Of the male disciples, only the disciple Jesus loved was there with them. When Mary goes to the tomb the following day, the darkness has not yet given way to light. Jesus calls her name in a familiar way and she recognizes him. He is risen from the dead. She goes to the disciples with the news: "I have seen the Lord!" Mary Magdalene is the first of Jesus's followers to witness to the resurrection of Jesus from the dead. She shares the good news that she has seen the Lord.

---

47. See Thompson, *John*, 409; she provides a nice summary of the passages in which the disciples appear together.

The Resurrected Lord and the New Community (21:1–25)

On the evening of that day, Jesus appears to the disciples who were still hiding for fear of the Jewish authorities. He offers them peace and then commissions them: "'As the Father has sent me, I am sending you.' And with that he breathed on them and said, 'Receive the Holy Spirit'" (John 20:21–22). The coming of the Spirit is a critical part of the transition from Jesus's earthly ministry to the mission of his disciples. They now are empowered to bear witness to him. He appears to Thomas a week later and shows him the puncture wounds in his hands and sides. He then states: "Because you have seen me, you have believed; blessed are those who have not seen and yet have believed." This, of course, is how people will come to believe in the future. They will not encounter Jesus directly but will believe solely on the basis of the disciples' witness. The presence of the Holy Spirit and the witness of the disciples represent a new chapter in the story of the spread of the gospel. Two more things need to occur.

First, the disciples need to learn anew that they must continue to "abide" in Jesus if they are to carry out their mission. A final resurrection appearance takes place by the Sea of Tiberias. Seven disciples have returned to their old trade of fishing. Perhaps they feel the lure of simply resuming their lives where they left off before their time with Jesus. Jesus appears on the beach, but they do not recognize him. Nevertheless, they follow his instructions and are rewarded with a miraculous catch of fish. If they continue to follow their Lord's guidance, their catch of women and men will be abundant as well. The meal they share likely alludes to the Lord's Supper, which Jesus has mentioned in his discourse on the bread of life (John 6:53–56). Jesus is the host who offers them bread and then fish. They will continue to encounter him as the bread of life in the future.

The second and final thing that must occur is that Peter must be reinstated. Jesus asks Peter three times whether he loves him, recalling his threefold denial (John 18:17, 25–27). The first time, Jesus asks whether Peter loves him "more than these" (21:15). He is not asking whether Peter loves him (Jesus) more than the other disciples do but whether his love for Jesus is greater than his love for anything else, even life itself. He failed this question earlier. Only if he answers this question affirmatively will he be in a position to take on a shepherding role parallel to that of the Good Shepherd who is willing to lay down his life for his sheep. He then alludes to Peter's martyrdom and calls him once again with the classic words of the Synoptic Gospels: "Follow me."

For Further Reading

Appold, Mark L. *The Oneness Motif of the Fourth Gospel: Motif Analysis and Exegetical Probe into the Fourth Gospel.* Eugene, OR: Wipf & Stock, 1976. Though I disagree with some of its conclusions, a stimulating treatment of the in-one-another theme in John.

Bauckham, Richard. *The Gospel of Glory: Major Themes in Johannine Theology.* Grand Rapids: Baker Academic, 2015. As title suggests, a treatment of different themes in John in a clear and highly suggestive manner. Leaves me wanting a commentary on John by the author.

———. *The Testimony of the Beloved Disciple: Narrative, History and Theology in the Gospel of John.* Grand Rapids: Baker Academic, 2007. Overview of recent approaches to John, followed by an altogether new and different perspective. Highly readable and fascinating.

Brown, Raymond E., SS. *The Gospel according to John*, vol. 1, *I-XII*, and vol. 2, *XIII-XXI.* The Anchor Bible Series vols. 29 and 29A. Garden City, NY: Doubleday, 2003. In terms of covering the background of all things related to John, a very helpful work. However, it relies on form and tradition criticism in ways I no longer agree with after reading Bauckham.

Keener, Craig S. *The Gospel of John: A Commentary.* Vols. 1 and 2. Grand Rapids: Baker Academic, 2003. This book is incredibly helpful in terms of covering background issues and history related to John and other Gospels.

Thompson, Marianne Meye. *John: A Commentary.* Louisville: Westminster John Knox, 2015. A very insightful commentary on John, excellent for academics, congregational leaders, and students.

PART II

Evangelism in Dialogue with Karl Barth

In the next two chapters, we engage Karl Barth as a dialogue partner. It may be helpful at the outset to note that the translation of *Church Dogmatics* uses the term "evangelisation," not "evangelism" or "evangelization," which are more common in American English. All of these terms draw on the Greek New Testament term *euangelizō*, to announce good news, and it is the theological framework in which they are placed that determines the meaning of this ministry. I will retain "evangelisation" in quotations from Barth but use "evangelization" for my own constructive proposal, following Darrell Guder.[1] I will continue to use "evangelism" to refer to the general field, with the caveat that most people in the United States understand this to refer to evangelism as conversionism.

Karl Barth was a Swiss theologian teaching in Germany when Adolf Hitler came to power. He provided intellectual leadership for the Confessing Church, which resisted efforts to unify Protestant congregations into a pro-Nazi Reich Church. While Barth is much admired for his courage during this period and for the brilliance of his theology, American evangelicals and progressives usually do not think of Barth's thought as a live theological option today.

Many evangelicals view Barth as too close to universalism in his understanding of salvation.[2] In their view this undercuts the motive and mission of evangelism. Many progressives view Barth as focusing too exclusively on Jesus Christ as the center of God's revelation and salvation. In their view, this

---

1. Darrell L. Guder, *Be My Witnesses: The Church's Mission, Message, and Messengers* (Grand Rapids: Eerdmans, 1985), 133-40.

2. An early critic of Barth was Cornelius van Til, *The New Modernism* (Philadelphia: P & R, 1947). See also G. C. Berkouwer, *The Triumph of Grace in the Theology of Karl Barth* (Grand Rapids: Eerdmans, 1956); and Donald Bloesch, *Jesus Is Victor! Karl Barth's Doctrine of Salvation* (Nashville: Abingdon, 1976).

undercuts the church's engagement of culture and interreligious dialogue. These perceptions are based on half-truths.

Barth does indeed offer a new motive and mission for evangelism based on the representative and substitutionary nature of God's salvation of the world in Jesus Christ. As we shall see, the theme of Christ in our place is central to his theology. But he does not eliminate the importance of a subjective response to God's objective, finished work in Christ. He understands faith along the lines promulgated by the Reformation. Likewise, Barth is highly Christocentric in theology, but he also is deeply contextual in his ethics and practical theology. He develops the first comprehensive missional theology of the church since the Reformation, portraying congregations as living in solidarity with the world and witnessing to the gospel in their own particular times and places.

In many ways, Barth may appear to be an unlikely dialogue partner for a book on evangelism. But I believe it is precisely the doesn't-quite-fit-anywhere quality of Barth's theology that makes him so intriguing today. It always has been difficult to locate Barth on the map of American theology and politics, especially when this is based on the topography of white evangelicalism and liberalism. He was not an evangelical as Americans have defined the term in the past, and he was a fierce critic of theological liberalism. Yet, the older theological dichotomies of evangelicalism and liberalism must be questioned today, including the ways they portray evangelism. Too often we fall into stereotypes in our polarized culture.

Contemporary evangelicalism is highly diverse. One prominent historian of American religion is reported to have said that it is no longer possible to define American evangelicalism in even semi-precise terms. The theology and practices of evangelical networks, congregations, and denominations are too varied. This variety is especially evident if you take into account that evangelicalism includes many African Americans, Hispanics, Asian Americans, immigrants, Pentecostals, urban activists, and members of mainline congregations.

The same is true of Christian progressivism today. Here too, racial and ethnic diversity make it impossible to pin down what progressivism means in terms of the theology and practices of white liberals. Many congregations, denominations, and church leaders transcend the dichotomies commonly used to define progressivism. Some are conservative theologically but progressive on social justice issues related to race and economic inequality. Others are on the forefront of social transformation but have no problem with evangelism aimed at the transformation of individuals' lives.

The diversity of evangelicalism and progressivism makes it difficult to sort them into clear-cut categories. But too often we are led in this direction by social scientists. Truth be told, their survey research often requires them to construct overly simple understandings of American religion in order to make claims about voter preferences, family structures, and attendance patterns of evangelicals and progressives.[3] While survey findings can be helpful for some purposes, the reality of American Protestantism today is far messier and more complex than can be captured in survey research. At the very least, qualitative and quantitative research must be combined to gain an approximation of what is going on in contemporary American religion. Good research builds on theories of structures and events to develop explanations of why actions and patterns are occurring in particular contexts.[4]

Barth has something to contribute to fresh thinking about evangelism in our present context. If he does not fit the theological and social science maps of American Protestantism, so too many congregations, church leaders, and individual Christians do not fit these maps either. Moreover, the role Barth plays in this book and for me as a practical theologian might be played by someone else for you. Barth is not the only helpful theologian, though I personally believe that he is the most significant Protestant theologian since the Reformation. I find him compelling in rethinking evangelism.

There are times, however, when I find myself wincing at Barth's highly critical evaluations of Roman Catholicism, theological liberalism, pietism, and many other Christian traditions. These often are found in the small-print sections of the *Church Dogmatics*. While I will not hide the tone and critiques in Barth's theology when I summarize his positions, I will not follow him by adopting this tone when articulating my own positions.

I realize Barth believed some theological issues were so important that he had to destroy his interlocutor's position. His *Nein!* to Emil Brunner is a case in point. Barth believed that he needed to forcefully reject Brunner's

3. Robert Wuthnow, *Inventing American Religion: Polls, Surveys, and the Tenuous Quest for a Nation's Faith* (Oxford: Oxford University Press, 2015). Cf. Conrad Hackett and Michael Lindsay, "Measuring Evangelicalism: Consequences of Different Operationalization Strategies," *Journal for the Scientific Study of Religion* 47, no. 3 (2008): 499–514.

4. M. S. Archer, *Critical Realism: Essential Readings* (New York: Routledge, 2001); B. Danermark, M. Ekstrom, and L. Jakobsen, *Explaining Society: An Introduction to Critical Realism in the Social Sciences* (New York: Routledge, 2001); Christian Smith, *What Is a Person? Rethinking Humanity, Social Life, and the Moral Good from the Person Up* (Chicago: University of Chicago Press, 2010).

understanding of natural theology, because that sort of theology was being used by German Christians to support the Nazis' takeover of the church. Fair enough. Christian truth and practice were at stake in a time of crisis; the church was in a *status confessionis*, a time to confess the faith in the face of heresy placing the identity of the church at risk.

But what about times that are not moments of crisis? When Barth began the *Church Dogmatics*, he made it clear that his engagement of Protestant liberalism and Roman Catholicism was not just a matter of plural and complementary ways of thinking about the same faith.[5] It was a matter of the struggle between faith and unbelief, between faith and *heresy*. It is difficult to hold this position without adopting a polemical tone toward one's interlocutors. As time passed, however, Barth softened his tone toward both traditions. He became less preoccupied with breaking away from liberal theology, a stance he held as a student. After Vatican II, his tone toward Roman Catholicism softened; he engaged Catholic theologians such as Hans Küng and Hans Urs von Balthasar, and they in turn engaged him.

One of the foremost scholars of Barth today, George Hunsinger, develops a way of thinking about these issues in terms of ecumenical theology.[6] Being an ecumenical theologian is like being a "troublesome friend," the way Eberhard Busch describes Barth's relationship to Pietism.[7] Hunsinger spells out ecumenical theology by contrasting it with two other positions. Barth encountered both of these positions himself over the course of his career, and this may have softened the sharpness of his polemics.

The first is what Hunsinger calls *enclave theology*. It is based narrowly on a single tradition that seeks not to learn from other traditions but rather to defeat them or at least to withstand them. It is polemical to the point of not really being interested in dialogue, only proclaiming the one true theology. This was the stance of Cornelius van Til toward Barth. Barth refused an invitation by Geoffrey Bromiley to meet with van Til because he believed that van Til did not really want to engage him and had not even bothered to read his theology.

---

5. See Kimlyn Bender's fine discussion of this point in *Reading Karl Barth for the Church: A Guide and Companion* (Grand Rapids: Baker Academic, 2019), 28.

6. George Hunsinger, *The Eucharist and Ecumenism: Let Us Keep the Feast* (Cambridge: Cambridge University Press, 2008), 1–6. At points I paraphrase Hunsinger and at others quote him explicitly.

7. Eberhard Busch, *Karl Barth and the Pietists: The Young Barth's Critique of Pietism and Its Response*, trans. Daniel W. Bloesch (Downers Grove, IL: InterVarsity, 2004), 316; cf. 286.

In a letter to Bromiley, Barth writes: "But these people have already had their so-called orthodoxy for a long time. They are closed to anything else, they will cling to it at all costs, and they can adopt toward me only the role of prosecuting attorneys, trying to establish whether what I represent agrees or disagrees with their orthodoxy, in which I for my part have no interest!"[8] In contrast, Barth was quite willing to engage G. C. Berkouwer, who raised thoughtful criticisms of Barth in *The Triumph of Grace in the Theology of Karl Barth*.[9] Today, examples of enclave theology are rampant on the theological left and right in America's highly polarized culture. Enclave theology is no longer the theology of sectarian churches. It is the theology of identity politics which will not address, much less listen to other groups.

A second type is *academic liberal theology*. It lacks allegiance to any Christian tradition or confessional norms like the ecumenical councils of Nicaea and Chalcedon. The latter are portrayed as full of contradictions and absurdities.[10] Similarly, Scripture is interpreted from every point of view—historical, literary, sociocultural, philosophical, and psychological—except the perspective of Christian theology, which affirms Scripture as the sacred text of a particular community of faith. The intrusion of theology is portrayed as compromising scholarship. No real discussion of theological norms is needed as long as modernist or postmodernist norms prevail.

Theologies rooted in the traditions of particular religious communities are dismissed as mythological, arbitrary, and even oppressive. Religion is taught in terms of other fields, such as psychology, sociology, or history. The different paths taken by Barth and Rudolf Bultmann illustrate these differences. Early in their academic careers they collaborated on the journal, *Zwischen den Zeiten* (*Between the Times*, 1923-33). But as Bultmann's project of "demythologizing" the Bible became more prominent, translating it into the categories of modern, existentialist theology, Barth came to view him as allowing the "alien" frameworks of the modern academy to overwhelm commitment to the theological interpretation of Scripture. In turn

8. This letter is found in *Karl Barth: Letters, 1961-1969* (Grand Rapids: Eerdmans, 1981), 7-8. Available online at https://postbarthian.com/2014/04/29/karl-barths-letter-in-response-to-cornelius-van-tils-questions/.

9. Berkouwer, *Triumph of Grace*. See Barth's detailed and respectful response in *Church Dogmatics*, ed. Geoffrey W. Bromiley and T. F. Torrance (Edinburgh: T. & T. Clark, 1956-75), IV/3, first half, 173-80.

10. As Hunsinger notes in *Eucharist and Ecumenism* (2), this is the position of Paul Tillich. See Tillich's *Systematic Theology*, vol. 2 (Chicago: University of Chicago Press, 1957), 142.

Barth has come under fire from academic liberal theologians right up to the present.

Ecumenical theology represents an alternative to enclave and academic liberal theology. Hunsinger briefly portrays it as follows:

> Ecumenical theology . . . presupposes that every tradition in the church has something valuable to contribute even if we cannot yet discern what it is. The ecumenical movement will succeed not when all other traditions capitulate to the one true church. . . . It will succeed only by a deeper conversion of all traditions to Christ. Ecumenical theology, though properly grounded in a single tradition, looks for what is best in traditions not its own. It seeks not to defeat them but to respect and learn from them. It earns the right to speak only by listening, and it listens much more than it speaks.[11]

In an age of religious, cultural, and intellectual pluralism, it is very important to affirm the kind of openness that Hunsinger is advocating here. Theologians cannot afford to immediately assume that others are wrong on the basis of their own tradition or the norms of the academic community to which they belong. I intend to learn from evangelical and progressive traditions, though I locate myself in the traditions of the Reformation as recast by Barth. Theology (*theologia*), as discourse (*logos*) concerning God (*theos*), always involves a commitment to truth, truth of the highest order. But precisely because it is truth of the highest order, it must be ecumenical as Hunsinger describes it. That is the approach I hope to embody even though I sometimes let Barth's polemical tone stand.

Since Barth's corpus is so large and examines doctrines in great depth and length, I have decided to structure our examination of his theology in terms of themes. His theology lends itself to this approach. It often is compared to a symphony that introduces many different motifs in the overture and returns to them again and again in different movements.[12] Discussion of a theme in one part of his theology is unlikely to be definitive of the whole. It often appears again in new material. This is what makes Barth so difficult to read

---

11. Hunsinger, *Eucharist and Ecumenism*, 2.

12. George Hunsinger, *How to Read Karl Barth: The Shape of His Theology* (New York: Oxford University Press, 1991), 28-30; and Theodore Gill, "Barth and Mozart," *Theology Today* 43 (1986): 403-11. See also John Webster, *Karl Barth* (New York: Continuum, 2000), 50.

and summarize.[13] For our purposes, focusing on themes allows us to keep our constructive purpose in view: reimagining evangelism in dialogue with key elements of Barth's Reformation theology.

In chapter 4, we focus on the themes of the being of the church and the church as witness. The first is Barth's way of talking about the relationship between Jesus Christ and the church. His discussion of this theme often compares his own position to that of Roman Catholicism and Protestant liberalism. Barth makes use of what Hunsinger calls the Chalcedonian paradigm to describe Christ's relationship to the church. Building on this theme, we then examine Barth's missional ecclesiology in which the church is described as a witness to the gospel of Jesus Christ. The theme of church as witness provides the theological context in which Barth discusses evangelism as a particular ministry of the church.

In chapter 5, we also focus on two themes: Christ in our place and the Holy Spirit as the mediator of communion. The first brings together a number of *leitmotifs* in Barth's theology: the relationship between election and reconciliation, his soteriological objectivism, and sin as revealed in humanity's response to Christ. By soteriological objectivism, we mean that God's salvation of the world is accomplished by Jesus Christ on humanity's behalf and in its stead—hence Christ in our place. Moreover, it is universal in scope and complete *in toto*. Barth develops this theme by drawing on and reworking the theologies of Martin Luther and John Calvin. It is one of the keys to a Reformation theology of evangelism.

The second theme, the Holy Spirit as the mediator of communion, allows us to examine Barth's understanding of how human beings participate in salvation. Obviously, this is a key issue in evangelism. In the introduction we portrayed the religious toolkit of conversionistic evangelism as including: (1) people are saved when they convert, (2) individuals have the freedom to decide whether they will convert or not, and (3) conversion is life-changing

---

13. Hans Frei once warned that any attempt to summarize Barth turns the material to dust. Close readings solve some of the problems but often lose a sense of the whole. Focusing on themes can provide a sense of the whole but often loses texture and context. Even books that deal exclusively with Barth run into these problems. Moreover, our engagement of Barth is not to explicate his thought but to engage him as a dialogue partner. We thus acknowledge the problem raised by Frei but also acknowledge there is no one right way of dealing with it. Thematic focus works best for our purpose in this particular book. For the comment by Frei, see Timothy Gorringe, *Karl Barth: Against Hegemony*, Christian Theology in Context (Oxford: Oxford University Press, 1999), ix.

and accompanied by a dramatic experience at a particular moment in time or over a short period of time. Barth's description of the relationship between Christ's work of reconciliation and the Spirit's work of mediating communion represents an alternative to the view of human agency found in conversionistic evangelism. Our discussion of this theme explores the relationship between Christ's finished work "there and then" and the subjective appropriation of this gift "here and now." It also points us to the future of reconciliation when the Holy Spirit will redeem all things, bringing them into communion with God. Until then, the mission of the church is witnessing to God's reconciliation of the world and the redemption yet to come.

CHAPTER 4

Evangelization and the Church as Witness

To understand Karl Barth's theology, we must appreciate his relationship to the Reformation of the sixteenth century. Kimlyn Bender points out that Barth wrote the *Church Dogmatics* to provide "an answer to the question of what the Reformation was truly about in its protest against the medieval church, and how its decisive insights were lost even to those who carried on the Reformation tradition in name up to and into the modern period."[1] Above all other dialogue partners (and there are many), Barth builds upon the legacy of the Reformation to write a contemporary theology for the church. Luther is the longest entry in the index of the *Church Dogmatics*, and Calvin is a close second.[2] This is especially germane to the American theological scene, which Dietrich Bonhoeffer characterized as Protestantism without Reformation after his second visit to this country in 1939.[3]

Like Luther and the other Reformers, Barth refers to the tradition he is seeking to retrieve as "Evangelical Protestantism." Since this may be confusing to readers who think of evangelicalism as a stream of Christianity emerging from the awakening movements coming *after* the Reformation, I will use the terms "Reformation Protestantism" and "Reformation theology" instead. While Barth's commitment to the Reformation is present in all of the themes we examine, it comes to the fore in the following chapter as we examine Christ in our place. We will highlight the Reformation roots of this theme at that point.

1. Kimlyn J. Bender, *Reading Karl Barth for the Church: A Guide and Companion* (Grand Rapids: Baker Academic, 2019), 27.

2. George Hunsinger, *Disruptive Grace: Studies in the Theology of Karl Barth* (Grand Rapids: Eerdmans, 2000), 279.

3. Dietrich Bonhoeffer, "Protestantism without Reformation," in *No Rusty Swords*, ed. Edwin H. Robertson (London: Fontana Library, 1970), 88–113. As Hunsinger notes, in this edition the title is misrepresented as "Protestantism with Reformation." *Disruptive Grace*, 70.

Our focus in this chapter is Barth's depiction of the mission of the church as bearing witness to the gospel, with evangelism as one of the ways this witness is carried out. It makes sense, then, to begin with Barth's understanding of the "being of the church."[4] By this, he means the way Christian traditions portray the relationship between Jesus Christ and the church. He contrasts his own position with those of other traditions.

The Being of the Church: The Chalcedonian Paradigm

Barth's Critique of Roman Catholicism and Protestant Liberalism

Barth develops his theology of the being of the church in dialogue with and contrast to Roman Catholicism and Protestant liberalism (which he sometimes calls Protestant modernism).[5]

Roman Catholicism, he believed, invests human and historical institutions of the church with the divine authority of Christ. It seeks "to understand and set up itself, the Church, as a direct representation of Jesus Christ, its existence as a vicariate, its action as a direct repetition and continuation of his."[6] In the end, Roman Catholicism confuses the relationship between Christ and the church. The voice of Christ and the voice of the church cannot be distinguished: "Jesus Christ is no longer the free Lord of its [the church's] existence."[7]

Barth therefore cannot agree with the way evangelism traditionally has been portrayed in Roman Catholicism. The "classical" Catholic view portrayed mission as the extension of the church, not the spread of the gospel. It focused on "establishing the visible church and its hierarchical structure" in territories where there was not yet an organized Catholic church.[8]

---

4. Karl Barth, *Church Dogmatics* (hereafter *CD*), ed. Geoffrey W. Bromiley and T. F. Torrance (Edinburgh: T&T Clark, 1956–75), I/1, 32.

5. Barth, *CD* I/1, 27. See Bender's very helpful discussion in *Reading Karl Barth for the Church*, excursus, 27–38, Kindle Edition. By Protestant liberalism, Barth has in mind the tradition of theology that stretches back to Friedrich Schleiermacher. He finds contemporary expressions of this tradition in Rudolf Bultmann and Paul Tillich. See Barth, *CD* I/1, 36.

6. Barth, *CD* IV/3, second half, 836.

7. Barth, *CD* I/1, 40.

8. Stefan Paas, *Church Planting in the Secular West: Learning from the European Experience* (Grand Rapids: Eerdmans, 2016), 19.

During the Middle Ages, this sometimes involved armed conflict. After Charlemagne conquered the tribes of what is now northern Germany, the tribal leaders converted, the people were baptized *en masse,* and bishops and priests were sent to establish the church and Christianize the people. This was described as "the planting of the Lord's Vineyard."[9] In fairness, this was not all that different from Protestant missions during colonialism, which often apportioned foreign territories to different European and American denominations that viewed themselves as extending Western civilization along with Christianity.

Following Vatican II, the link between Christianization and evangelism was eliminated, and today, new Catholic congregations reflect many aspects of local culture. Yet the idea of mission as planting the Catholic church remains. As the decree *Ad Gentes* (1961) puts it: "The proper purpose of missionary activity is evangelization, and the planting of the Church among those peoples and groups where it has not yet taken root" (1.6). There is no question, however, that Vatican II ushered in new interest and thinking about evangelization among Catholics. As Avery Dulles notes, evangelization was a prominent topic in the documents of Vatican II.[10] Its documents mention the gospel 157 times, the word "evangelize" eighteen, and the word "evangelization" thirty-one.

This opened the door for the "new evangelization" in Roman Catholicism. This portrays evangelization as taking place in three settings: (1) the regular pastoral ministry in an attempt to awaken the hearts of the faithful, (2) ministry among Catholics who are lapsed or no longer live up to the demands of Christian discipleship, and (3) outreach to those who do not know Christ.[11] This has similarities to Barth's view of evangelization, though his focus always remained on the sharing of the gospel and never on the extension of the church.

9. Paas, *Church Planting,* 20.
10. Avery Dulles, SJ, *Church and Society: The McGinley Lectures, 1988-2007* (New York: Fordham University Press, 2008), 546.
11. Pontificium Consilium de Nova Evangelizatione Promovenda, *Compendium on the New Evangelization: Texts of the Pontifical and Conciliar Magisterium, 1939-2012* (Washington, DC: Libreria Editrice Vaticana, 2015); Avery Dulles, *Evangelization for the Third Millennium: 1918-2008* (Mahwah, NJ: Paulist, 2009); William Houck, *John Paul II and the New Evangelization: How You Can Bring the Good News to Others* (San Francisco: Ignatius Press, 1995). See Scott Hahn's bibliographical references found online at http://www.scotthahn.com/newevangelization, accessed June 2021. See also Scott Hahn, *Evangelizing Catholics: A New Mission Manual for Evangelizing Catholics* (Huntington, IN: Libreria Editrice Vaticana, 2014).

Barth was invited to be an observer at Vatican II, but his work responsi-
bilities made it impossible to attend. Throughout the latter part of his life,
he engaged a variety of prominent Catholic theologians, such as Hans Küng,
Hans Urs von Balthasar, and others. His view of Catholicism began to change
as the Catholic Church itself began to change. He even began to exert some
influence on Roman Catholicism through dialogue with theologians including those mentioned above.[12] He went so far as to write: "We are witnessing
a complete reinterpretation of Roman Catholic dogma. The thoughts ex-
pounded by Hans Küng and other modern theologians in Germany, Holland,
France, and elsewhere are no longer views of a small spearhead minority, but
form the very ground swell of Catholic renovation."[13] It is not clear that Barth
would continue to hold this view if he were still alive. Küng later was stripped
of his *missio canonica*, his license to teach as a Roman Catholic theologian,
and many of the reforms of Vatican II have come under fire.

Yet the new evangelization is indicative of an openness to the world that
has continued to the present. It also is reflective of the large number of Roman Catholics in the United States who have left the church in recent decades. According to the Pew Research Center, "Catholicism has experienced
a greater net loss due to religious switching than has any other religious tradition in the U.S."[14]

Barth leveled his most ferocious attacks on Protestant liberalism. Not
only was he breaking with the theological liberalism of his university years,
but he also was shocked that many of his former liberal professors, such as
Adolf von Harnack, were signatories of the *Manifest der Intellektuellen* (the
Intellectuals' Manifesto) which supported Germany's entry into World War I.
He was very critical of liberalism's understanding of the relationship between
Christ and the church and the suspicions of evangelism it fostered.

Protestant liberalism emphasizes the humanity of Christ and the historically situated nature of the church. In the tradition of Friedrich Schleiermacher, it begins by first identifying a religious, ethical, or spiritual capacity possessed by all human beings—for example, self-transcendence,
ultimate meaning, compassion for others, longing for justice and liberation, and absolute dependence (Schleiermacher's term). Christ is por-

12. Philip J. Rosato, "The Influence of Karl Barth on Catholic Theology," *Gregori-
anum* 67, no. 4 (1986): 659–78.

13. "Barth in Retirement," *Time* magazine, May 31, 1963, cited online at https://
content.time.com/time/subscriber/article/0,33009,896838,00.html.

14. "7 Facts about American Catholics," online at https://www.pewresearch.org
/fact-tank/2018/10/10/7-facts-about-american-catholics/.

trayed as fulfilling such capacities in a supreme way, offering an example of what a spiritually fulfilled life looks like and functioning as a symbol that evokes an analogous response among his followers in the church. The expression and form of this response in the church are shaped by historical and social contexts. Theology thus has the important task of correlating Christianity with contemporary experience, language, problems, and questions. Unless the church can reinterpret Christ for the present, Christianity will become irrelevant.

Barth argues that what is lost in all this attention to present experience and relevance is God—the otherness of God as Creator and the particular events by which God is known through revelation and Christ's reconciliation of the world. Protestant liberalism ends up being highly anthropocentric. As Barth puts it: "Modernist dogmatics is finally unaware of the fact that in relation to God the human being has constantly to let something be said to him or her, has constantly to listen to something, which he or she constantly does not know and which in no circumstances and in no sense can he say to himself. Modernist dogmatics hears human beings answer when no one has called them. It hears human beings speak with themselves."[15]

In light of this understanding of Christ's relationship to the church, Protestant liberalism is deeply ambivalent about evangelism. There are two reasons: the historically situated nature of the church and its commitment today to religious inclusivity. Both come to the fore in Robert Wuthnow's research on inclusive and exclusive Christianity.[16]

Almost all contemporary participants in Protestant liberalism reject the tendency of some nineteenth-century liberals to portray Christianity as the highest form of religion and morality and Western culture as the apex of civilization. In this older, historically situated view, the spread of Christianity through mission was part of the West's civilization of other cultures. Contemporary liberal Christians view this as a terrible mistake. It turned Christianity into a tool of colonial oppression.

This continues to shape Protestant liberals' understanding of mission and evangelism. They are willing to share their faith when asked but are not willing to take the initiative in sharing the gospel with others such that God might bring them to faith. They are especially opposed to converting the members

---

15. Barth, *CD* I/1, 61–62. Alterations of translation are my own.
16. My characterization of liberal Protestantism draws on Robert Wuthnow, *America and the Challenges of Religious Diversity* (Princeton: Princeton University Press, 2005), ch. 5.

of other religions. In the words of a participant in Wuthnow's study: "God is working with these people."[17]

A commitment to inclusivity stands at the heart of contemporary Protestant liberalism, reflecting the increasingly pluralistic context of contemporary America. It starts with the idea that all people share a common religious, ethical, or spiritual capacity that is shaped by their historical and religious contexts as well as their individual life journeys. There are many paths to God. For those who are Christian, Christianity happens to be the path they were born into or have chosen. It is an individual preference, largely accepted because it "works" for them. There is no need to view evangelism as part of the church's mission, for there is nothing exclusive or unique about Christ. N. T. Wright's astute insight cited in the introduction to part I is completely absent from Protestant liberalism: "Why then did early Christianity spread? Because early Christians believed that what they had found to be true was true for the whole world."[18]

Barth strongly disagrees with liberalism's understanding of evangelism and with theological liberalism across the board. While affirming with certainty that God loves all people and has died to save them, Barth believes that we can only know this to be true through Jesus Christ. There really are not many paths to God. God is known only through God, through the incarnation of God's Son, the Second Person of the Trinity. And to know God is to know and experience his reconciliation. The church's mission is to witness to him and share the good news of God's reconciliation of the world through him. The church should be open, patient, and compassionate. It should fight against all forms of oppression, as Christ did. It must be glad that there are many good and spiritual people in other religions or in no religion at all. It must leave judgment to God and not set itself up in God's place. It must recognize, as Barth explicitly does, that Christ is the *hope* of all people, Christians and non-Christians.[19] But the church cannot be ambivalent about its mission, for this is its very reason for being. This mission is to bear witness to Christ, through whom the love of God is revealed and enacted in Christ's work of reconciliation. Evangelism is an essential part of this mission.

17. Wuthnow, *Challenges of Religious Diversity*, 149. The quotation comes from an interview in the Wuthnow study and is described as representative of his findings.

18. Wright's insight rests on the perspective of critical realism, not the highly relativistic and skeptical position of postmodernism.

19. Barth, *CD* IV/3, first half, 364.

The Being of the Church in Barth: The Chalcedonian Pattern

So how does Barth understand the relationship between Christ and the church? He seeks to avoid Roman Catholicism's portrayal of the church as possessing divine authority, on the one hand, and Protestant liberalism's portrayal of the church as fulfilling human spirituality in a Christian way, on the other. In forging his own understanding of the being of the church, Barth is deeply influenced by the Council of Chalcedon. This council was convened to focus on the question: As the Word made flesh, how can Jesus Christ be both divine and human at the same time? This was a point of conflict in the early centuries of Christianity and began to divide the church. The Council of Chalcedon was convened to settle this controversy. In 415, the council offered the Chalcedonian Definition, which described Christ as truly God and truly human, one person in two natures.[20] It portrays the relationship between Christ's divinity and humanity in terms of three elements:

> *Unity:* In Christ the divine and human cannot be divided or separated.
> *Distinction:* But their unity is a differentiated unity in which the divine and human are not mingled and their integrity not compromised.
> *Asymmetry:* They exist in an ordered and irreversible relation; Christ's divinity is superior to his humanity.

The formula is minimal. It describes two terms (human and divine) and their relationship (unity-in-distinction and asymmetry).[21] This leaves room for a variety of Christologies, as long as they meet these minimal requirements. Obviously, Barth is not the only Christian theologian to develop a Christology on the basis of Chalcedon. Luther, Ulrich Zwingli, and Calvin were Chalcedonians, as are all orthodox Roman Catholic theologians and even so-called evangelical liberals.[22]

20. Philip Schaff, *The Creeds of Christendom*, vol. 2 (New York: Harper & Row, 1931), 62–65.

21. Hunsinger, *Disruptive Grace*, 134.

22. The term "evangelical liberals" was used by H. Shelton Smith, Robert T. Handy, and Lefferts A. Loetscher in *American History: An Historical Interpretation with Representative Documents*, vol. 2 (New York: Charles Scribner's Sons, 1963). Today, it is sometimes used journalistically to describe a subset of evangelical congregations in mainline denominations that are typically classified as liberal by sociologists.

But few theologians have developed the potential of this pattern like Barth. He uses it to describe not only the relationship between the humanity and divinity of Christ but also other relationships in which Christ and human beings are involved. As Bender points out, this is especially the case in Barth's description of the church, individuals, and, with modification, the church's solidarity with the world.[23]

There are numerous places in the *Church Dogmatics* where the Chalcedonian pattern guides Barth's description of the being of the church.[24] Two that stand out are Barth's interpretation of the church as the body of Christ and its visibility and invisibility.[25] Paul's description of the church as the body of Christ is an especially nice example, for the Chalcedonian pattern draws out the theological logic implicit in Paul's image.

Christ lives as the head of the church, and the church lives as his body, the "earthly-historical form" of his existence in the world. Unless the church is united to Christ it does not exist, for Christ through the Holy Spirit calls it into being, builds it up, and sends it. It is this invisible, spiritual relationship between Christ and the church that constitutes the being of the church, moment by moment, day by day. There can be no confusion between the head and the body; they are clearly distinguished. Christ alone is both human and divine and as such is the only one capable of mediating between God and humanity. The church is not the mediator of salvation; it is the instrument Christ uses to re-present himself through word and sacrament. It is a witness pointing beyond itself to Christ and as such stands in an asymmetrical relationship to his person and work. As it is united to him it participates in his righteousness, obedience, and mission—even as it remains part of a sinful world. Thus Barth consistently describes the church and its members in dialectical terms. They are simultaneously justified and sinful, sanctified and disobedient, given a vocation and turned in upon themselves. When the church is united to him as the body to the head, it proclaims in provisional ways the Word of God.

In short, Barth portrays the being of the church along the lines of the

23. Kimlyn Bender, *Karl Barth's Christological Ecclesiology* (Eugene, OR: Cascade, 2013), 6–10.

24. For examples and discussion see Hunsinger, *Disruptive Grace*, ch. 6. See also Bender, *Barth's Christological Ecclesiology*, introduction.

25. Barth, *CD* IV/1, 662–68. The entire section, "The Being of the Community," 650–725, is relevant here. Also Barth, "The Church—the Living Congregation of the Living Lord Jesus Christ," in *God Here and Now*, trans. Paul M. van Buren (New York: Harper & Row, 1964), 61–85.

Chalcedonian pattern. This allows him to affirm a wide variety of institutional expressions of the church, as long as they maintain the unity of Christ and the church, their differentiation in unity, and the asymmetrical nature of their relationship. While he writes of the church as a universal fellowship spread out across time and space, he tends to think of the church as a community of believers in a specific time and place. He even prefers the term "community" to "church," for it emphasizes the specific fellowship of a particular community of people who are united to Christ and one another. This brings us to a second theme in Barth's theology.

The Church as Witness

Two areas where the Reformers betrayed the potential of their own theologies were evangelism and mission. As Barth points out, these points of emphasis emerged from churches that broke with the Reformation and believed in adult baptism following an individual's conversion.[26] In contrast, Calvin's position in *The Institutes* is representative of the Reformers.

Drawing on Ephesians 4:4-7, which offers a list of ministries, Calvin describes the role of each ministry in the apostolic church and its role in his context. Apostles, prophets, and evangelists were very important in the early church, he contends, but their time has passed: "These three functions were not established in the church as permanent ones, but only for the time during which churches were to be erected where none existed before."[27] Only in times of special need, Calvin continued, does God raise up persons to fill these ministries. He refers to them as "extraordinary" ministries.[28] He believes the ministry of Luther was extraordinary in this sense, and Calvin praises him as "a distinguished *apostle* of Christ by whose ministry the light of the gospel has shone."[29]

Barth's attention to mission and evangelism thus breaks new ground in Reformation theology. It is not that ministers, missionaries, and laypeople in Reformation churches have neglected evangelism since the sixteenth century. They have not. Typically, however, they have adopted some version of evangelism as conversionism to carry out this ministry. Yet many lay-

26. Barth, *CD* IV/3, first half, 22-26.
27. John Calvin, *The Institutes of the Christian Religion*, vol. 2, ed. John T. McNeill and trans. Ford Lewis Battles (Philadelphia: Westminster, 1960), 1057.
28. Calvin, *Institutes*, vol. 2, 1057.
29. Calvin, *Institutes*, vol. 2, 1057n4.

people, pastors, and theologians of Reformation churches have felt uneasy about this. They have wondered if focusing on an individual's conversion at a given point in time coheres with central beliefs, like bondage of the will, infant baptism, and *sola gratia* (grace alone). Barth is the first major theologian building on Reformation theological traditions to place such importance on the mission of witness and to affirm evangelism as a ministry of the church. As Darrell Guder points out, Barth is a key source of recent thinking about the missional church and how the church must change in a post-Christendom context.[30]

Barth first introduces the church as a missional community in *The Doctrine of Creation*, volume 3 of the *Church Dogmatics*: "The Church is either a missionary Church or it is no church at all."[31] In section 72 of the *Church Dogmatics* volume 4, *The Doctrine of Reconciliation*—titled "The Holy Spirit and the Sending of the Christian Community"—he spells out more fully what this means. By nature, Barth contends, the church is a sent community. Apart from this it has no other reason for being. It is sent into the world by Christ: "As the Father has sent me, I am sending you" (John 20:21). This is portrayed along the lines of the Chalcedonian pattern described above.

The congregation shares in Christ's mission as it is *united to and participates in* him. Christ's mission and the church's mission are clearly *distinguished*. Christ is the one Savior and Reconciler of the world; the church is a witness to Christ's work. The church accompanies Christ in his work, serving as an instrument of his call to come and follow him. The relationship is asymmetrical. The church cannot bring people to faith.[32] Only Christ and the Spirit can do this. But it can bear witness by pointing to him.

Going beyond the Classic Answer of the Purpose of the Church

By describing the church as a sent community whose mission is to bear witness to the gospel, Barth is breaking with what he calls the "classic" theological answer to the questions: Why do Christians exist? What is their purpose?[33] There are many permutations of the classic answer to these questions, but they all come down to this:

---

30. Darrell Guder, *Called to Witness: Doing Missional Theology* (Grand Rapids: Eerdmans, 2015), 9-12.

31. Barth, *CD* III/3, 64.

32. See Barth, *CD* III/4, 504.

33. Barth, *CD* IV/3, second half, 557.

Christians, we are told, are those who are the recipients of grace. They are illumined and awakened by the work of the Word and Spirit of the Lord. They are born again and converted. They have peace with God.... They have their own personal share in the fruit of this divine action—a share that is effective in their lives and experienced by them.[34]

While there is something "true and important" in this, Barth continues by asking whether it is really the case that "my gracious visitation and salvation, the saving of my soul . . . my reception, possession, use and enjoyment of the *beneficia Christi* (benefits of Christ) is the only thing important."[35] He becomes more pointed:

Can it really be the inner end, meaning and basis of my Christian existence . . . that I should be blessed, that my soul should be saved, that I should participate in all the gifts of reconciliation, that my life should be one of reception, possession, use and enjoyment of these gifts, that I should finally attain to eternal bliss, that I should not go to hell but to heaven? . . . Does not this wholly possessive being seem to smack of the sanctioning and cultivating of an egocentricity which is only too human for all its sanctity, of a self-seeking which in the light of what is at stake renders every other form of self-seeking quite innocuous?[36]

He then makes the Christological point:

Did the Son of God clothe Himself with humanity, and shed His blood, and go out as the Sower, simply in order that He might create for these people—in free grace, yet why specifically for them and only for them?— this indescribably magnificent private good fortune, permitting them to obtain and possess a gracious God, opening to them the gates of Paradise which are closed to others? Can this really be the goal of His calling and therefore of his ongoing prophetic work?[37]

Repeatedly throughout this section, Barth uses the language of "pious egocentricity" to refer to the classic answer. It portrays the goal of the Chris-

34. Barth, *CD* IV/3, second half, 561–62.
35. Barth, *CD* IV/3, second half, 563–64. My translation of the Latin.
36. Barth, *CD* IV/3, second half, 566–67.
37. Barth, *CD* IV/3, second half, 567.

tian life as gathering with other Christians to enjoy together the benefits of Christ's grace. This focuses on what is secondary, what is a by-product of the church's mission. The goal of the Christian life and the mission of the church are to bear witness to the gospel. It is to share God's love for the world, to set up signs pointing to this reality, and to serve this love in its relationships and causes. As Barth succinctly puts it at one point: "What the community owes the world, and each individual within it, is basically that in its life, and in the lives of all its members, there should be attempted an imitation and representation of the love with which God loved the world."[38] To bear witness to the love of God in Jesus Christ is its mission. This is the love revealed in God's sending of his only Son to reconcile the world. It is wonderful and terrible, attractive and fearsome, for it partakes of the cross and resurrection.

Barth was fond of using Matthias Grünewald's depiction of John the Baptist in the Isenheim Altarpiece as an image of the church's witness.[39] Just as the Baptist points away from himself to Christ, so too must the church. In his discussion of this image, Barth often added John's words: "He must become greater; I must become less" (John 3:30). He is making a point that is central to his entire theology, discussed more fully in the next chapter. Christ stands in our place in the work of reconciliation; our role as the church is to point to what he has done on our behalf and in our stead. But this pointing, this mission of witness asks us to offer a visible but provisional representation of God's reconciling love. In word and deed the church is to point to him by living as a reconciled and reconciling people. Every ministry of the church—not just evangelism—is a form of witness. This leads us to Barth's understanding of the ministries of the church.

Evangelism as a Ministry of the Church

Barth develops a description of the "enduring" ministries of the church, based on a simple distinction in Jesus's ministry: "He preached the gospel of the kingdom and healed every sickness and every disease among the people"

---

38. Barth, CD III/4, 502.
39. Matthias Grünewald, "The Crucifixion of Christ," one of the panels of the Isenheim Altarpiece. Pictures are readily available online.

(Matt. 9:35).[40] So too, the church has ministries of word and deed, work of the lips and also of the hands.[41] Ministries of word include:

(1) the praise of God
(2) the proclamation of the gospel
(3) instruction in Scripture and faith
(4) evangelization to the surrounding culture
(5) mission to the nations
(6) the discipline of theology

Ministries of deed consist of:

(7) prayer
(8) the cure of souls
(9) the production of exemplars of Christian life
(10) the rendering of service (the diaconate, which addresses material needs in church and community and offers social criticism)
(11) the prophetic action of the community based upon the discernment of current events
(12) the establishment of fellowship[42]

Each and every one of these ministries is a form of witness to the gospel. Before describing them in detail, Barth explains what this means. As a form of witness, every ministry of the church should include three elements: "declaration, exposition and address, or the proclamation, explication and application of the Gospel."[43] In my view, these sets of terms seem to come from teaching and preaching respectively, making it difficult to discern how they might come to expression in other forms of ministry. Thus, I first will explain them and then offer an illustration.

Declaration means that each ministry introduces the content of the gospel in conjunction with its words or deeds. Ministry is done in the name of Jesus,

40. Barth, *CD* IV/3, second half, 859. Barth is aware that the church's ministries have a contextual dimension and that some ministries may be quite important in a particular context but not represent ministries that are enduring.

41. Barth, *CD* IV/3, second half, 862–63. Barth goes on to add that this division is not hard and fast, for it is "differentiated, though not divided, into speech which is also action . . . and action which is also speech."

42. Barth, *CD* IV/3, second half, 865–901.

43. Barth, *CD* IV/3, second half, 843.

serves as a sign that points to him, and is a way of declaring his reality. Why are you doing this action or saying these words? Because I am loved by Jesus Christ; I trust and follow him. Exposition attempts to explain the meaning of the gospel in ways that are understandable. Who is this Jesus? Why do you trust him? When you say he is God's Son, what do you mean? No one knows in advance how the gospel will need to be explained to this person or group in these circumstances. But Barth is confident that "the Gospel gives itself to be understood, and wills to be understood."[44] In his discussion of these three elements, Barth calls the final one "evangelical address." It "sets the truth of the Gospel before the world in such a way that invites decision and action. As such, it is an *invitation* for people to the Gospel."[45] The gospel is not just true for Christians; it is true for the entire world. But its claim does not come in the form of abstract, timeless truths. It comes to people as personal address "in such a way that they come to see its crucial application to them."[46]

Barth's description of the diaconate illustrates how these three elements might be part of this ministry. By diaconate, he means rendering service and material aid to the needy: "caring for the sick, the feeble, and the mentally confused and threatened, looking after orphans, helping prisoners, finding new homes for refugees, stretching out a hand to stranded and shattered fellow-men of all kinds."[47] Barth recognizes that this assistance is little more than "drops in a bucket" and challenges the church to call the world to address the social injustices that put people in such circumstances. The diaconate and Christian community "become dumb dogs, and their service a serving of the ruling powers, if they are afraid to tackle at their social roots the evils by which they are confronted in detail."[48] The diaconate, thus, is a ministry of advocacy and social criticism as well as direct service of the needy. Both are needed, and woe to the church that believes one can take the place of the other.

In the ministry of diaconal service, the Christian community explicitly accepts solidarity with the "least of the little ones" living in obscurity and on the margins of society. In face-to-face encounters, they are recognized to be brothers and sisters of Jesus Christ as indicated in the parable of the last judgment in Matthew 25. Without this "concrete witness to Jesus the

44. Barth, *CD* IV/3, second half, 846.
45. Bender, *Barth's Christological Ecclesiology*, 252.
46. Barth, *CD* IV/3, second half, 852–53.
47. Barth, *CD* IV/3, second half, 891.
48. Barth, *CD* IV/3, second half, 891, 893.

Crucified, who is the Neighbour of the lost, its witness may be ever so pure and full at other points, but it is all futile."[49]

Though the diaconate is a ministry of action, it is clear that Barth believes its connection to the compassion of Jesus for the least of these should be declared and explained, not only to the church and surrounding community but also to those receiving assistance. Ultimately, it must become a word of personal address, especially to those who need to hear of God's love and may be most ready to receive it. They too should be called "urgently and explicitly to God . . . who is the primary and proper Deacon," "though the distinctive action here is to hold out a helping hand . . . causing the good deed which corresponds to the good Word to be tasted and felt."[50]

Clearly, Barth works with a rich and multilayered understanding of witness. It includes some of the things we normally associate with evangelism. What then is the specific contribution of evangelism as Barth defines it? We turn now to the *Church Dogmatics*, volume 4, part 3, section 2.4, titled "The Ministry of the Community," where Barth discusses each of the ministries of the church, including evangelization.

He defines the ministry of evangelization as sharing the gospel in words with those "who stand in the more immediate environs of the community."[51] Obviously, Barth wrote long before the advent of social media. Today evangelism reaches far beyond the immediate environs of a congregation through digital social networks.[52] Yet Barth's starting point remains a good one, for he begins where most of us start. Evangelization is directed to people who are not Christians and seeks to share the gospel in words.

In the United States and Europe we might say it is directed to the "unaffiliated" sector of the population: people who neither identify with nor participate in any religious community. Many identify themselves as spiritual but not religious, not affiliating with a religious institution. This is one of the fastest growing groups in the American population and includes large numbers of young people.

Using words, evangelization declares, explains, and applies the gospel to people who are not members of the Christian community. The emphasis on words is important. Evangelism is a ministry of the word. This does not pre-

---

49. Barth, *CD* IV/3, second half, 891.
50. Barth, *CD* IV/3, second half, 893.
51. Barth, *CD* IV/3, second half, 872.
52. Archbishop's Council on Mission and Public Affairs, *Mission-Shaped Church: Church Planting and Fresh Expressions in a Changing Context* (New York: Seabury Books, 2004), ch. 1.

clude acts of hospitality, compassion, friendship, and kindness. As we have seen in the case studies, creating a relational context is crucial in evangelism. You have to show as well as tell. But words are essential. Why?

To encounter Jesus and begin fellowship (*koinōnia* in Greek) with him is to begin to know him. How can we know who Jesus is and what he means to us and our world unless he is described, narrated, talked about, read about, and related to the specific circumstances of our lives? Knowledge shared through words in evangelization is knowledge of a person, not a set of ideas or laws. In this sense, evangelization might be described as facilitating an encounter with Jesus. It is a personal meeting on the basis of words.

In his description of evangelization as a ministry, Barth gradually expands the circle of those to whom evangelization is directed. When he wrote the *Church Dogmatics* volume in which his discussion of ministry appears (the German edition was published in 1962), he was part of a Christendom context that already was showing signs of becoming post-Christendom.[53] The former is a context in which the large majority of people in a nation are affiliated with Christianity and baptized into the church as infants or adolescents. Many, Barth contends, "seem to belong to the [Christian] community and yet do not really belong to it to the extent that they have no obvious part in either the knowledge or the resultant ministry of the community."[54]

This trend has only intensified during the past sixty years in the United States and Germany, to take one of the most religious and economically strong countries in Europe. Survey research in 2017 by Pew found that 70 percent of the German population still identify as Christian but most are nonpracticing, attending worship services only a few times a year.[55] Twenty-four percent of the German population state they have no religion. The unaf-

53. Throughout the *Church Dogmatics*, Barth makes reference to the likelihood that Christianity will soon become a shrinking minority. He believes that this could be a positive development if the distinction between church and culture were strengthened in ways that allowed the church to better bear witness to the gospel. Indeed, he argues that the church should always be a minority and that this is especially likely to be the case in the West after centuries of growth. See, for example, *CD* III/4, 484–85, 504–5.

54. *CD* IV/3, second half, 872. Throughout this section, I am drawing on material found in Barth's discussion of evangelization as a ministry of the church, found in *CD* IV/3, second half, 872–74. I footnote all quotes and material from other parts of the *Dogmatics*.

55. "Being Christian in Western Europe," https://www.pewforum.org/2018/05/29/being-christian-in-western-europe/.

filiated sector of the population increased dramatically after East and West Germany were reunited at the end of the Cold War.

While conducted three years earlier, Pew's Religious Landscape Research (2014) provides more detailed data about congregational participation in the United States. At that time, Christians represented 70.6 percent of the American population, a drop of nearly 8 points in seven years. During the same time period, the religiously unaffiliated jumped more than 6 points, representing 22.8 percent of the population. Nearly 40 percent of millennials fall in this group.[56] The decline of Christianity has continued at a rapid pace.[57]

The Pew Landscape research also provides insight into the participation of people who belong to congregations. Using a more sophisticated measure of church involvement than worship attendance, the 2014 research found that 33 percent of Christians are highly involved in their congregations, 58 percent have a medium level of involvement, and 12 percent fall in the low category.[58]

Over sixty years ago, Barth argued that both nominal Christians and the unaffiliated are "strangers to the Gospel."[59] The former belong to the church in name only. They ought to have heard, accepted, and responded to the gospel long ago but have not really done so. How is the church to present the gospel in words to people who are in the church but not really of the church? Part of the task of evangelization in this context is "to awaken this sleeping Church."[60]

I was surprised that Barth uses the language of *nominal* Christians in his description of the recipients of evangelization. Usually, he dislikes this term

56. Yonat Shimron, "Is the Rise of the Nones Slowing? Scholars Say Maybe," Religion News Service, February 11, 2020, accessed online at https://religionnews .com/2020/02/11/is-the-decline-in-religious-affiliation-slowing-some-scholars-say -maybe/.

57. See "In U.S., Decline of Christianity Continues at Rapid Pace: An update on America's changing religious landscape," Pew Research Center, October 17, 2019. https://www.pewforum.org/2019/10/17/in-u-s-decline-of-christianity -continues-at-rapid-pace/.

58. See Alexandra Sandstrom, "Church Involvement Varies Widely among U.S. Christians," Pew Research Center, November 16, 2015, accessed online at https:// www.pewresearch.org/fact-tank/2015/11/16/church-involvement-varies-widely -among-u-s-christians/. Their scales were based on membership, frequency of attendance at worship services, and frequency of attendance at small group religious activities like a prayer group or Bible study.

59. Barth, *CD* IV/3, second half, 872.

60. Barth, *CD* IV/3, second half, 873.

because it smacks of the spiritual elitism that often accompanies forms of Christianity that focus on individual piety and morality. But he adds a real twist with significant implications for evangelization:

> Those countless nominal Christians are undoubtedly the immediate neighbours of the community as the assembly of serious Christians. Do not even the latter continually find that they themselves are nominal Christians and urgently need to receive the Gospel afresh? The concern of evangelisation is precisely to sound out the Gospel on this shifting frontier between true and merely nominal Christians.[61]

The distinction between highly involved and nominal Christians is a "shifting frontier." All Christians find themselves needing "to receive the Gospel afresh." In his discussion of evangelization as a ministry, Barth explicitly singles out worship, preaching, and teaching as ministries that "must have the character of evangelisation."[62] These are ministries of the gathered community. Evangelization is to take place through them. It is not just directed at the few non-Christians or backsliders who happen to be present at church on a given Sunday. It is directed at "serious" and "true" Christians as well. All Christians need "to receive the Gospel afresh." Why is this the case? To answer this question we must examine Barth's soteriology, his understanding of salvation. We will take this up in the next chapter.

Before moving on, let's sum up some of the things we have learned by examining the church as witness and evangelization as one of its ministries.

1. The congregation is a missional community.
2. The mission of the congregation is to bear witness to the gospel: the good news of God's reconciliation of the world in Jesus Christ.
3. Every ministry of the congregation is a form of witness with the task of declaring, explaining, and applying the gospel to the people it serves.
4. The enduring ministries include ministries of words and deeds. Evangelization is a ministry of words.
5. Evangelization's task is to share the gospel in words with people who are not affiliated with congregations, inviting them to respond to God's gift of salvation in Jesus Christ.

61. Barth, *CD* IV/3, second half, 873.
62. Barth, *CD* IV/3, second half, 873.

6. But the task of evangelization involves more than this. It also presents the gospel afresh to nominal and serious Christians. This may take place in conjunction with other ministries like preaching, teaching, the cure of souls, and diaconal service. While it is clear why nominal Christians might need evangelization, we have left it an open question why Barth thinks "serious" and "true" Christians need to hear the gospel again and again. We will return to this in the next chapter.

A Case of Evangelistic Practice: Sharing the Gospel in a War Zone

We turn now to a case study. As you read it, try to identify the ways an understanding of evangelism as conversionism influences the responses of the people involved. Then consider how viewing the church as a witness to the gospel and evangelism as one of the ministries of the church might change the ways Sylvester (the case writer) and others interpret and respond to what is going on. The case was written by a student from Africa in one of my classes on evangelism. I have retained his first-person perspective and only changed enough details to maintain confidentiality.

My home is Liberia, a small country located on the west coast of Africa. We have a long and complicated history with the United States, which I will not share in detail here. Suffice it to say that many freed slaves who were Christians returned to Liberia with the support of the American church in hopes of evangelizing Africa. English remains the official language, but there are at least seventeen different ethnic groups, speaking twenty indigenous languages. The last two decades of the twentieth century and the first part of the twenty-first were periods of great strife in my country. Coup followed coup. Two civil wars were fought. Between 1989 and 1996, over two hundred thousand Liberians died and a million were displaced from their homes. Many ended up in refugee camps in neighboring countries. During this period, the infamous John Taylor came to power. He later was charged and convicted of crimes against humanity and war crimes by the Special Court in Sierra Leone and the United Nations. Much of my early life was spent seeking refuge. We experienced times of starvation and lived in constant fear of violence.

As a young adult, I became the pastor of a Pentecostal denomination. I was assigned to a congregation in a rural area that was predominantly Muslim. This was unusual because Liberia was about 80 percent Christian at the time and experienced very little religious violence. The civil wars were mostly based on ethnic divisions. In the community where the church was located, however, conflict between two businessmen—one a Christian and the other a Muslim—turned into a larger conflict. The (local) Muslim majority intensified the violence and even went so far as to burn down several church buildings. This included the one where I was pastor. Many in the church were already giving a "widow's mite" to support God's work, so the loss of the building was very bad for us. The violence only ceased with the arrival of peacekeepers. It took several years to rebuild the church, costing $75,000. This might not sound like a lot to Americans, but it was a huge sum of money for us.

Several years later, a new period of political unrest broke out at the national level. Five different factions were unhappy with the government. Everyone knew that war was imminent. Rural areas like ours were especially vulnerable to massacres, starvation, and rapes. War broke out when a group of rebels took a portion of the nation's capital, Monrovia. My case recalls events that took place when the war came to our community.

We learned by radio that a faction of the rebels, composed of a different ethnic group than our own, was moving in the direction of our community. My wife and I decided that it would be best if we took our baby boy to the church and opened it for others. Isolated families were vulnerable to terrible treatment by soldiers. It is true that in the past some church buildings had been burned with people inside, but we decided there was less risk coming together than being by ourselves. As word got out that the church was open, people began to gather. Some were members; others belonged to different churches.

I soon faced a problem. Muslims left their large mosque and sought refuge in our church. As I have mentioned, they were a majority in our community but a minority in Liberia as a whole. They were afraid of being singled out by the rebels who were approaching. The Christians already gathered in the building were furious when the Muslims showed up. One man said what everyone was thinking, "How can you seek refuge in a church that you once burned down?" Those already in the building refused to let the Muslims in. As the tension began to build, the members called for the pastor to come and decide what they should do. I was much younger than the elders of my congregation. I worried about the safety of my wife and baby boy. But I took on the pastoral role and pondered my decision. I knew that Muslim families (like everyone else) were more vulnerable in isolation and that many lived in huts that could be easily penetrated by flying bullets. The church building was made of cement bricks and was a good place of refuge. The Muslim group also had many children and elderly people. It was the rainy season, making it difficult to hide in the woods for any length of time.

The members of my church knew that I had been affected more than most by the burning of the church. I lost my entire library of books and personal items in the office. During the time of rebuilding, I heard mockery and sarcastic references to Christ as I went about my work. On a practical level there were a lot of Muslims seeking refuge. The church would be very crowded. Not only would it be less comfortable, but this kind of congestion sometimes led to the spread of tropical diseases.

So there I stood, squarely between the two groups. I remembered the many times I had sought refuge as a child. The Holy Spirit reminded me that Jesus told his followers to love one another as I have loved you and to love your neighbor as yourself. In a loud voice, I said, " We offer you refuge in the name of Jesus Christ." The crowd murmured. Not everyone agreed. I heard a church member tell a Muslim, "You heathen are blessed. Had it not been for our pastor, we would have driven you away, and even God would have understood." I also overheard one of our elders tell a member, "We know what Pastor is thinking, but he will be disappointed. These people will come right into the church they burned and start praying to their Allah." Later, a group of church elders approached me with several requests. They didn't want Muslims near the altar lest they desecrate the holy place. I told them to leave the people alone and allow them to sleep where there was room. They also told me that the Muslims were praying to Allah and using the house of God as a mosque. I told them, "Let it be, we are at war."

The one rule I made was that every evening at 8:00 the entire group was to be seated with no movement or talking. I'd offer a brief exhortation, prayer, and then would leave time for everyone to pray silently. During the three weeks we stayed in the church, this is what we did. I intentionally didn't preach a message of salvation or make an altar call. This message, along with healings and speaking in tongues, are the heart of evangelistic services and gatherings. [In class, Sylvester explained that by "message of salvation" he meant a sermon that challenged people to convert by confessing their sins, asking for forgiveness, and placing their faith in Christ as the only way to salvation.] I stayed away from topics like superiority or which religion is the way to God. My exhortations were rather on the love of Christ and how Scripture teaches us to treat our fellow humans. I intentionally avoided Scriptures such as Jesus is the way, the truth, and the life, no one goes to the Father, but through him (John 14:6). To be sure, I believe without a shadow of doubt that Jesus is the only way by which one can be saved, for there is "no name under heaven or on earth by which anyone can be saved" (Acts 4:12). Some of my church members wondered why I was not using this opportunity to "lead people to Christ." Some saw it to be a sort of fear that had settled in me.

Finally, the rebels approached. We could hear the sound of heavy mortar shells growing nearer and nearer. When a mortar round struck just beyond the church, the people panicked. They ran out of the church in all directions. It was unsafe to stay; it was unsafe to go. It took six months to restore order in our area. This only happened after the arrival of African peacekeepers and then United Nations troops. God spared the lives of some of us, and we slowly returned home. Most lived in refugee camps, for their homes were burned. Our church was heavily looted but remained standing.

My ordeal was not over. Some elders from my congregation traveled to church headquarters and spoke to a committee of denominational leaders. They offered different perspectives on my leadership during the crisis. When I was finally invited to share, I received mixed reactions from the denominational leaders. Some said I did the right thing by allowing the Muslims in, while others thought that I was wrong and risked polluting the sanctity of the holy place of worship. Almost unanimously, they agreed that it made no sense to allow Muslims into the church but not proclaim the message of salvation to them. They contended that I had a perfect opportunity for evangelism but "wasted" it, quoting the scripture that we ought to "preach in season and out of season" (2 Tim. 4:2). I was told that it was my responsibility as a pastor to proclaim the gospel and give the Muslims a chance to convert before they died. The rebels were advancing and death was a real possibility. Before the meeting ended, one of the senior leaders of the denomination stood up and brought the meeting to a close. He seemed to be addressing all of us: "Best remember, my friends, none of us can convert anybody. Only the Holy Spirit can do that. All we can do is plant the seed and leave the rest to God."

Reflection on Evangelistic Practice

In precept discussion, several issues came to the fore. Most of the students in Sylvester's precept disagreed with the denominational leaders who accused Sylvester of "wasting" an opportunity for evangelism. They believed that trying to convert Muslims in this kind of situation would have been unethical. People were gathering together for safety in a time of war. As one person put it, "Trying to convert people in these circumstances almost guarantees their decision won't be genuine. They'd have been coerced."

They also wondered why Sylvester did not consider other ways of sharing the gospel besides preaching the "message of salvation." One student framed this in terms of *doing* the gospel, not just *saying* the gospel. She put it this way: "Sylvester and some of the Christians were sharing the gospel through their actions. They were loving the very people who had burned their church. They were offering them refuge and forgiveness. Isn't this *doing* the gospel? This was sending a more powerful message than a 'message of salvation' trying to pressure Muslims to convert."

Another student built on this idea: "Why can't Sylvester's evening exhortations be used as a form of indirect evangelism? When one of the church members told a Muslim that they would have driven them away if not for their pastor, it is pretty clear that *he* needs to hear the gospel again. He's sharing a gospel of revenge, not forgiveness and love. He's fallen for a 'different gospel' as Paul puts it in Galatians." Another student added: "And this might be a really good way of approaching them. The Muslims would get to overhear the gospel when Sylvester exhorted the Christians to love their neighbors and enemies as Christ loves them. Instead of trying to convert them on the spot, he would present the gospel indirectly. This might plant a seed and turn out to be a more effective way of evangelizing them in the long-run than a frontal assault."

These comments are quite insightful, and I feel certain that is why I wrote them in my notes as I listened to the precept discussion. But they are still operating within the framework of evangelism as conversionism, which focuses on converting people in order to save them. Barth's alternative to this view of salvation comes to the fore in the next chapter. At this point, let us reflect on the case in terms of Barth's depiction of the church in terms of the Chalcedonian pattern and as a witness to the gospel.

We could hardly have a more vivid image of the common plight of all human beings caught in sin and death than that of human beings seeking refuge in a war zone out of fear of atrocities at the hands of soldiers. Muslims, Christians—it does not matter. They are human beings in solidarity with one another in sin and suffering. It would not be difficult to extend metaphorically different dimensions of this image to capture many aspects of the human condition: rape of women, rape of the earth, rape of workers by greedy corporations, and so on. In the face of sin and death, the mission of the church is to bear witness to the gospel, the love of God revealed in Jesus

Christ. Earlier we quoted Barth as writing that the church owes the world "an imitation and representation of the love with which God loved the world." Within the framework of conversionism, love appears to mean trying to get Muslims saved as soldiers advance. As the denominational leaders put it, Sylvester had the responsibility of giving them the chance to choose Jesus before they faced possible death. Otherwise they would be lost. He wasted this opportunity. In marked contrast, I believe the class was right. Trying to convert people under these circumstances would be unethical. But even more importantly, it would represent a failure to witness to the gospel, to love your neighbor as yourself, to extend forgiveness to those who have hurt you in the past, to love the vulnerable as Jesus did.

Viewing the case through the lens of witness, also, opens up opportunities to communicate the gospel through ministries other than evangelization. When witness occurs through all the ministries of the church, then evangelization no longer must serve as salvation central, the primary ministry through which people are invited to respond to the gospel. One of the students pointed to this when she asked why Sylvester did not use his nightly exhortations (encouragement and teaching) to declare and explain Jesus and to relate him to the situation they were facing. Evangelization is not the only way to bear witness. Teaching can serve this purpose as well. This does not need to be viewed as an "indirect" form of evangelism, for all ministries should bear witness to the gospel.

The student who pointed out that evangelization takes place through doing the gospel and not just saying the gospel made a closely related point. I frankly am ambivalent about the way Barth stresses the use of words in evangelization. Actions often speak louder than words. We saw this again and again in our dialogue with Scripture. Acts of courage and compassion often are the starting point of a relationship in which the gospel is shared. We can recall the case of Ariana Diaz in stark contrast to the words-only approach of "from scratch" evangelism in a mall.

Yet I am reluctant to let go of the point Barth is making. Actions can be ambiguous and need words to interpret them to others. The student who made this point was certainly right to note that welcoming into the church the very people who burned it down would have embodied the gospel in a wonderful way. But those who have had no exposure to the significance of the cross, loving one's enemies, or sacrificial love might not get the point. Words are necessary to describe who Jesus is and why Christians try to follow in his way. Certainly, Sylvester would have done well to keep this in mind.

Finally, Barth's depiction of the church in terms of the Chalcedonian pattern in which the relationship between Christ and the church is one of unity, differentiation, and asymmetry might frame everything taking place in this case. The church's role is to serve as a witness; it is not the savior of the world. Its words and deeds are not a way of glorifying itself and acting as if it is somehow more moral and more blessed, the recipient of the benefits of salvation. No, the church is to point beyond itself to Christ. In these circumstances, it will do this best by showing hospitality and welcome to its neighbors. Moreover, during the meeting in which Sylvester was called on the carpet, the denominational elder who ended the event not only had the last word then, but the last word now: "Best remember, my friends, none of us can convert anybody. Only the Holy Spirit can do that. All we can do is plant the seed and leave the rest to God."

For Further Reading

Introductions to Barth

Barth, Karl. *Evangelical Theology: An Introduction.* Garden City, NY: Anchor Books, 1964. An excellent "first read" of books by Barth as a point of entry into his theology.

Bender, Kimlyn J. *Reading Karl Barth for the Church: A Guide and Companion.* Grand Rapids: Baker Academic, 2019. A companion to the first volume of the *Church Dogmatics* written by an exceptionally clear and incisive interpreter of Barth's theology.

Bromiley, Geoffrey W. *Introduction to the Theology of Karl Barth.* Grand Rapids: Eerdmans, 1979. A section-by-section summary of every part of the *Church Dogmatics.*

Busch, Eberhard. *The Great Passion: An Introduction to Karl Barth's Theology.* Grand Rapids: Eerdmans, 2004. Written by one of Barth's closest colleagues and considered by many scholars to be the best introduction.

———. *Karl Barth: His Life from Letters and Autobiographical Texts.* Philadelphia: Fortress, 1974. Draws extensively on Barth's own words from letters and other documents to depict and interpret events in his life and his historical context. A masterful work.

Hunsinger, George. *How to Read Karl Barth: The Shape of His Theology.* New York: Oxford University Press, 1991. For those with some acquaintance with Barth's theology. Provides analysis of key motifs running through his theology that help readers recognize patterns of thinking and substantive themes.

———, ed. *Thy Word Is Truth: Barth on Scripture*. Grand Rapids: Eerdmans, 2012. Overview essays of Barth's view of Scripture. Includes Hunsinger's summary of Rudolf Smend's essay, "Postcritical Scriptural Interpretation," a landmark in how Barth interprets the Bible.

Jüngel, Eberhard. *Karl Barth: A Theological Legacy*. Philadelphia: Westminster, 1986. An introduction to Barth from a theologian who would later draw on Barth in his own constructive work in ways that are compelling.

Mangina, Joseph. *Karl Barth: Theologian of Christian Witness*. Louisville: Westminster John Knox, 2004. Clearly written overview of Barth's theology as a whole. Quite helpful.

Molnar, Paul. *Divine Freedom and the Doctrine of the Immanent Trinity: In Dialogue with Karl Barth and Contemporary Theology*. 2nd ed. London: Bloomsbury T&T Clark, 2017. In clear language, this book explores the importance of maintaining the theological distinction between the immanent and economic Trinity, that is, God's antecedent and inner being apart from creation and God's being in revelation and salvation. Points to weaknesses of theologies failing to maintain this distinction and the contrasting strengths of those that do.

Nimmo, Paul T. *Being in Action: The Theological Shape of Barth's Ethical Vision*. London: T&T Clark, 2007. Focuses on the importance of actualism in Barth—God's being is in God's action—relating it to his ethics.

Webster, John. *Karl Barth*. Outstanding Christian Thinkers. 2nd ed. London: Continuum, 2000. A clear, insightful overview by a master interpreter of Barth's ethics.

Interpretations of Barth

Bender, Kimlyn J. *Confessing Christ for Church and World: Studies in Modern Theology*. Downers Grove, IL: InterVarsity, 2014. Brings Barth's theology into conversation with contemporary theological issues and traditions.

———. *Karl Barth's Christological Ecclesiology*. Eugene, OR: Cascade Books, 2013. One of the best overviews of Barth's understanding of the church and its Christological foundation.

Busch, Eberhard. *Karl Barth and the Pietists: The Young Karl Barth's Critique of Pietism and Its Response*. Downers Grove, IL: InterVarsity, 2004. As the title indicates, much attention is focused on young Barth's relationship with Pietism, but the epilogue explores the relationship of the mature Barth with Pietism and raises issues relevant to Barth's evaluation of contemporary evangelicalism.

Ford, David. *Barth and God's Story: Biblical Narrative and the Theological Method of Karl Barth in the "Church Dogmatics."* Eugene, OR: Wipf & Stock, 1985. Early book on Barth's distinctive approach to Scripture. Remains helpful.

Gorringe, Timothy. *Karl Barth: Against Hegemony.* Christian Theology in Context. Oxford: Oxford University Press, 1999. Overview of Barth's determined resistance to all forms of political and social oppression, in spite of major problems in his interpretation of male/female relationships and homosexuality, which he later corrected.

Hunsinger, George. *Disruptive Grace: Studies in the Theology of Karl Barth.* Grand Rapids: Eerdmans, 2000. Excellent select essays on aspects of Barth's thought.

McCormack, Bruce L. *Karl Barth's Critically Realistic Dialectical Theology: Its Genesis and Development, 1909–1936.* Oxford: Clarendon, 1995. Upends standard interpretations of Barth since Balthasar's *The Theology of Karl Barth.* Of major significance.

McKenny, Gerald. *The Analogy of Grace: Karl Barth's Moral Theology.* Oxford: Oxford University Press, 2010. Prominent Notre Dame moral theologian probes Barth's ethics.

Webster, John. *Barth's Ethics of Reconciliation.* Cambridge: Cambridge University Press, 1995. One of two brilliant books by Webster on Barth's ethics.

———. *Barth's Moral Theology: Human Action in Barth's Thought.* Grand Rapids: Eerdmans, 1998. The second book by Webster exploring Bath's ethics with great insight and lifting up its constructive potential.

CHAPTER 5

Evangelization and Salvation

What is the relationship between salvation and evangelism? This question has come up again and again as we have reflected on cases, theology, and traditions of evangelistic practice. Evangelism as conversionism makes the question unavoidable. It claims that human beings are not saved until they convert, which alters their status before God from lost to found. They have the freedom as human beings to make a choice: they will either give themselves to Christ or not. A pattern of human experience is often linked to this model. Being saved through conversion takes place at an identifiable time and place, dividing experience into a before and after. Frequently, conversion takes the form of a dramatic experience like the apostle Paul's as portrayed in Acts 9.

In this chapter, we identify two ways of thinking about salvation. One is soteriological existentialism, the other soteriological objectivism.[1] Barth's theology revolves around the latter; theologies of conversionism, the former. It is defined as follows: "Soteriological existentialism is characterized by the view that salvation in itself and as such is not constituted or complete until something decisive takes place in one's human existence. To that extent, what took place in Christ does not acquire validity and efficacy until something decisive also comes to take place in us."[2]

There are many versions of soteriological existentialism among Roman Catholic and Protestant theologians. For our purposes, we are especially interested in how this understanding of salvation is related to the dominant view of evangelism emerging during the modern period. Obviously, in evangelism as conversionism salvation is dependent upon an individual's

---

1. George Hunsinger, *How to Read Karl Barth: The Shape of His Theology* (New York: Oxford University Press, 1991), ch. 5.
2. Hunsinger, *How to Read Karl Barth*, 106.

conversion, however this is defined. Whether this is personal acceptance of Jesus Christ as Lord and Savior or confessing one's faith publicly followed by full immersion baptism, salvation becomes real and effective for individuals only when they convert. Salvation is conditioned upon conversion. Evangelism is thus about saving people. It seeks to trigger the soteriological moment, summoning people to move from the lost to the found. The pattern of soteriological existentialism is so fused with evangelism as conversionism that it is very difficult for people to think of evangelism in any other way. Yet the relationship between this understanding of salvation and evangelism largely emerged out of awakening movements and new churches appearing after the Reformation.

The two themes of Karl Barth's theology to be explored in this chapter articulate a different understanding of salvation. This leads us to a new understanding of evangelism. These themes are Christ in our place and the Holy Spirit as the mediator of communion. In the first of these, Barth portrays Christ as taking our place in every aspect of salvation: we are justified, sanctified, and called in him. As he puts it: "The work of atonement, the conversion of humanity to God, was done for all. The Word of God is spoken to all. God's verdict and direction and promise have been pronounced over all. To that extent objectively, all are justified, sanctified, and called."[3]

Christ offers us salvation by taking our place, fulfilling the broken covenant on our behalf and in our stead. Salvation is not dependent on us in any way. This is a form of *soteriological objectivism*, defined as follows: "Soteriological objectivism . . . signifies that Jesus Christ is regarded as the sole Mediator not only of revealed truth, but also of saving truth. . . . [It] means that there is finally no other truth about us than the truth of who we are before God in Jesus Christ."[4]

What takes place in us is not constitutive of our salvation nor is it the final step we must take in order to make salvation effective. Barth was fond of telling the story of H. F. Kohlbrügge, who once was asked, "When were you converted?" and responded, "On Golgotha."[5] We are saved through the reconciling work of Christ alone. It is complete, perfect, and unsurpassable. It is not conditioned on something we do. We receive salvation as a free gift *in toto* and add nothing to it.

3. Karl Barth, *Church Dogmatics* (hereafter *CD*), ed. Geoffrey W. Bromiley and T. F. Torrance (Edinburgh: T&T Clark, 1956-75), IV/1, 148.
4. Barth, *CD* IV/1, 103.
5. Barth, *CD* I/2, 709.

Barth's soteriological objectivism, moreover, portrays Christ's salvation as universal in scope. Christ has died and risen for all. Does this mean all will be saved at the consummation? Barth does not claim to be a universalist in this sense. Though we may hope and pray for the salvation of all, God does not owe eternal patience to those who persistently resist the truth of who they already are in Christ Jesus. The threats of final judgment are real. God is a jealous God. But judgment remains in God's hands, not ours.

Moreover, Barth's comments about the objectivity of God's salvation of the world in Jesus Christ lead directly to our second theme: the Holy Spirit as the mediator of communion. Immediately after the passage quoted above, Barth continues:

> But the hand of God has not touched all in such a way that they can see and hear, perceive and accept and receive all that God is for all and therefore for them . . . they do not know their justification, sanctification, and calling as they have already taken place in Jesus Christ. But the hand of God has touched and seized Christians in this way—which means the Holy Spirit.

The Spirit is the way Christ's objective work impacts the existence of people. More properly, we should say, the Spirit joins us to Christ, for his person and work cannot be separated. The Holy Spirit imparts salvation to us by joining us to Christ and allowing us to participate in him.[6] The key words in describing the saving work of the Spirit are participation, communion, *koinōnia*, and even union.

It is helpful to recall the Chalcedonian pattern, for it determines the way Barth views our participation in Christ through the Spirit. We are united to him: he is in us, and we are in him. But it is a differentiated participation. Each retains their own identity. The relationship is asymmetrical. Christ is Savior and Lord; we are those who are saved by him, receive a new direction for our lives, and participate in his self-witness.

As we shall see, the Holy Spirit mediates other forms of communion. The Spirit not only joins us to Christ, but also brings us into communion with the Triune God and other Christians in our congregations and around the world. The Spirit brings us into solidarity with the world to which we are sent as Christ was sent to us. Obviously, two major questions emerge from this

---

6. George Hunsinger, *Disruptive Grace: Studies in the Theology of Karl Barth* (Grand Rapids: Eerdmans, 2000), 165.

understanding of salvation. First, is God everything and humanity nothing? What happens to human freedom when salvation is so objective and our subjective appropriation portrayed as the work of the Holy Spirit? Second, what happens to evangelization when it is based on a form of soteriological objectivism? Our answer to the second question will emerge over the course of the chapter. Since the first question is so vexing for many people, I want to address it briefly here.

Barth's soteriological objectivism takes its bearings from Martin Luther's understanding of justification by grace through faith, found in Paul's letters. Salvation is the outcome of God's gracious action in Jesus Christ. It is a free gift, undeserved and unmerited. We receive it in faith, by trusting in God's grace through the Holy Spirit. Luther often used the image of an open hand to portray our reception of this gift. As we shall see, Barth builds on this theme in his portrait of the way Christ takes our place in salvation.

In terms of human agency, Barth rejects modern understandings of freedom that center on human autonomy. Here, human beings are viewed as free to be "self-legislating," making their own choices and judgments on the basis of their own reason, morality, or interests. Freedom in this sense portrays human beings as situated in a neutral place with the ability to choose between this option or that. Barth sometimes portrays this understanding of freedom with the image of Hercules at the crossroads, the mighty hero free to choose whether he will travel down the road of vice or the road of virtue.[7] This image of freedom is one of the most seductive illusions of modernity, Barth contends. It is an illusion because we are caught in sin and death. Like Luther, he believed our will is in bondage, and we are not even free enough to realize how trapped we are.

In sharp contrast, Barth portrays freedom and agency as emerging from an objective change in the conditions in which we live. This is what happens in God's salvation of the world in Jesus Christ. Sin and evil are defeated and the Holy Spirit is sent into our midst. We might explore this way of thinking with images.

As a child living in St. Louis, I remember my parent taking our family to nearby caverns to see the stalactites and stalagmites. After walking in the caverns for a ways, we got in boats and continued to go deeper. Just before we entered one large cave, our guide turned off the lights. We were in total darkness. The boats came to a stop. After a few minutes, he turned on the boat lights, and we were surrounded by twinkling, quartz-like stalactites hanging

---

7. Depictions of this image are easily found online.

from the top of the cave. We had no idea they were there until the light broke into the darkness and gave us the ability to see. So too John's Gospel portrays Christ as the light coming into the darkness and illuminating the reality of our situation. An objective change has taken place in our conditions. The boat lights have been turned on; we can see.

Or suppose we are in prison sentenced to death. A passionate legal aid lawyer has discovered old DNA evidence that exonerates us. Our case is dismissed by a judge. The jail warden is notified. He sends a guard to release us. The cell door is unlocked. All we have to do is get up and walk out.

This is the kind of freedom that Barth believed Christians are granted by God's salvation in Christ. A change in our objective conditions has taken place and our freedom is a by-product of this. It is not the result of capacities we already have, as if we are autonomous beings with the freedom to choose this way or that. Our ability to see or walk out of our jail cell emerges in response to things done for us. Christ has taken our place and the Holy Spirit shines his light on our lives, establishing our true place and our freedom, not annulling them. Let's explore further what this means.

Christ in Our Place

I first came upon this phrase in the title of Paul van Buren's book on John Calvin, *Christ in Our Place: The Substitutionary Character of Calvin's Doctrine of Reconciliation*.[8] This originally was van Buren's dissertation for the theological faculty at the University of Basel, where he studied under Karl Barth. While the focus of the book is Calvin's theology, van Buren offers his professor's appreciative critique of Calvin throughout, a critique that comes to expression in the *Church Dogmatics*.

It is worth commenting on the use of "substitutionary" in the subtitle of van Buren's book. A substitutionary understanding of the atonement means that Christ dies in our place. But it implies more. As Simon Gathercole puts it, "In a substitutionary theory of the death of Jesus, he did something, underwent something, so that we did not and would never have to do so."[9] In other words, *substitution means instead of us*. As I interpret

8. Paul van Buren, *Christ in Our Place: The Substitutionary Character of Calvin's Doctrine of Reconciliation* (Eugene, OR: Wipf & Stock, 2002; previously published by Oliver and Boyd in 1957).

9. Simon Gathercole, *Defending Substitution: An Essay on Atonement in Paul*, Acadia

the theme of Christ in our place in Barth's theology, I want to be clear that it means Christ does something on our behalf and in our stead so we will never have to do it. Indeed, he does for us what we are incapable of doing ourselves. For Barth, this does not preclude other ways of thinking about reconciliation that are also found in Scripture, like representation. Christ does represent God to us and us to God. But the language of substitution does clarify the strength of what is meant by *in our place.*

In his discussion of evangelism as a ministry of the church, Barth offers a short summary of the gospel.[10] The language of "place" appears, as it often does, in his explanations of reconciliation. We will start here to look closely at the way this theme comes to expression in a particular passage in the context of evangelism. We then will step back and look at the way the theme structures the entirety of Barth's doctrine of reconciliation. We then will turn to the theme of the Holy Spirit as the mediator of communion. This focuses on how God's objective salvation accomplished in Christ intersects the lives of communities and individuals.

Evangelization Bears Witness to the Gospel in Words

In the previous chapter, we examined Barth's understanding of the mission of the church as witness, pointing beyond itself to Christ like John the Baptist. Evangelization is only one form of witness, but it is an essential part of the church's mission. As Barth puts it at the very end of his discussion of this ministry: "Certainly a Church which is not as such an evangelising Church is either not yet or no longer a Church, or only a dead Church, itself standing in supreme need of renewal by evangelisation."[11] As we have seen, Barth portrays evangelization as directed to people outside the church, nominal Christians, and even serious Christians who need to awaken to the gospel again and again.

What does Barth mean by the gospel? He offers a short summary in the midst of his discussion of evangelization. He begins with a comment on the European context in the middle of the twentieth century. Evangeliza-

---

Studies in Bible and Theology (Grand Rapids: Baker Academic, 2015), Kindle edition, loc. 184.

10. For other examples of summaries of the gospel, see Barth, *CD* IV/2, 181–83, 195–97.

11. Barth, *CD* IV/3, second half, 874.

tion encounters an obstacle in countries where most people are Christians. Whether nominal or serious Christians, church members believe they have already arrived at the "*place* to which they are summoned by the Gospel."[12] Yet Christian respectability in a Christian nation is not the place where they are called to stand. Nor is it the place where they actually are standing. This attitude is a form of pious self-deception in which Christians fail to discern the ways their religion is compromised by class, race, economic structures, and other "lordless powers," as Barth puts it.[13] They have not arrived. As Christians, they are simultaneously saved and sinful. They live between the "already" and "not yet," between Christ's triumph over sin and evil and its full realization in the consummation. They are caught up in the eschatological "turn" of the ages.

If the Christian religion is susceptible to this kind of self-deception in countries that are majority Christian and have long Christian histories, it is very tempting to start with judgment or the law in evangelization and then move to the gospel. This is the norm in evangelism as conversionism, though it normally does not involve a critique of social sins. It focuses more on complacency and nominalism fostered by Christian respectability and institutionalism. Revivalistic conversionism excels at this. "The more one heats up hell for them, the more they come running," Barth commented after hearing Billy Graham preach.[14]

But God's judgment is not the first and most important word of the gospel:

In evangelisation, the concern must be, not so much to engage negatively in the necessary criticism and destruction of this notion, but rather, to disclose positively that both neighbours without and those within are at this *place* as seen by God in Jesus Christ, that the love and grace of God apply to them from the very beginning, that their salvation is assured and present to them, and that on this basis they are *invited*, not to pass by this reality in their blindness and deafness, but to accept it from their hearts and with all its consequences, in other words to believe and to obey, coming to this *place* in practice and becoming in practice what they already are, not just in theory, but according to the resolve of

12. Barth, *CD* IV/3, second half, 873.
13. See the section "The Lordless Powers" in Barth, *CD* IV/4, 213–33.
14. Eberhard Busch, *Karl Barth: His Life from Letters and Autobiographical Texts* (Philadelphia: Fortress, 1976), 446.

God and on the basis of his act of reconciliation, namely, those who are also called, who also know, who also witness, who also have a part in the responsibility of the community.[15]

This is one sentence. It is typical of Barth's writing. It is complex and demanding of the reader. You have to read it four or five times just to get the basic ideas. Even then, unless you know other parts of his theology, the meaning is hard to grasp. Although Barth was a citizen of Switzerland, he writes like a German theologian and philosopher of his period. So let us look at this sentence closely.

As we saw in the previous chapter, Barth extends evangelism to include "both neighbours without and those within." They are portrayed as standing "at this place as seen by God in Jesus Christ." When God looks at us in mercy and judgment he sees us "in" Jesus Christ who has taken our place. What Barth means by this is captured in the *locus classicus* of this theme in the *Church Dogmatics*:

> "In Christ" means that in him we are reconciled to God, in him we are elect from eternity, in him we are called, in him we are justified and sanctified, in him our sin is carried to the grave, in his resurrection our death is overcome, with him our life is hid in God, in him everything that has to be done for us, to us, and by us, has already been done, has previously been removed and put in its place, in him we are children in the Father's house just as he is by *nature*.[16]

In his summary of the gospel as he discusses evangelization, Barth goes on to write: "the love and grace of God apply to them from the very beginning, that their salvation is assured and present to them." "From the beginning" could mean from the beginning of the lives of the people Barth has been referring to, neighbors without and within the church. This signals the universal scope of Barth's understanding of reconciliation. All are included—those within the church and those without. Christ has taken the place of all. Or it could mean from the beginning of creation itself, indeed, in eternity. I believe it is likely that "from the beginning" here is referring to election. This appears to be indicated a bit further on by his use of the word "resolve," which is associated with election. In either case, before any of us know it,

---

15. Barth, *CD* IV/3, second half, 873.
16. Barth, *CD* I/2, 240.

God loves us in Jesus Christ; his grace is ours; "our salvation is assured and present." This is the word with which we begin evangelization. God's love and grace are primary; judgment comes later and always is in the service of God's salvation.

This is one of the ways Barth helps us respond to scholars who dismiss the atonement by portraying it along the lines of "sinners in the hands of an angry God." God does hate sin and evil. What kind of God would we be worshiping if a divine blind eye were turned to the social sins of economic injustice, racism, and the rape of the earth? These are the by-products of a more fundamental turning of humanity away from God and against itself. The earth is bloodied, and this must be paid for with blood. But the first word always is God's love of the world in Jesus Christ. Because God loves us, God provides the means of reconciliation: "But God demonstrates his own love for us in this: While we were still sinners, Christ died for us" (Rom. 5:8). This is "resolved" in eternity.

Barth continues his summary of the gospel by writing that in evangelization we are "invited" to become who we "already are" in Jesus Christ. We are persons who already have been saved in him. This is who are. We are invited to respond to God's salvation of the world in Christ with faith and come under the direction of Christ as his disciples, a prominent topic in Barth's discussion of sanctification.[17]

Barth regularly makes the distinction between our salvation in Christ and our participation in his salvation with the terms *de jure* (by right or law, in principle) and *de facto* (in fact).[18] Human beings are "in" Christ *de jure* before they even know it. They are invited to respond to this reality *de facto*, in fact, not just in principle. As Barth's summary of the gospel implores: Don't pass this by in "blindness and deafness" but receive this good news from the heart—believe and obey.

Clearly, Barth is pointing to a subjective response to God's salvation of the world in Jesus Christ.[19] By "subjective," he means the activity of the Holy Spirit who imparts Christ's salvation to us and brings us into communion

---

17. Barth, *CD* IV/2, 533–52.

18. See, for example, Barth, *CD* IV/2, 521.

19. By "subjective," Barth never means inward or internal experience of the self. He always thinks of human beings as "existing" persons, who exist in and are determined by their relationships, actions, responses, decisions, and so forth. It always is the total self in the totality of existence-with-others who is responding to God, who is an "object" or person independent of us evoking our responses. Moreover, our responses include every part of our personhood: our intellect, our emotions, our

with Christ and through him with God the Father. This includes our active participation in Christ's salvation. We are not robots with God at the controls. Rather, the conditions in which we exist before God are changed both objectively and subjectively, setting us free to participate. The subjective change in conditions is the work of the Holy Spirit. Before turning to the Spirit as the mediator of communion, I want to say a bit more about the relationship between election and reconciliation in salvation. This will allow us to see how the theme of Christ in our place runs across the *Church Dogmatics*, as well as its influence on the arrangement of material within *The Doctrine of Reconciliation*.

We often think of election in terms of God's choice of a people to be his covenant partner (the election of Israel) or God's determination of those people who will be saved or "passed by" in eternity (for example, double predestination in Calvin). Both are correct, Barth contends, in portraying God as the subject of election and God's people as the object of election. Moreover, Calvin was correct in portraying election as involving both God's grace and judgment. But these traditional ways of portraying election neglect the Christological basis of this doctrine as found in Scripture.[20]

Election focuses on God's decision in eternity to be for the world in Jesus Christ.[21] Barth directs our attention to passages like Ephesians 1:4-6: "For he chose us in him before the creation of the world to be holy and blameless in his sight. In love he predestined us for adoption to sonship through Jesus Christ, in accordance with his pleasure and will—to the praise of his glorious grace, which he has freely given us in the One he loves." This passage is interpreted in different ways, and Barth does not rely on it alone. However, he believes we should take seriously the various references in the New Testament of God's decision in eternity to be for humanity in Jesus Christ.

In Barth's view, Christ is both the electing and elected one. As a member of the Trinity, Christ participates as a subject of election. He resolves to be for humanity and to accept the mission he is given to reveal and enact God's love for humanity in reconciliation. He also is the object of election, the elected human being who serves as God's faithful covenant partner in humanity's place. The movement here is from the particular to the universal, from Jesus Christ as the electing God and elected human being to all human beings who

---

imagination, and so forth. One human capacity cannot be singled out as having a privileged position in openness to, participation in, and responding to God.

20. Barth, *CD* II/2, 55-58, 60-76.

21. Thus Barth locates election in the doctrine of God. It is "the basis of all the relationships between God and humanity." *CD* II/2, 52 (my translation).

are elect in him. It is little wonder that Barth frequently refers to election as the "sum of the gospel." As he puts it at one point, "Of all words that can be said or heard it is the best: that God loves human beings, that God is for humanity."[22]

If election is the event of God's decision to be God for us in eternity, then reconciliation is the fulfillment of this decision in time.[23] As fully divine and fully human, only Christ is in a position to serve as the mediator between God and humanity, representing God to humanity and humanity to God. This leads Barth to bring together in his doctrine of reconciliation material that usually is treated separately in dogmatic theology. Here is a brief summary:

OVERVIEW OF BARTH'S DOCTRINE OF RECONCILIATION

The Son of God	The Son of Man	The God-Human
Christ's priestly office	Christ's royal office	Christ's prophetic office
Divine atonement for sin	Human covenant fidelity	Glory of the Mediator
Humiliation of Son of God	Exaltation of Son of Man	Christ's self-attestation
Pride and fall	Sloth and misery	Falsehood and condemnation
Justification	Sanctification	Vocation (calling)
Holy Spirit's gathering of Christian community	Holy Spirit's upbuilding of Christian community	Holy Spirit's sending of Christian community
Christian faith	Christian love	Christian hope

Salvation, sin, the church, and the individual are treated in their relationship to Jesus Christ and one another. This overview helps us grasp the way Christ is portrayed as taking our place in this doctrine. In what follows I italicize key ideas that are found in the overview.

As the *Son of God* (fully divine), Christ alone is in a position to take our place as those caught in sin and death, who have rebelled against God and thus have ruined our relationships with our fellow human beings and ourselves. We are in no position to save ourselves from this situation, for we are both caught in and blinded by our *pride*. But God is for us. He makes our situation his own, takes our place, and *justifies* us. As Barth puts it: "What took

---

22. Barth, *CD* II/2, 3.
23. Barth, *CD* IV/2, 31–37.

place is that the Son of God fulfilled the righteous judgment on us human beings by Himself taking our place as humans and in our place undergoing the judgment under which we had passed."[24]

Barth brings out four dimensions of Christ in our place in our justification before God: (1) he takes our place as we, in pride, set ourselves up to judge in God's place;[25] (2) he takes our place as the judged, exchanging his righteousness for our sinfulness; (3) he takes our place in the judgment, atoning for our sin in his death on the cross; (4) he takes our place in establishing the justice of God, repentant on our behalf in his baptism by John and resisting temptation in the wilderness and passion. The imagery throughout is forensic. Barth realizes the atonement can be presented in other ways, especially with the priestly concepts of offering and sacrifice. No matter how it is expressed, reconciliation is the fulfillment of election. God is for us in Jesus Christ, who maintains the justice of God while justifying us before God by taking our place.

We have noted the influence of Luther's understanding of justification by grace through faith on Barth's theology. It was for Barth one of the greatest theological achievements of the Reformation. Luther characterized the Christian life with the phrase *simul iustus et peccator*, simultaneously righteous and sinner. What is remarkable about Barth's development of this theme is his portrait of *sanctification* and *vocation* along the same lines. We are sanctified and called "in him," in Jesus Christ, who has taken our place as the Son of Man (fully human) and as the Mediator between God and humanity. Barth even coins the phrase *simul peccator et sanctus*, simultaneously sinner and saint.[26] In a very real sense, Barth is bringing together Luther and Calvin.[27] Calvin portrays sanctification and justification as taking place simultaneously. To underscore this point, Calvin deals with sanctification first in the *Institutes of the Christian Religion*.[28]

24. The "in our place" theme is especially prominent in *CD* IV/1, 222–28. The quote is from 222.

25. Barth means, not only our willingness to pronounce final judgment on others or to judge them in everyday life, but our tendency to set ourselves up as judge in the capacity to determine good and evil. Pride appears to have a special place in Barth's famous statement that the "general conception of ethics coincides exactly with the conception of sin." *CD* II/2, 518.

26. Barth, *CD* IV/2, 575.

27. See George Hunsinger, "A Tale of Two Simultaneities: Justification and Sanctification in Luther, Calvin, and Barth," in *Evangelical, Catholic, and Reformed: Doctrinal Essays on Barth and Related Themes* (Grand Rapids: Eerdmans, 2015), ch. 10.

28. John Calvin, *The Institutes of the Christian Religion*, 2 vols., ed. John T. McNeill, trans. Ford Lewis Battles (Philadelphia: Westminster, 1960).

In Barth, Christ is portrayed as taking our place by entering into our human and adamic nature, but unlike us living as the faithful, obedient, and true human being in covenant partnership with God. As such, he is exalted to God, the upward and Godward dimension of a human life that corresponds to God. As Barth puts it: "The covenant broken by Israel and the whole of humanity, but never repudiated or destroyed by God, is maintained in the life-act of this one human being. He does that which is demanded and expected in the covenant as the act of human faithfulness corresponding to the faithfulness of God."[29]

Christ's exaltation does not exclude the humiliation of the cross. Indeed, as we saw in the Gospel according to John, the cross is the climax of Christ's revelation of God's glory in the form of self-giving love. It is the epitome of Christ's human correspondence to his Father who loves humankind and summons it to right-relatedness in which justice reigns among communities and love in relations with others and oneself. Christ goes to the cross in part because of his faithfulness to God's reversal of worldly values by favoring the weak and lowly, not the high and mighty.[30] And he is vindicated by God who raised him from the dead; he is "not only the suffering Son of God but also the victorious and triumphant Son of Man . . . in our place. . . . We are not saints and sanctified because we make ourselves such. We are saints and sanctified because we are already sanctified, already saints, in this One."[31]

In living as the faithful covenant partner in correspondence to God, Christ takes our place. We are drawn down by the pull of *sloth*, failing to do and be all that we can as God's covenant partners—not just as individuals but as communities, nations, organizations, and so forth. He alone is the Holy One, the one true sanctified human being. He is exalted on our behalf, and we are exalted in him. Holiness is not our doing; it is his doing: "It is not a matter of knowing ourselves but of knowing ourselves in Christ."[32] But our *de jure* sanctification in him becomes *de facto* as we are redirected by him through the Holy Spirit. We are disturbed from our sleep and lift up our heads to look at the sanctified one. We are raised and liberated for obedience. In Barth's view, however, the struggle between the old person and the new in Christ Jesus, the old creation and the new, is ongoing. We are simultaneously both sinners and saints.

29. Barth, *CD* IV/2, 167; see also 514-15.
30. Barth, *CD* IV/2, 168.
31. Barth, *CD* IV/2, 516.
32. Barth, *CD* IV/2, 283.

Before we move to the third part of Barth's doctrine of reconciliation—vocation—we must describe Barth's understanding of conversion. He locates conversion in his discussion of sanctification. The section is called "The Awakening to Conversion," and it picks up the image of human beings falling asleep, dragged down under the weight of sloth, sleepwalking through life without seeing the extent of the world's rebellion against God and failing to do and be all that is possible in "revolting against the disorder" this creates.[33] The saints are jolted awake by God and begin to turn around and walk in a new direction. But their walking is both a proceeding and halting. They are still sinners, but they are disturbed sinners. They will fall asleep again but hopefully will be awakened again. This way of putting it tells us a lot about Barth's understanding of conversion:

> We cannot, therefore, define Christians simply as those who are awake while the rest sleep, but more cautiously as those who waken up in the sense that they are awakened a first time and then again to their shame and good fortune. They are, in fact, those who constantly stand in need of reawakening and who depend upon the fact that they are continually reawakened. They are thus those, who, it is to be hoped, continually waken up.[34]

Hence, Barth's image of the awakening to conversion, a turning around and proceeding in a new direction, a movement toward God marked by renewal and regeneration. But this is not a linear or incremental process. We awaken and fall asleep. Thus, "We cannot understand the conversion of human beings as a matter for only one period in their life.... It is neither exhausted in a once-for-all act, nor is it accomplished in a series of such acts.... But sanctification in conversion is not the affair of these individual moments; it is the affair of the totality of the whole life-movement of human beings."[35]

The work of salvation is Christ's alone. We are justified and sanctified in him. He alone has taken our place. There is nothing we can contribute. But Barth adds a third dimension to his depiction of reconciliation: *Christ the Mediator* between God and humanity. What he has accomplished on our behalf must be revealed to humanity. For Barth, reconciliation and revelation go hand in hand. We do not really grasp reconciliation until we are grasped

33. Barth, *CD* IV/2, 553–84. The revolt against disorder is found in *CD* IV/4, 205–12.
34. Barth, *CD* IV/2, 555.
35. Barth, *CD* IV/2, 566.

by reconciliation, which brings us into fellowship with Christ and through him to his Father in the power of the Holy Spirit. The one who reconciled us to God was raised from the dead and is our contemporary who continues to call human beings to himself.

As we have seen, the mission of the church is to accompany Christ in this work. This is the church's *vocation*. We are called, built up, and sent as a community to bear witness to him. Even here there is a substitutionary dimension to Christ's work. Christ is the true witness.[36] He alone is in a position to break through human *falsehood* and speak into the lives of all people in all times and places. In contrast, we are caught in falsehood as human beings and as the church. I do not think Barth coined the phrase *simul peccator et martyr*, simultaneously sinner and witness, but he certainly could have on the basis of his theology.

How often are the worst evils justified in the name of religion? We have only to look at America today to see many striking examples of this. The pious lie is often the most seductive. It is not just a matter of the worst-case scenarios—the German Christians supporting Hitler, for example. It is the hidden, taken-for-granted assumptions of our everyday lives that blind us to evils that are not even in the outer reaches of our consciousness. Not only do they blind us, they lead us to perpetrate evil, often, in the name of goodness and Christianity. Christ alone is the true witness. Only when we are joined to him and accompany him in speaking his Word into the lives of people do we serve as his witnesses.

The Holy Spirit as the Mediator of Communion

How then are we to understand the relationship between the objective and subjective dimensions of salvation? How is what occurs in Christ related to what occurs in us?[37] These are crucial questions for evangelization. Barth consistently describes our subjective appropriation of Christ's objective work in terms of the Holy Spirit. The Spirit imparts Christ's salvation to us and brings us into communion with Christ and through him with God the Father. As we see in Paul and John, moreover, "in Christ," "fellowship" (*koinōnia*), "in-one-another," and other expressions are used to describe various forms of communion created by the Holy Spirit. This ranges from communion

36. Barth, *CD* IV/3, first half, 368–434.
37. Hunsinger, *How to Read Karl Barth*, 105.

within the Trinity, between Christ and individual believers, among Christians, and many other relationships. I believe it would be very difficult if not impossible to describe our subjective appropriation of salvation in a straightforward way as simply a matter of human choice or freedom. To do so would be to have more in common with modern understandings of freedom than the interplay of divine and human action as depicted in the New Testament. It is the saving work of the Holy Spirit to join us to the saving work of Christ and in the process to bring into being our freedom to respond in faith to God's love in Jesus Christ.

The Spirit's role in our subjective appropriation of Christ's salvation of the world has a number of implications for evangelization. First, it decenters human agency from the central role it often occupies in this ministry of the church. We are not preaching for decision so people might be saved. It is not their decision that saves them. It is Christ's saving work and the Spirit's action upon them that makes it possible to respond in faith. How can we help others begin to grasp and respond to God's love as found in Jesus Christ? Barth uses the language of mystery and miracle to describe how the Holy Spirit gives us eyes to see and ears to hear so we no longer pass the gospel by. He is adamant that this cannot be reduced to human techniques or methods and that our response in faith should never be reduced to a particular pattern of experience. It is a mistake, a huge one, to think of our response to the gospel in terms of decision alone. It is much more than this and takes many forms. It may take the form of acknowledging our vulnerability before God after a near-death experience or a self-transcending experience in worship through music. What is important is an acknowledgment of the love of God in Jesus Christ. This is the Spirit's doing, and to confine it to one kind of human action is to both reduce and control the Spirit's freedom.

Second, acknowledging the Spirit's role in evangelization decenters human agency in another way. It places our reliance on the Spirit through prayer more at the center. We pray for the people we evangelize because we cannot control their response. Nor should we try. This is the Spirit's doing. This should keep us away from all forms of manipulation in evangelization. These have long been a staple of evangelism as conversionism. Revivalism relied on various forms of mass psychology to gain conversions. Even gentler forms like positive peer pressure or sleep deprivation go too far in the direction of trying to take over the job of the Holy Spirit.

Third, the guidance of the Spirit should play a much larger role than it often does. We cannot evangelize everyone. How do we decide where we invest our time and energy? This should be a matter of prayer and ongoing discernment. Moreover, in relational evangelization particularly, we would do well to learn from the posture of prayerful listening encouraged in spiritual companioning. We listen to the person, but we also listen for the Holy Spirit at the same time. We are seeking guidance; we are praying for the other person; we are trying to discern openings for evangelization as they emerge in conversations. The posture of prayerful listening is a radical shift away from evangelism as trying to make a sale or close the deal. It is a matter of talking less and listening more, of having less of a set agenda and more being open to God's presence in the conversation. The Spirit is present to help both of the participants in the conversation come to know the love of Jesus in a new and deeper way. We have to trust this more than our own resources. It seems to me that when we do so, we are evangelized too, receiving as much, if not more, than we give.

Three Patterns of the Christian Life

As we reach the end of our discussion of four themes in Karl Barth, we now are in a position to answer a question left hanging in the previous chapter: Why does Barth believe the congregation should address all Christians—both nominal and serious—with the gospel again and again? George Hunsinger offers a set of distinctions that help us answer this question and, at the same time, continue to clarify the differences between Barth's understanding of evangelization and evangelism as conversionism. They represent different patterns of the Christian life in the subjective appropriation of salvation: once-and-for-all, more-and-more, and again-and-again.[38]

In evangelism as conversionism, once-and-for-all tends to refer to the event of conversion, the moment when a person moves from being lost to being saved. More-and-more has to do with incremental growth in the Christian life. Again-and-again is only relevant if people are backsliders and lose their faith. Presumably, they need to be reconverted. Again-and-again may also apply to people who are members of a church and gradually become nominal Christians. Research on Billy Graham's crusades, for example, found that they were mostly effective in helping people who were nominal Christians become committed Christians.[39] But Graham's orientation

38. Hunsinger, *Disruptive Grace*, 167n23, and 300–301n34. See also Hunsinger, "A Tale of Two Simultaneities," 189–215.

39. Richard Peace, *Conversion in the New Testament: Paul and the Twelve* (Grand Rapids: Eerdmans, 1999), 288–91.

to decision was found to have a major weakness. Follow-up research after one Graham crusade discovered that only 15 percent of those who signed a decision card were incorporated into a church one year later.[40] Without a congregation to support them, perhaps, they would show up at another crusade again (and again?) in future years.

Barth views these three dimensions of salvation very differently. Once-and-for-all refers to God's reconciliation of the world in Jesus Christ. Christ takes our place in reconciling us to God. The soteriological event is not the individual's conversion, but Christ's once-and-for-all life, death, and resurrection on our behalf and in our stead. We awaken to who we already are in Jesus Christ. This may have the character of a dramatic experience but not necessarily. As we have seen above, Barth rejects turning once-and-for-all into a pattern of Christian experience that marks our movement from the lost to the saved. The gospel is infinitely rich in speaking into the life-situations of individuals and groups in different times and places, as well into the situations of individuals at different moments of their lives.

Again-and-again is the way Barth describes our response to Christ's complete and perfect work. It is why the church needs to communicate the gospel anew to all Christians. This was another insight Barth learned from Martin Luther. Luther believed we never move beyond our need for the gospel, for we remain caught in sin the entirety of our lives. As we noted above, we are simultaneously righteous and sinful, sinful and sanctified.[41] We stand in need of the gift of God's grace again-and-again.

More-and-more is not really developed in Barth's theology. Just as we are not made righteous (justified) by degrees, we do not become holy (sanctified) by degrees. Barth is particularly suspicious of the role soteriological gradualism plays in pietism, evangelicalism, and other traditions portraying growth in holiness as an incremental process. Too often this leads to viewing justification as God's work and sanctification as our work as we cooperate synergistically with God. In sharp contrast, Barth portrays salvation as a matter of receiving God's gift of grace in Christ again and again. We receive it as a whole in perfect form, not as partially finished and gradually completed by us.

Barth's perspective is rich, but it also is demanding. Let us see what light it throws on the first part of another case study coming from one of my classes on evangelization.

---

40. Some of the "decisioners" were already members and, thus, did not need to be incorporated into a church, but this does not account for all of them.

41. Barth, *CD* IV/2, 515, 575.

A Case of Evangelistic Practice: I'm Gonna Do a Bad Thing

Jamal Parker and Tyrone Smith are African American men who worked side by side in the food and nutrition department of Jefferson Hospital in Philadelphia, washing dishes and preparing food. Jamal was only twenty and a part-time university student. Tyrone was forty-four and had dropped out of high school. But they had a lot of time to talk while working together on the "iron horse," a dish machine in the back of the kitchen that was so large it took two men to operate it. "I kind of gravitated to the people my age," Jamal said, "but Tyrone and I got along just fine. He always wore this huge gold cross on a large chain around his neck. When the kitchen heated up and steam from cooking and the dishwasher filled the room, that cross would shine bright. It was like a beacon of light, drawing people to Tyrone to talk about their problems. I'm not sure that he even went to church. He always worked on Sundays." Little did Jamal know that Tyrone would turn to him at one of the darkest and most dangerous moments in his life.

Tyrone was a fun-loving, heavyset man. In Jamal's words, "He did it all in the kitchen, working long hours, cooking, cleaning, and joking around with everybody." Tyrone was open about his past. He had a drinking problem that caused him to lose his driver's license for a year after his second DUI. Over the years, he'd had a few brushes with the law but nothing that landed him in jail, except after his second DUI. Most of all, he talked about his problems with his former wife. It bothered him that she refused to work, living off the meager child support he provided. Tyrone also believed that she was "jealous" of his relationship with their children. As Jamal put it, "Tyrone was always talking about those kids. Right before Christmas, he started working hundred-hour pay periods. He kept talking about how he was going to buy great presents for his kids and give them the best Christmas ever. It seemed like the only way he could enjoy Christmas was through his kids' excitement." But as Christmas drew near, Tyrone's dreams were suddenly dashed, and he reached out to Jamal in a desperate plea for help.

It was on the second Saturday in December. The weather was cold and rainy. Jamal was trying to sleep in because he had just finished his exams and he didn't have to work. He remembers rolling over in bed and feeling the vibrations of his cell phone "going crazy." He turned over and tried to go back to sleep. But his curiosity got the best of him, and he answered the phone. "Hello, hello," he said, while trying to stifle a yawn. Silence. Then, he heard a mumbled sobbing of his nickname at work: "Nas, Nas, I need you to come get me or I'm going to do something real bad." Jamal responded, "Who is this? Where are you?" All he could hear was "It's Tyrone" before the line went dead.

Jarred out of sleep, Jamal frantically called the number on his cell phone several times before Tyrone finally picked up. He asked Tyrone what was wrong, but all Tyrone would say, over and over, was that he was going to do a bad thing. Jamal finally got him to share where he was and told him he'd be there as soon as possible. He threw on his clothes and dashed down to his car. It took him thirty minutes to finally locate Tyrone on a street corner—a hooded, shaking figure drenched by the rain. He pulled up and rolled down the window. Jamal recalls, "I could see that his eyes were bloodshot, and when he got in the car he reeked of liquor. It wasn't until we drove off that I noticed a plastic bag in his hand. There was a black gun inside." The two drove for a while in silence. Then Jamal asked Tyrone: "What's going on?" Tyrone responded, "My wife got full custody of the kids. She's going to take them away permanently. I might as well be dead." Jamal couldn't help glancing down at the gun and feeling very, very nervous. He started praying silently for God's guidance.

Jamal pulled into the parking lot of a McDonald's and turned off the motor. He turned to Tyrone and said, "Tyrone, you're one of my best friends at work. I really don't want you to hurt yourself." He told Tyrone that he could appeal the custody decision and offered other reasons he shouldn't give up hope. But nothing he said seemed to have any impact. Jamal's own words tell us what happened next:

> Finally I said—and I think it was the Holy Spirit that told me to say it—Tyrone, do you really want your kids to remember Christmas as the time their father killed himself? This seemed to get through. I asked him if we could get rid of the gun, and he gave a feeble smile, handing me the plastic bag. I rolled down the window and threw it out of the car. I wondered if Tyrone would attack me when I did that. But he made no response. I leaned over and placed my arms around him and began to pray, telling him that Jesus loved him and asking the Holy Spirit to comfort him and stay with him. After a while I leaned back. I gave him the pocket Bible I had with me and told him that not killing himself was the best Christmas present that anyone had ever given me. Every Christmas I still remember this. I told him that I thought it would be a good idea if I took him to his brother's house. As I drove him there over the broken roads, the tires sounded like horse hoofs: "Clipity, clap; clipity clap."

It was the only sound breaking the silence inside the car. To this day, I believe it was the power of the Holy Spirit that guided me that day. It wasn't anything I could have done myself.

When Jamal shared this with my class, he added that these events still haunted him. He asked us to reflect with him on the ministry he offered to Tyrone at a terrible moment in his friend's life. He also asked the class to reflect with him on what he might have done after the crisis was over. Tyrone was back at work the next day.

One question is whether this situation called for evangelization. Jamal rightly focused on deterring Tyrone from an act of violence—toward himself, his family, or innocent bystanders. He managed the crisis and offered care to his friend. Yet it is also clear that in many ways—in what Jamal said and did—the gospel was shared with Tyrone. He told Tyrone that Jesus loved him and asked the Holy Spirit to comfort him. He gave him a pocket Bible. His willingness to get out of bed on a rainy day and put himself in danger was analogous to God's love in Christ. Why should we resist calling this evangelization? I do not think we should. The new evangelization no longer thinks in terms of conversion in order to save someone. Rather, its focus is on communicating the love of God in Jesus Christ in order that a person might have a chance to respond to this through the Holy Spirit. Jamal did this in his words and actions in this incident. It is a mistake to think that this was not evangelization because Jamal did not try to convert Tyrone on the spot.

Jamal asked the class to explore what he might have done after the crisis was over. He continued to work alongside Tyrone at Jefferson Hospital throughout the Christmas season and into the following months. Several people asked Jamal why he did not take Tyrone with him to church. This led him to share more about his church background. As a member of a congregation in the holiness tradition, Jamal had been taught that Christians have the right to *say* the gospel to others only if they *do* the gospel in their everyday lives. This influenced the way he related to people at work. Though he was much younger than Tyrone and better educated, he worked alongside him as a friend. Of all the people Tyrone might have turned to, he chose Jamal. Sharing the gospel is only credible if it comes from a church or person who in some ways embodies the gospel. While Barth is a long way from the holiness tradition, he does agree that the gospel should become visible, embodied, and even incarnate in the church and its members.

Yet how we think of the visibility of the gospel in the church is worth considering carefully. Jamal shared in class that he was hesitant to invite Tyrone to his church. He wasn't sure how the "good and holy people" (his words) of this community would react to a person with a drinking problem who owned guns and harbored violent fantasies. Moreover, he wasn't sure if his church could really help Tyrone with his legal problems. It did not see these kinds of social services as part of its mission.

Barth would invite us to see these issues differently. He would remind us that the church is a witness to the gospel. It points beyond itself to Christ. It must acknowledge its solidarity in sin with Tyrone. We all are recovering sinners. We never get over this. If we cannot welcome people who are not "good and holy" like Jesus did, it is unclear if we are really witnessing to him. Moreover, Barth has a rich understanding of witness as something that should take place through all ministries of the church. He probably would want to know more about the diaconal ministries of this church and whether they view them as part of their mission to accompany Christ in sharing the reconciling love of God.

Most of us would flinch at the idea that Jamal should have threatened Tyrone with God's judgment as he helped his friend. Tyrone did not need to be brought to his knees. He already was on his knees. We are glad that Jamal starts and ends with God's Yes to Tyrone. He needed to hear the good news of God's gracious love in the face of the bad news of his wife's efforts to cut him off from his children right before Christmas. This is a good example of Barth's understanding of the relationship between the law or judgment and the gospel in evangelization. Gospel takes priority over judgment. This is typically where evangelization should begin. Yet this is not the whole story.

Barth has a rich understanding of sin and evil, and we will give it more attention in the following chapter. He portrays sin as impacting every level of life—from individuals to relationships to social institutions to the environment. Instead of leading Jamal to approach Tyrone in a judgmental fashion—you made your own bed, now you've got to sleep in it—Barth encourages us to take account of the complexity of Tyrone's plight. He is an African American who grew up in poverty. He dropped out of high school and now has limited economic prospects. The social sins of racism and economic injustice are important factors in what is going on here. Surely, the No of God's judgment falls on these institutional patterns and should impact the ways the gospel is communicated to Tyrone. His plight is not entirely of his own making, and the gospel offers hope to those who are oppressed by institutional forms of sin and death. It offers hope for the future; Christ's judgment at the consummation will be the coming of justice. It also offers hope in the present, as this future already breaks into the present to create signs and parables of God's justice-bringing judgment and the healing of the earth.

Yet it also is true that Tyrone made bad choices in the past. He lost his driver's license for a year after his second DUI. He owns a gun. He participated in the breakup of his family. Evangelization communicates God's judgment in the face of our particular sins. It offers us forgiveness and new life, the foundations of new beginnings. It invites us to face and confess the concrete ways we have turned away from God and hurt our neighbors. In Tyrone's case, the No of God's judgment on his personal life must be encompassed by the gracious affirmation and hope God offers people who suffer the legacy of slavery.

One of the most dramatic parts of this story is Jamal's struggle to break through the black shroud of despair that surrounds Tyrone. Jamal tells him that he can appeal the court's decision to give his wife full custody of his children. He tells Tyrone that he is his friend, and he doesn't want him to kill himself. None of these are persuasive. Jamal finally gets through when he says: "Tyrone, do you really want your kids to remember Christmas as the time their father killed himself?" Only at this point does Tyrone hand over his gun.

Jamal is effective in persuading Tyrone away from a terrible outcome. But he attributes the effectiveness of his words to God. At three points in his written account, he points to the guidance of the Holy Spirit. As he puts it near the end of the case: "To this day, I believe it was the power of the Holy Spirit that guided me that day. It wasn't anything I could have done myself." With these words, Jamal joins hands with Karl Barth and Christians everywhere who affirm the present power of the Holy Spirit to save people from sin and death and bring them back to life.

Further Reading

Texts on Barth and the Christian Life

Barth, Karl. *Learning Jesus Christ Through the Heidelberg Catechism*. Grand Rapids: Eerdmans, 2004. Excellent way of gaining an initial understanding of Barth's Christology and its relationship to the Christian life.

Deddo, G. *Karl Barth's Theology of Relations—Trinitarian, Christological, and Human: Towards an Ethic of the Family*. Bern: Peter Lang, 1999. Clear presentation of Barth's dynamic, relational theo-ontology of persons.

Explores its impact on his view of various forms of human community, especially the family.

Flett, John G. *The Witness of God: The Trinity,* Missio Dei, *Karl Barth, and the Nature of Christian Community.* Grand Rapids: Eerdmans, 2010. A major work dispelling standard interpretations of Barth's influence on the *missio Dei* and opening space for a fuller appropriation of his influence on the contemporary missional church discussion.

Hunsinger, George. *Evangelical, Catholic, and Reformed: Doctrinal Essays on Barth and Related Themes.* Grand Rapids: Eerdmans, 2017. A collection of brilliant essays that open up the background and potential impact of Barth's thinking. Not to be neglected.

———. *Karl Barth and Radical Politics.* 2nd ed. Eugene, OR: Cascade Books, 2017. The single best book in English that explores Barth's commitment to radical politics, from his work as a pastor to his role as a leader of resistance to Hitler to a world-famous theologian.

Mangina, Joseph L. *Karl Barth on the Christian Life: The Practical Knowledge of God.* Issues in Systematic Theology, vol. 8. New York: Peter Lang, 2001. Provides insight into Barth's understanding of the Christian life.

Molnar, Paul. *Faith, Freedom and the Spirit: The Economic Trinity in Barth, Torrance, and Contemporary Theology.* Downers Grove, IL: InterVarsity, 2015. Explores the relationship between Barth and T. F. Torrance, a major constructive theologian who draws on and "corrects" Barth's theology.

Price, Daniel J. *Karl Barth's Anthropology in Light of Modern Thought.* Grand Rapids: Eerdmans, 2002. Excellent overview of Barth's theological anthropology. Explores interdisciplinary issues.

Thompson, John. *Christ in Perspective in the Theology of Karl Barth.* Edinburgh: Saint Andrew Press, 1978. Very clear comparative overview of Barth's Christology.

———. *The Holy Spirit in the Theology of Karl Barth.* Princeton Theological Monograph. Eugene, OR: Pickwick, 1991. Very clear overview of Barth's understanding of the Holy Spirit.

PART III

The New Evangelization

In this part, we return to evangelistic practice and begin to reimagine what evangelism might look like on the basis of our dialogues with Scripture and the dogmatic theology of Karl Barth. I have made the case that the way we typically think of evangelism—evangelism as conversionism—is transformed when Scripture is taken seriously. Often the Bible is approached in ways that simply seek justification for evangelistic practices that already are taking place. This verse or that is cited. Instead, I have looked at Paul's letters to discern his strategy and practices, his understanding of the content of the gospel, and his calling as an apostle to the nations. I have also looked at Mark and John, two Gospels that tell the story of the good news of God's salvation of the world in Jesus Christ. I have tried to show that new ways of thinking about evangelization emerge when we approach Scripture with openness. Let us suppose that we do not know in advance what evangelization means. What do we see if we look anew at the announcement of the kingdom of God in Jesus's words and deeds and even more at the way his mission as God's Son is narrated.

I also have engaged dogmatic theology in the form of Karl Barth. I placed the ministry of evangelization in a theological framework informed by the Reformation of the sixteenth century. In doing so I also have attempted to show the importance of the dialogue between dogmatic and practical theology. By redefining evangelization on theological grounds, we discovered a new way of thinking about the purpose of this ministry. Now we consider what this might look like in practice. There is no question that reimagining evangelism in terms of Reformation theology implies the transformation of evangelistic practice. This is the new evangelization. It represents a fundamental shift in soteriology—from being saved by conversion on the basis of human choice to affirmation that we are saved *in toto* by Jesus Christ who takes our place in justifying and sanctifying us before God. As we are joined to him through the Holy Spirit, we receive the free and unmerited gift of salvation in faith and are led to follow him as his disciples among a community of disciples. We become sent ones who bear witness to him as we join in his continuing work of self-revelation.

My primary contribution in part II was lifting up four themes in Barth's theology that have the potential to transform our understanding of evangelistic practice: the Chalcedonian pattern, the church as witness, Christ in our place, and the Holy Spirit as the mediator of communion. Unlike evangelism as conversionism, the new evangelization in this framework is not a matter of saving people who are lost, going to hell, and outside the scope of God's love. Rather, it is a matter of inviting people to become who they already are in Jesus Christ: justified, sanctified, and called in him. They are loved by God before they even know it. Their vocations and identities are found in him. They are invited to become a part of a reconciled and reconciling community.

To signal this shift in understanding I use "evangelization" instead of "evangelism" to refer to this ministry. Darrell Guder uses the language of "evangelization" for the same reasons. We both are trying to signal to others that a shift has taken place in our understanding of evangelism, and we should not automatically think about this ministry in the ways we have during the modern period. I remember hearing Roberta Hestenes lecture at Princeton and asking her afterward why her title at Fuller was director of Christian formation and discipleship instead of director of the School of Christian Education, my title at Princeton Theological Seminary at that time. She responded that her title made people pause and ask the question that I was asking: What does that mean? That is exactly what I am hoping will happen by adopting the language of "evangelization" and "the new evangelization" instead of "evangelism." What does that mean? If you begin to think of the purpose of this ministry in new ways, what implications does this have for practice? How can you help your congregation reimagine this ministry in new ways?

CHAPTER 6

Evangelization as a Ministry of the Church

My purpose in this part of the book is to support a process of practical theological reflection by congregational leaders. Bonnie Miller-McLemore and Rod Hunter argue persuasively that practical theology includes a special kind of knowing and reasoning.[1] This involves learning from experience, gradually building up knowledge relevant to practice in different situations as well as developing expertise and even wisdom over time. In part, I have used case studies to support this kind of reflection and knowing in relation to evangelization. The pragmatic dimension of practical theology, which Miller-McLemore and Hunter explore, is very important.[2]

Evangelization and the Missional Church

The shift from evangelism to evangelization is part of a broader transformation of the church from an established part of Western culture to a missional community. A missional community is called together by God, built up, and sent into the world to bear witness to the gospel. This is its mission. Its purpose is not to serve as the chaplain of the culture, help parents raise

1. See Rod Hunter's early articles, "The Future of Pastoral Theology," *Pastoral Psychology* 29 (1980): 58-69, and "A Perspectival Pastoral Theology," in *Turning Points in Pastoral Care: The Legacy of Anton Boisen and Seward Hiltner*, ed. LeRoy Aden and Harold J. Ellens (Grand Rapids: Baker Books, 1990), 53-79. A more fully developed perspective is found in Bonnie Miller-McLemore, *Christian Theology in Practice: Discovering a Discipline* (Grand Rapids: Eerdmans, 2012).
2. In general, I locate Hunter's and Miller-McLemore's emphasis on practical knowing in the pragmatic dimension of practical theology. It does not replace empirical research, normative reflection, and so forth. See Richard Osmer, *Practical Theology: An Introduction* (Grand Rapids: Eerdmans, 2008).

moral children, keep young people out of trouble, meet the spiritual needs of adults, support civil society, and so forth. These are all important, but they are secondary goals or by-products of the church's primary mission: to bear witness to the gospel of Jesus Christ.

One of the most important insights of the missional church discussion is the shift from viewing the church as *having* a mission to *being* a mission. What does this mean? As Barth clearly saw, the very being of the church is a dynamic relationship with Jesus Christ through the Holy Spirit. It is like a marriage. It is not just two individuals interacting; a marriage is the relationship between them; it has a life of its own that exists at a different level of reality than that of individuals. So too the church exists in its relationship with Christ. It is joined to him in faith and love as it responds to his finished work of reconciliation. It accompanies him as he continues to make God's love for the world known. He will abide in them and they in him through the Holy Spirit. The church's very being as a community subsists in this relationship and mission. The church does not merely have a mission. It is a mission shaped by its participation in the mission of God. As we begin to understand the implications of this shift to a missional ecclesiology, it is time to begin thinking about evangelization in new ways as well.

What Are We Learning?

In parts I and II, we have focused on case studies in dialogue with Scripture and the dogmatic theology of Karl Barth. As we move into part III, it will be helpful to return to the definition of evangelism I offered in the introduction. What would you change or add to this initial definition in light of what you have learned in different chapters? Below are some of the things I have learned, and I would encourage you to develop your own insights as well. I have offered some guidelines along with my insights. These are not fully developed programs or models of evangelization. One of the things I have learned from Barth is a certain amount of skepticism toward such things. Evangelization, like other forms of ministry, will work in different ways in different contexts. Guidelines inform the kind of practical knowledge and judgment that mediates between the purpose of evangelization and its practice. Working as a practical theologian, I have attempted to reflect on practice in the form of case studies and contemporary evangelistic traditions in dialogue with Scripture and dogmatic theology. The telos is not a program or model but a new understanding of the purpose of evangelization. This will take shape in practices and programs in specific contexts. The guidelines I offer are pointers to your own thinking about what this ministry might look like in your own setting.

How might we begin to think about the ministry of evangelization in new ways? Here is the initial definition offered in the introduction.

> Evangelism is the invitation to respond to the gospel, the good news of God's salvation of the world in Jesus Christ, which is offered to others as part of the witness of the church under the guidance and persuasive power of the Holy Spirit.

I think this definition is fine as far as it goes, but it does not go far enough. Several insights occur to me in light of our dialogue with Mark and John, with side comments by Paul. Guidelines emerge in tandem with these insights.

Jesus calls the disciples to come and follow him. Responding to this call is an act of obedience on their part. The disciples are asked to trust in Jesus and respond to his call. This involves leaving their families, work, and social obligations. It is an event taking place at a moment in time. At the same time, it is the beginning of a process. Following Jesus takes the disciples from one place to another; it involves learning over time; the disciples fail to understand what Jesus is teaching them as often as they succeed. It is safe to say that they do not really acknowledge who Jesus is until the very end of his time with them. The initial definition above focuses solely on calling, an event. It does not include the process of following. Calling and following go hand in hand. It is inviting people to come, but also to see.

Guideline: It is important to move beyond thinking about evangelism focused on a single point-in-time event in which a person is converted. Responding to Jesus's call and following him involves both significant moments of change and a longer process of coming to trust in him and follow in his way.

The initial definition does not mention anything about community. Yet Jesus called people to follow him by becoming a part of a community of disciples. This was not just the Twelve, but also others who followed him, including women as well as a larger group. Some of Jesus's disciples lived at home and served him when he was in their areas. After Jesus departed, congregations began to form in Jerusalem and, later, Antioch. By the time we reach

Paul, Christianity is spreading around the Mediterranean, and new congregations are being formed in many urban areas. In Paul's letters, baptism is portrayed as both participation in Christ and initiation into the Christian community. Moreover, his communities attracted people because of their diversity, their inclusion of women in leadership roles, their members' love of one another, and their other concrete and visible expressions of the gospel. The church evangelized as a community and invited others into community. In John, Jesus washes his disciples' feet and tells them to love one another as he has loved them. Other people will know they are Christians by the way they love each other. The community as a whole is a witness to Jesus, salt and light. Lesslie Newbigin put it like this: "The only hermeneutic of the Gospel is a congregation of men and women who believe it and live by it."[3]

Guideline: The congregation is the first witness to the gospel. It points to Christ by loving as he did. The love of Christ must be embodied in its fellowship, its welcome of people into the community, and its outreach to the world. This is the context in which evangelization takes place. The church must embody visibly, if provisionally, the love of God in Jesus Christ for evangelization to share the gospel with others in a credible way.

Mark and John tell their stories of Jesus in different ways. There is something to learn from this. We have four Gospels for a reason. All four were widely used in the early church. They were included in the canon because of the cumulative choices of congregations and individuals who used them in worship, studied them, prayed them, and copied them so they could be passed on to others.[4] The decision to include these four was not imposed from above. It was a matter of Gospel reception. Francis Watson speaks of a "fourfold gospel," and Martin Hengel titled one of his books, *The Four Gospels and the One Gospel of Jesus Christ.*[5] The one gospel is told in four different ways.

So too evangelization must tell the gospel story in different ways to communicate with different individuals and groups while remaining true to the

---

3. Lesslie Newbigin, *The Gospel in a Pluralistic Society* (London: SPCK, 1989), 227.
4. Francis Watson, *The Fourfold Gospel: A Theological Reading of the New Testament Portraits of Jesus* (Grand Rapids: Baker Academic, 2016), Kindle edition, loc. 82.
5. Watson, *Fourfold Gospel*; Martin Hengel, *The Four Gospels and the One Gospel of Jesus Christ: An Investigation of the Collection and Origin of the Canonical Gospels* (Harrisburg, PA: Trinity Press International, 2000).

one gospel. Too often the "message of salvation" has been reduced to the theology of one part of Scripture, like Paul's letter to the Romans or Acts. The richness of Scripture's witness to Christ should serve as a guide to the richness of our own witness. The definition of evangelism with which we began needs to pay more attention to this. The calling and following of the disciples look different in Mark and John.

Guideline: Evangelization must develop a variety of ways of sharing the gospel to reach different people and groups. In doing this, it corresponds to the witness of Scripture.

Mark's story focuses on the messianic secret, the theme that Jesus will be a suffering messiah, failing to meet the expectations of Israel. He attracts huge crowds early in his ministry while he heals and teaches around Galilee. But as he travels toward Jerusalem and the cross, the crowds drop away. Even his closest disciples do not understand why he must suffer and die on the cross. Three times on the way to Jerusalem, Jesus shares that he will suffer, die, and be raised from death. Each time the disciples fail to understand him, amid arguments about matters like who will sit at his right hand or left. When Jesus is arrested, the disciples fall away, except for Peter who follows him to the courtyard of the high priest where he denies him three times. Jesus appears to be powerless before the religious and political authorities, but all is proceeding according to Scripture. At last he is crucified, his blood poured out for many and as a ransom for many. Of his disciples, only the women go to the tomb to anoint his body with spices. They find an angel who tells them that Jesus has risen and gone before them to Galilee. They are to share this good news with Peter. Instead, "Trembling and bewildered, the women went out and fled from the tomb. They said nothing to anyone, because they were afraid" (Mark 16:8).

There is no question in Mark about Jesus's resurrection from the dead. Repeatedly Jesus tells his disciples this will happen, and the readers would not be reading Mark's story if this had not occurred. Why is the failure of the disciples highlighted? Why does the story end with such a strong sense of incompletion? Why does Jesus go to the cross alone, even asking God why he has forsaken him? The story is a powerful telling of the gospel story in terms of God's entry into the suffering and death of the world, crucified at the hands of the authorities, abandoned by the crowds and his own disciples, and even forsaken by God. Yet in handing himself over to suffering and death,

Jesus has ransomed "the many" captive to sin and evil, inviting them into a new covenant with God based on God's grace.

This story goes hand in hand with evangelization that enters into the suffering and pain of others. As with Ariana Diaz, it may be the suffering of a woman recovering from breast cancer; or as with George, it may be the suffering of a soldier living with PTSD for a long time, who also suffers from the guilt of inflicting pain on others; or as with James and Ivy, it may be the suffering of an older woman who was raped as a child.

The content of Mark's story tells us something about the process of communicating the gospel to others: close listening, empathizing in order to enter into the experience of others, not shying away from painful experiences, sharing one's own suffering and failures, and pointing to Jesus's entry into the suffering and pain of the world, dying in our place, and rising to new life in anticipation of the healing of all creation. Christ enters fully into the world's suffering and brings salvation. Christ still enters the suffering of our lives through the Holy Spirit and touches it with the salvation he has accomplished. Our words and our actions must bear witness to this as instruments of the Holy Spirit. This is the kind of evangelization I see Mark as encouraging. What do you see as you reflect again on this story?

Guideline: Evangelization involves entering into the suffering and pain of other people in order to share the good news of God's participation in and care for their plight. Salvation involves healing and consolation now, but also hope in God's promised future for creation when the Spirit will manifest the healing and reconciliation of the world.

John's story of the gospel is very different than Mark's. It focuses on Jesus's revelation of the glory of God: God's power, majesty, beauty, and splendor. It turns upside down the meaning of glory as it was understood in the Greco-Roman world and, to some extent, in Israel's Scripture. In John, the high point of the revelation of God's glory occurs when Christ is lifted up on the cross, revealing God's sacrificial and self-giving love as the Lamb of God who takes away the sin of the world. If Mark's Gospel communicates meaning through the plot, John uses the plot to introduce symbolic meanings that invite readers to go deeper and deeper into the mystery of God's self-revelation in Christ's mission. The signs are followed by dense and evocative discourses. Jesus's trial, crucifixion, and resurrection draw on images and stories of God's glory in Israel's Scripture. At last, God's glory is incarnate in human flesh, culminating in his death on the cross. The church is to bear witness to him, pointing beyond itself to the one who takes away the sin of the world, while simultaneously embodying his love as a community.

More than any of the Synoptic Gospels, John portrays the witness of the church as grounded in the mutual indwelling of the Triune God. Just as the Father, Son, and Holy Spirit are in one another, so too those born from above by the Spirit are in Jesus and he is in them; they are in one another as a community. Unless they abide in the vine, they will bear no fruit. Unless they love one another as Jesus has loved them, the world will not see Christ in them.

John includes themes mentioned already that take us beyond thinking of evangelization solely in terms of calling: the interplay of calling and following Jesus and the importance of the witness of the community *qua* community. But John's distinctive story evokes new insights as we think about evangelization. If Mark invites us to see God's full embrace of the suffering of the world, John invites us to see the glory of God in his death on our behalf. The joy of the resurrection and the Word's ascension to the glory he shared with the Father before his incarnation reaches backward into the story as a whole and especially the cross. It is a story of the majesty, beauty, and splendor of God's salvation of the world through his sacrificial and self-giving love.

Guideline: The gospel celebrates the glory of God and God's beauty, splendor, and might in the form of self-giving love. Evangelization invites people to live in the light of God's glory right now, for life abundant begins in the present and continues into eternity. This is a life of participation in the Triune God, a life of joy, intimacy, and fulfillment as we live in one another through the Holy Spirit, who joins us to Christ and through him to the Father.

We have already mentioned some of the insights emerging from our dialogue with Paul. He adds a great deal to our rethinking of evangelization. Like John, he emphasizes the universality of God's salvation of the world in Jesus Christ. He also emphasizes the substitutionary and representative nature of the atonement, our participation in Christ through the Holy Spirit, and our continuing struggle with sin and evil as people who live between the "already" and "not yet" of Christ's reconciliation of the world. Christ in our place is a consistent theme in Paul's letters, articulated mainly in his discussion of justification by grace through faith. God's justification of the world is a free gift and its power to save is manifested in our response of faith. Faith is not a precondition of salvation, which would turn it into a work of the law. It is a response to God's grace made possible through the Holy Spirit.

In the form of epistles, not extended gospel stories, Paul contributes much to thinking about the content of the gospel. If the gospel is the message of salvation through which God reaches out to people, then Paul helps us think through the meaning of the gospel. In his letters, he does not communicate meaning through narrative but primarily through theological reflection on issues facing his congregations. This is a key part of equipping Christians to share the gospel with others. Learning to understand what we believe theologically and relate this to the events of our lives and world enriches our ability to talk with others about our faith. Sharing our faith story is important, but some people have hard questions about the church and religion. Brian McLaren is surely right when he observes that "Good evangelists are people who engage others in good conversation about important and profound topics."[6]

I doubt that Paul evangelized by sharing the kind of the theology he uses in his letters to communicate with people he has already catechized. But I do believe that he evangelized on the basis of his theology. This prepared him to talk with Jews, gentiles, and "God-fearers" (gentiles associated with Hellenistic Judaism). Michael Green believes certain theological themes in Acts and Paul's letters were developed in order to "translate" the gospel into terms understandable to the Hellenistic world.[7] Here again, it was not so much a matter of using theology to talk about the gospel as theologically thinking through how best to share the gospel in terms that would make sense to people from a culture that is different from Palestinian Judaism.

Our examination of Paul led us to believe that he had a clear strategy guiding his missionary work and evangelization. He spent much of his time in urban centers that were linked by roads and shipping routes. He would establish a congregation, catechize new members, teach them basic practices and moral standards of the Christian life, develop a cadre of local leaders, and then move on. Paul was one of the first and most effective Christian missionaries to the Hellenistic world. He had no other choice than to plant new churches. Today, as Europe and North America become more plural-

6. Brian McLaren, *More Ready Than You Realize: The Power of Everyday Conversation* (Grand Rapids: Zondervan, 2003), 16.

7. Michael Green, *Evangelism in the Early Church*, rev. ed. (Grand Rapids: Eerdmans, 2003), ch. 5.

istic and secular, church planting as a form of evangelization has become an important option once again. Thus I would like to make a short detour in our reflection on Paul to think about church planting as a strategy of evangelism today.

The research is ambiguous on the effectiveness of this strategy, and there is not much quality research available.[8] It is not clear that planting new churches actually attracts people who would not otherwise be involved in a congregation. Some members of church plants are people who have been nominally involved in other congregations or have switched from other churches. Moreover, many church plants do not grow numerically. They stay small. On the positive side, there are indications that church plants are younger, more diverse, and attract more converts than older, established churches.

Stefan Paas argues that the age of a church alone does not determine growth (contradicting the assumption that newer congregations are more apt to grow).[9] Many older congregations are revitalized and grow. Three factors seem to be more important than the age of the church: (1) location (in areas with population growth), (2) missionary focus (with participants who are committed to evangelization, social action, and outreach to their neighborhoods or specific populations—they have a missional orientation), and (3) leadership (church planters are much more entrepreneurial than pastors of older churches).[10] In the end, Paas notes, church planting may be more important for innovation in the church than attracting converts. It discovers new ways of being church that appeal to young adults or others who are unlikely ever to participate in established congregations.

Paas also makes an observation about a possibility for evangelization that was not really available to Paul. Some churches—old and new—appear to be much more effective at attracting children and keeping them involved through adolescence. The decline of young people's participation in church in both Europe and the United States and the dim prospects of their involvement in the future when this is the case should serve as a wake-up call. Even if people leave the church during emerging adulthood, they are much more likely to be open to evangelization later in life if they had prior involvement

---

8. For a thoughtful overview of research on church planting in Europe, see Stefan Paas, *Church Planting in the Secular West: Learning from the European Experience*, Gospel and Our Culture series (Grand Rapids: Eerdmans, 2016).

9. Paas, *Church Planting*, ch. 3.

10. Paas, *Church Planting*, 175–76.

with the church. Paas draws out the implication: "Trying to attract children may be the best long-term missionary strategy."[11]

Guideline: New forms of evangelism will only emerge in congregations with missional orientations, whether these are church plants or established congregations in the process of revitalization. It is important for established congregations with financial resources to support church plants and to learn from their innovations. It is equally important for many church plants to move beyond their anti-establishment postures, which sometimes come across more as adolescent than as innovative.

Guideline: Focusing on children's experience of church must become a priority for evangelization. It represents a long-term missionary strategy in the present context of Europe and North America. In this context many emerging adults move through a prolonged period of identity exploration and distance themselves from the institutional church but later are more open to returning if they had a positive experience of the church during childhood.

Karl Barth offers a comprehensive theological framework in which to understand the church as a missional community and the role of evangelization in such a community. We explored only four themes, but they are central to Barth's theology as whole:

1. *The being of the church along the lines of the Chalcedonian pattern:* the unity of Christ and his church (the church has its being in a relationship of mutual indwelling), the distinction of Christ and the church (the head and the body), and their asymmetrical order (as Savior and Lord on the one side, and witness on the other).
2. *The church as witness:* The church as a whole is to bear witness to the gospel; evangelization is only one of the ministries through which this takes place.
3. *Christ in our place:* Christ takes our place in order to accomplish our objective justification, sanctification, and calling to a vocation. Our salvation is accomplished in him and is accepted by us as free gift of grace.

11. Paas, *Church Planting,* 179.

4. *The Holy Spirit as the mediator of communion:* The Spirit accomplishes our subjective appropriation of the objective work of salvation in the form of our participation in Christ. Christ's salvation becomes a reality in our existence. We know it and allow our lives to correspond to it in the obedience of faith, love, and hope. The Spirit also brings us into communion with the Triune God, other Christians, and the world in solidarity.

These four themes have the potential to completely transform the dominant model of evangelism as conversionism. They offer us a different understanding of salvation, human freedom, sin and evil, and other theological doctrines that have shaped evangelism throughout the modern period. Here I highlight three shifts that need to take place if the church is to move from evangelism to evangelization as part of broader turn toward a missional ecclesiology.

Become Who You Already Are in Christ Jesus

The theological logic of evangelism as conversionism rests on a change in status when people convert. They move from the status of unsaved to saved, from lost to found. Barth's soteriology transforms this logic. All people are saved in Jesus Christ because he took their place in the history of reconciliation; they are justified, sanctified, and sent in him. There is nothing people can do to complete or finish their salvation. This is God's work, and it has been accomplished.

Evangelization invites them to acknowledge who they are already in Jesus Christ, loved by God before the world was even created and reconciled to God, their neighbor, and themselves through his Son, the realization of God's eternal love in history. Their reality is who they are in Christ Jesus. Evangelization invites them to acknowledge this reality. This good news is difficult to believe for two reasons. One is sin, which we speak about below. The other is the modern understanding of freedom that portrays human beings as freestanding with the ability to choose between this option or that.

John Webster summarizes nicely the alternative Barth offers: "Rather, freedom is consent to a given order of reality which encloses human history, an order which is at one and the same time a loving summons to joyful action in accordance with itself, and judgment against our attempt to be ourselves by somehow escaping from or suspending its givenness. Freedom is the real possibility given to me by necessity."[12] We are loved by God. This is the nature of ultimate reality, which surrounds and encloses all of our loves. This is why Barth says again and again that all witness to the gospel of Jesus Christ must begin with God's Yes. God's love is the "real possibility" that confronts us, judges us, and saves us.

Evangelization does not set out to save people from sin by converting them; it invites them to give consent to the love of God in Jesus Christ, which is our true reality. This changes everything in terms of the way missional churches share the good news with others. We start with these realities: human beings are loved by God; they are saved by God; the Holy Spirit already is working in their lives to allow them to acknowledge this. Our task is to communicate joy and gratitude, the freedom that comes with obedience, the loving care of God and God's people, and all the ways we consent to the reality of God's steadfast and certain love revealed and enacted in Jesus Christ.

Guideline: Evangelism is the good news of God's salvation of the world in Jesus Christ. It is the story of God's love for the world, from election to reconciliation to the consummation. Our message is: God loves you; Christ has saved you out of love; if you trust this love your life will be transformed. Come and see.

The Reality of Sin Is Much Greater and Much Less Than We Think

Evangelism as conversionism starts with sin and then moves to grace. Barth rejects this in the strongest of terms. Eberhard Busch shares that Barth met Billy Graham two times and liked him as a person. But he responded very negatively after hearing him preach in one of his crusades: "It was the gospel at gun-point.... He wanted to terrify people. Threats, they always make an impression."[13] But this is common wisdom in evangelism. John Wesley is commonly portrayed as saying, "Before I can preach love, mercy, and grace, I must preach sin, Law, and judgment."[14] You must first make people thirsty for the water of life before they are willing to drink. Barth rejected the law-

12. John Webster, *Barth's Moral Theology: Human Action in Barth's Thought* (Edinburgh: T&T Clark, 1998), 112.

13. Eberhard Busch, *Karl Barth: His Life from Letters and Autobiographical Texts* (Philadelphia: Fortress, 1976), 446.

14. https://www.azquotes.com/quote/1311121.

to-gospel approach of Martin Luther and Reinhold Niebuhr, as well as the judgment-to-grace pattern of evangelism emerging after the Reformation. In a sense, awareness of sin must initially become less not more in the new evangelization. Only then will it play its proper role in Christian doctrine and evangelistic practice.

As we have seen, this is not because Barth did not take sin and evil seriously. He had a profound understanding of sin. But he believed we are only able to grasp the nature and scope of sin by taking seriously the way human beings responded to Christ in the incarnation and by seeing how far Christ had to go to save us. He had to die so our sins would be put to death along with him. He died in our place because sin renders us incapable of breaking free and making amends to God ourselves. It is not a matter of simply correcting a few bad tendencies in our character or building new relationships with better people or exercising more self-discipline. Our will is in bondage, as Luther put it. We are born into a condition that is not of our own making, and we very quickly begin to participate in it through our own actions and choices.

Moreover, Barth writes of various forms of sin—pride, sloth, and falsehood—and the way sin warps every level of life—from the individual level to the interpersonal to the familial to the institutional and cultural. In *The Christian Life*, he speaks of the "great disorder of life," which is created by sin in its various forms at various levels of life. Here he gives special attention to the "lordless powers," like mammon, ideologies, technology, and Leviathan.[15] Human beings create them to exercise greater control over life; yet inevitably these powers end up controlling them.

Capitalism was created, for example, to allow persons to break free of the late medieval stations of life into which they were born as cooks, farm owners, gentry, tradesmen, and so forth. It offered everyone the opportunity to compete to better themselves and their families in the marketplace. Yet national and global capitalism has become a way for the rich to become more prosperous while the poor become more disadvantaged. Today's wretched of the earth would be better off under the subsistence living of rural villages where they farm and barter than in the slums of the world's cities where most of them will live within decades. The sin and evil of the lordless powers are far more than the decisions of individuals, greedy corporate leaders or corrupt politicians. They are powers in their own right with systems of inter-

15. Karl Barth, *The Christian Life: Church Dogmatics IV/4, Lecture Fragments* (Grand Rapids: Eerdmans, 1991), 213-33.

connected networks and patterns of communication by which they maintain themselves and respond to their environment. Indeed, not all leaders of corporations are greedy nor are all politicians corrupt. It is not the decisions of individuals that control the lordless powers; these powers control them.

When we speak today of racism at a structural level, this too is the kind of reality Barth has in mind when he speaks of the lordless powers. Racism is not just a matter of interpersonal prejudice. It is a larger institutional structure or pattern that distributes life chances and resources according to race, which itself is a social construction created to denigrate a group of people and, often, to justify their enslavement. So real and powerful are these forces that Barth calls them the very "motors" of society and "the hidden wirepullers in humanity's great and small enterprises, movements, achievements, and revolutions."[16]

Barth calls on Christians and the church to revolt against the great disorder of life created by sin. When he addressed these theological concepts, he was one of the few theologians writing about revolution and liberation, though he used these terms in ways that are different from liberation and feminist theologies.[17] As long we live, he argues, we contend with sin within and sin without. The lordless powers will not be defeated by human revolutions; they will reappear in new forms. We are to revolt nonetheless—a sign of Christ's victory over the lordless powers as the one who "disarmed the rulers and authorities and made a public example of them, triumphing over them" (Col. 2:15) and a sign of God's promised future in which this victory will be manifest to all.

Barth's appreciation of the eschatological and apocalyptic frameworks of the New Testament allows him to realize that after Christ human beings live at the "turn" of the ages, caught between the old age and new creation. While not always obvious in Luther and Calvin, this is the foundation of the Reformation insight that we are simultaneously saved and sinners as reappropriated by Barth. Barth's appreciation of the continuing power of sin and evil in human life shapes his understanding of God's judgment. This should impact the way missional churches think about judgment in evangelization.

Barth firmly believes that God's No is in the service of God's Yes. In Scripture and dogmatic theology, judgment serves a redemptive purpose. Evangelization should not threaten people in order to save them. First and foremost,

---

16. Barth, *Christian Life*, 216.

17. George Hunsinger, *Disruptive Grace: Studies in the Theology of Karl Barth* (Grand Rapids: Eerdmans, 2000), ch. 2.

it should invite them to know the love of God in Jesus Christ. This is the good news it has to share. Barth believes, moreover, that as we come to acknowledge God's love in Christ, we will become more and more aware of our own sins and the sinful condition of the world around us. We live in darkness. As we come to the light, more and more of our condition is illuminated. We may turn our lives around and become genuinely better people. But we will live in awareness of the misery of our world, the terrible hubris of our leaders, and the many falsehoods that buttress our everyday lives.

The problem with conversionistic evangelism that starts with judgment is that it relies on conventional understandings of sin, often grounded in conventional notions of Christian morality and respectability. Since we know what sin is and how to overcome it, we can offer a remedy for our plight, returning outsiders to the fold of the good people, now saved, and sharing in the benefits of Christ's blessings. If only sin were so easy, Barth contends. But in truth, we remain caught in sin and death and participate in the eschatological turn of the ages as we are joined to Christ through the Holy Spirit. Only as we are joined to him do we come to recognize the extent to which sin and death are realities with which we continue to struggle both within and without, even as we participate in Christ's victory over them.

In short, habitually starting with judgment and then moving to God's grace in evangelism does not reflect the deepest theological pattern of the gospel. Grace is the first and last word; it takes priority over judgment and law. This does not mean that at the level of sermon arrangement or interpersonal conversations in relational evangelism sin and judgment can never be the first topics to emerge. The "logic" of practice is not determined in a straightforward way by the "logic" of dogmatics. It is not a simple matter of "application." Practical reasoning takes account of particular circumstances within an unfolding history. It relies on practical judgment, knowledge, and skills about the best courses of action in particular situations. But actions at the practical level must ultimately be guided by a dogmatic pattern. In the long run, grace takes priority over judgment and the law in sharing the gospel in evangelization. It can never become a rigid pattern of judgment to gospel or habitually rely on judgmentalism, guilt-inducement, and threats. God knows people better than they know themselves, and God loves, accepts, and forgives them. This is the heart of the gospel we share.

Barth adds one final dogmatic insight to our understanding of judgment in evangelization. This has to do with his understanding of the relationship between God's judgment and God's justice. The Day of the Lord will be the day God's justice is done and the cries of the oppressed and the suffering turn to joy. This kingdom was breaking in already in Jesus's earthly ministry, including his miraculous healings, feedings, and other physical manifestations of God's love.[18] Christ alone is the true witness to God's kingdom; in the present Christians can only set up signs and parables that point to him. But they can and must do so, involving them in actions and movements that point to the final triumph of God's justice. If evangelization invites people to hear the call of Jesus to come and follow him, then they will encounter judgment as the challenge to embody God's justice in anticipatory and provisional ways. This is a part of the Christian life that seeks to follow in Jesus's way, and it should be introduced as congregations introduce new members or converts to the life of discipleship. To repeat: this is far different from judgment as threats, inducing guilt, or judgmentalism. It is judgment as a commitment to embodying an alternate way of life that corresponds to God as revealed in Christ.

Guideline: Evangelism does not begin by shaming people, mocking them, making them feel guilty, or trying to manipulate them because their very salvation is at stake. It communicates through attitudes and words the high cost and depth of God's love. God knows who we really are; God knows us better than we know ourselves. Yet God loves us as we truly are; God loves us better than we love ourselves. This profound sense of being known for who we are and still loved is a good place to start in evangelization. Judgment serves this as Christians become aware of their participation in sin at all levels of life, within and without, and as part of the call to discipleship that anticipates provisionally the coming day of judgment when justice is established.

Evangelization to the Unaffiliated, to Nominal Christians, and to Responsible, Longtime Christians

I want to lift up one more way Barth transforms our thinking about evangelization in missional churches. He invites us to change the way we think about the people to whom evangelization is directed. Evangelism as conversionism focuses on people who have not yet had a conversion experience. They may be people who are unaffiliated with any Christian community, members of other

18. Barth, *Church Dogmatics* IV/2, 811-17. Barth, *The Christian Life*, 14-18.

religions, or people who were baptized as infants in families of mainline congregations. In each case, they need to be saved. Barth's soteriology changes the logic of evangelization from "Convert and be saved" to "Wake up and acknowledge who you already are in Christ Jesus; he took your place to save you and is calling you through the Holy Spirit to come and follow him."

As we have seen, Barth believes we need to encounter the good news *again and again.* We are asleep in sin; we are jolted awake by God; we fall asleep; we are jolted awake again. Barth places much less emphasis on the patterns of more-and-more, slow incremental growth in the Christian life, and once-and-for-all, which portrays salvation as a one-time event in our lives. Again-and-again is a pattern in which we need to encounter the gospel over the course of our lives. It is relevant to each of the groups to which evangelization is directed: the unaffiliated, nominal Christians, and responsible Christians involved in the ministries of the congregation.

The *unaffiliated* may have heard the gospel in the past and responded with hostility or indifference. Perhaps they hold a perception that they were hurt by the church or the religious convictions of their parents in the past. Maybe they left the church when they passed through a period of identity exploration or when their parents were divorcing and the church did not provide any support. Perhaps the gospel they heard in the past was narrow and rigid or flaccid and boring.

There are many reasons people have heard the gospel in the past and not responded. But those responsible for evangelization must not give up. They must keep reaching out to share the gospel. Understanding who a person or group is, taking time to develop a relationship, and sharing the gospel in ways and in settings appropriate to this relationship all improve the likelihood that it will be given a hearing. Barth emphasizes repeatedly that the church's role is to proclaim or share the gospel; it is God alone who is capable of opening the eyes and ears of the recipients.

One of the most serious challenges to evangelizing the unaffiliated is finding ways to meet them on their ground. Church members often are too churchy. They affiliate with persons like themselves and live in restricted social networks. For this reason it may be less important to volunteer for the next church responsibility you are offered than to coach a little league or soccer team. Any opportunities to get out into the community serve as chances to meet people. Building relationships with people who do not belong to the church is the all-important first step in evangelization of the unaffiliated.

Church members who take on this kind of evangelization need to be reminded that their job is not to convert or save people. It is to talk about their faith and church in ways that are genuine and natural to the context. It is to show the gospel in simple acts of kindness. Whether you call this servant evangelism or relational evangelism does not really matter. The real issue is developing relationships in which to share God's love with others as revealed in the gospel of Jesus Christ and to invite them to "come and see" at church.

Another way to reach the unaffiliated is for congregations to host gatherings that are directed at the needs of people in their neighborhoods. Some churches host musical events or plays that involve children who are not members of the church. Others make space available for diaconal ministries that bring people into the church. Still others host events that help people fill out tax forms, educate parents in how to keep their children away from drugs, or offer advice from experts during a pandemic. The issue in all of these kinds of events is how to walk the fine line between evangelizing people and making them feel unwelcome. In my view, evangelization in these kinds of situations involves welcoming, providing hospitality, offering participants the chance to be notified about future events, and following up with phone calls or visits to gain more information about the kinds of events that people might be interested in. Over time, the goal is to get to know participants personally and for them to get to know the congregation. In an era of pandemic, these kinds of events might take the form of Zoom meetings.

An important issue for congregations just learning to evangelize is raised by Martha Grace Reese.[19] It is easier to evangelize peers than people who are very different from either the evangelist or the congregation. Reese draws a helpful comparison with the bandwidths of radios that use different frequencies. Some bandwidths offer clearer transmission and reception than others. Reese describes a continuum of bandwidths moving from the clearest and easiest communication to the most difficult: children and youth of the congregation, children's friends, attenders who are not committed, transfers with a similar theology, transfers with a different theology, people far from

---

19. Martha Grace Reese, *Unbinding the Gospel: Real Life Evangelism*, Church Leaders' Study, Unbinding the Gospel Series (Danvers, MA: Chalice Press, 2008), ch. 7. See also her small group study aid and personal prayer journal, *Unbinding Your Soul: Your Experiment in Prayer and Community*, Unbinding the Gospel Series (Danvers, MA: Chalice Press, 2009). Broadly speaking, this excellent series is compatible with the understanding of evangelization developed in conversation with Barth. If a congregation is inviting people to move into a relationship with Christ or the Christian community, it is sharing the gospel. See *Unbinding the Gospel*, 88. This is what the series supports in the small group format it uses.

the church because they drifted away, people far from the church because they were hurt, people who aren't Christians but have similar backgrounds, people who aren't Christians but have different backgrounds. As Reese notes, churches that are just learning how to evangelize should start by using band-widths that allow for the easiest and clearest communication. Starting with people who never have been Christians and who come from backgrounds that are different from the congregation's is probably not a great idea.

Nominal Christians present their own set of challenges. These are church members who belong to churches but do not really participate in their min-istries or support them financially. They show up at Easter and Christmas. They may believe they already know what Christianity is all about, and they are not really interested. Many of the recommendations for evangelization to the unaffiliated apply to them as well: building relationships, learning their stories and the stories of why they lost touch with the church, trying to discover the kinds of activities and settings they gravitate toward. They too may have the perception that they were hurt or alienated by the church in the past.[20] Or they may simply have lost touch over the years.

This is especially true of emerging adults who tend to move more often, marry later than in the past, live in homes or apartments owned by others, and hold jobs they do not see as long term.[21] Life feels tentative for them, and getting involved in churches is often not a priority. People become nominal Christians for a lot of different reasons. The place to start is finding out why this has happened and building a relationship from there.

A second insight also applies to both nominal Christians and people who are unaffiliated. This is the role of crises and moments of transition among both groups on their openness to evangelization. A widely established find-ing of social science is the role of crisis in religious conversion.[22] Crises in-clude times of illness, loss of jobs, divorce, severe car accidents, deaths of children, and so forth. Crises often trigger periods of psychological disloca-tion and searching in people's lives. Some aspects of their lives or identities are called into question.

Many liberal Protestants view evangelization during moments of crisis as predatory, as taking advantage of people while they are vulnerable. Pastoral

20. David Kinnaman, *You Lost Me: Why Many Young People Are Leaving the Church . . . and Rethinking Faith* (Grand Rapids: Baker Books, 2011).
21. Jeffrey Arnett, *Emerging Adulthood: The Winding Road from the Late Teens through the Twenties*, 2nd ed. (New York: Oxford University Press, 2015).
22. Lewis Rambo summarizes much of this research. See *Understanding Religious Conversion* (New Haven: Yale University Press, 1993).

care is fine, but evangelization is not. This is based on a view of evangelism as the attempt to convert someone in order to save them. The kind of evangelization we have in mind is inviting people to realize they are loved by God already. Concrete care and support are demonstrations of this love. As shown by Ariana Diaz, sharing one's faith, praying for a person, and speaking of God's love in Jesus is not taking advantage of people. It is offering what the church believes is most needed when people begin to move to new places in their lives, whether they have never been a part of the church or are renewing their relationships to the church after times of absence.

Social science finds that people in crisis are looking for more than acts of caring. They are looking for meaning, ways to make sense of what they are experiencing. They want community, relationships that will support them, and help with establishing new friendships. As people begin to move into or renew their relationship to a religious community, they need a "plausibility structure," a group of people who actually embody and live out the new way of life newcomers are learning.[23] Moreover, many people in crisis or transition seek "techniques for living," practical tools to help them change and learn how to live in new ways.[24] In a Christian context, these may include methods of prayer, meditation, Scripture reading and interpretation, and other practical steps that help people establish new routines in their everyday lives. People passing through times of transition or crisis often want to change their lives but do not have the "know-how" to do this. Offering tools and careful instruction for their use is attractive to people who are seeking change. In all of these scenarios, the evangelist is much closer to a spiritual guide than a revival preacher. Yet these are precisely the kind of things that evangelists should pursue in their conversations with unaffiliated and nominal Christians who are in the midst of crises.

We end our reflection on Barth by exploring what he might mean by saying that even responsible, long-term Christians need to hear the gospel

---

23. The idea of plausibility structure was initially coined by Peter Berger and Thomas Luckmann in *The Social Construction of Reality: A Treatise in the Sociology of Knowledge* (Garden City, NY: Anchor Books, 1966). Erin Dufault-Hunter has found its continuing usefulness in her research on conversion. See *The Transformative Power of Faith: A Narrative Approach to Conversion* (Lanham, MD: Lexington Books, 2012).

24. This insight was offered many decades ago by Jacob Needleman, but it still holds true. See *The New Religions* (Garden City, NY: Doubleday, 1970). I paraphrase Lewis Rambo's discussion of this insight in *Understanding Religious Conversion*, 84, because I believe it is more broadly applicable than just to converts who have experienced crisis. It applies to persons in major life transitions as well.

again and again. What we have just said about crisis applies to them as well. Longtime Christians too will feel that their world has fallen apart when their spouse leaves them, they have a near-death experience from COVID-19, or their only child is killed in Iraq. Such moments of suffering and dislocation can challenge their faith. But such moments also can deepen their faith. Either way, it is the church's responsibility to share the gospel. As one older friend said to me after a funeral with four eulogies extolling the person being buried, "Please don't talk about me at my funeral. Preach the resurrection of Jesus Christ."

We also need to hear the gospel again and again as we move from one stage of life to another. Barth does not talk about this very much except briefly in his discussion of the human vocation in *The Doctrine of Creation*.[25] One of the finite limitations of our human lives is our particular age and stage of life. We should not allow some social scientific description of these stages to determine what we think our vocation is at this particular period of life, as if all children or youth share the same vocation. Rather, God's call comes to each of us in its particularity. Yet it is shaped and constrained by our stage of life and will change as we move through life.

I probably think this is more important than Barth did, based on my work on the Confirmation Project, a national study of confirmation in five denominations.[26] The research team came to realize that confirmation represented a significant opportunity for young people to hear the gospel anew. The large majority of confirmands were raised in the church and at the high end of church involvement. Now as they were entering adolescence, they were given the opportunity to begin responding for themselves to the faith handed down to them during childhood. In congregation after congregation, young people shared with us how mentors or time at confirmation camp or their small group Bible study or their service activity gave them a new and deeper understanding of God, the church, and the meaning of being a Christian. In some cases, these new insights were associated with awe-inspiring experiences such as baptism in a lake as the clouds began to gather for a storm. For others insights came out of the experience of living out the Christian way of life at a confirmation camp. Not one of us on the research team believed that confirmation would be the last time these young people would face difficult

---

25. Karl Barth, *Church Dogmatics*, ed. Geoffrey W. Bromiley and T. F. Torrance (Edinburgh: T&T Clark, 1956–75), III/4, 607–18.

26. Richard R. Osmer and Katherine M. Douglass, eds., *Cultivating Teen Faith: Insights from the Confirmation Project* (Grand Rapids: Eerdmans, 2018).

questions about their faith or encounter God. But it was right for this stage of their life, and it left enough of an afterglow that it could be fanned to life again in the future. While Barth does not tie the again and again pattern of the Christian life to moments of crisis or the journey through life, I believe it can be adapted in appropriate ways to both.

As noted above, this pattern emerges from Barth's affirmation of the Reformation insight that we are simultaneously saved and sinners. We are never beyond the grasp of sin and death or beyond the reach of the lordless powers. We do not grow beyond these realities. They are like the air we breathe and the water we drink. As long as we live, they will be around us and in us. Before we fall asleep in sloth or overreach in pride or succumb to the falsehoods that deceive us, we need to hear the gospel. We have been saved by God in Christ; let us become who we already are. This Word breaks into our experience to call us awake and lead us in a new direction. This will not happen every time we go to church, but it should happen some of the time. If not, the gospel is not being preached or taught or lived out.

Perhaps if Barth had written his planned final volumes on the consummation and eternal life, we would have heard more in his theology about the inbreaking of God's promised future, when Christ's reconciliation of the world becomes a cosmic reality through the saving work of the Holy Spirit. The gospel does not just address us in times of crisis. It breaks into our lives to offer us a foretaste of God's promised future for creation. We need this to sustain our hope, to celebrate in advance, to rest even now in the eternal Sabbath. We are saved by the God who loves us even more than we love ourselves. This is reason to feel joy and gladness again and again across our lives.

In light of the above insights, I think dialogue with Barth yields several guidelines for evangelization directed to the unaffiliated, nominal Christians, and responsible, long-term Christians.

Guideline: In evangelizing the unaffiliated and nominal Christians, understanding who a person is, taking time to develop a relationship, and sharing the gospel in words and actions improves the likelihood that it will be given a hearing.

Guideline: People in all three of these groups experience times of crisis, triggering experiences of dislocation and the search for meaning. Evangelization that shares the love of God in Jesus Christ through words and deeds is one form of the church's ministry to people at such times. It should pay special attention to their desire to make sense of what they are experiencing, to find supportive relationships and communities that embody the way of life they are learning, and "techniques for living," practical tools to help them begin to live in a new way.

Guideline: Responsible, long-term Christians need to hear the gospel again and again—in times of crisis and as they move from one stage of life to another, but most importantly of all because they live in the tension of being simultaneously saved and sinful. The gospel breaks into their experience to wake them up and send them in a new direction. It also provides them a foretaste of joy, peace, and celebration in anticipation of God's promised future for creation.

The Importance of Leadership

As mentioned above, I recently finished codirecting a national study of confirmation, which was funded by the Lilly Endowment.[27] It was the first study of its size in the United States to compare confirmation across five denominations. It even opened up the possibility of comparative research between findings about this practice in the United States and those of a larger, longitudinal study in Europe.[28] One of the most important findings of the American research is the importance of leadership. The very best confirmation programs almost universally have been transformed in recent years through the initiative of leaders willing to do the work, evoke the creativity, and take the risks of innovation. This is what we had to say about the importance of leadership:

> The driving force behind vibrant and creative confirmation programs are congregations and their leaders. . . . We discovered many different programs that are highly effective in working with young people. What

27. Osmer and Douglass, eds., *Cultivating Teen Faith.*
28. A summary of that study's early findings is found in Friedrich Schweitzer, Wolfgang Ilg, Henrick Simojoki, eds., *Confirmation Work in Europe: Empirical Results, Experiences and Challenges. A Comparative Study in Seven Countries* (Gütersloh: Gütersloher Verlagshaus, 2010). See also http://konfirmandenarbeit.eu/en/home-page/.

really matters is the passion and creativity that congregations and leaders put into confirmation and related discipleship ministries and their ability to design a program that fits their setting and young people.[29]

I am certain that this finding is true of new programs and practices of evangelization as well. It will take the hard work, passion, creativity, and practical wisdom of leaders to transform the ways their congregations think about evangelization.

Perhaps the greatest challenge facing many pastors, especially in mainline congregations, is convincing their members that evangelization is part of the mission of their church. In part, this will involve leading them to think about this ministry from a different theological perspective. I have attempted to contribute toward that aim by dialoguing with the thought of Karl Barth. But other theologians also might serve as worthy dialogue partners. Projecting a vision of what evangelization might be on biblical and theological grounds is critical to leading change. It is part of a broader transformation that needs to take place in American congregations if they are to be missional communities. At the end of this chapter I have included some books that will introduce you to the missional church discussion and, in some cases, propose ways that established churches can move toward becoming missional communities and ways church plants can make this a part of their DNA from the beginning.

I have very intentionally avoided creating a new approach, program, or model of evangelization. Rather, I have focused on looking anew at Scripture and tradition—tradition in the form of dogmatic theology—to reflect on the recent history of evangelistic practice and imagine new ways of thinking about this ministry. The next step needs to take place in congregations. Just as we saw in our research on confirmation, new approaches to evangelization will emerge as a result of the passion, creativity, and risk-taking of leaders who work with teams of church members to think about and practice this ministry in new ways. Here are some things leaders might do:

1. Read this book together. The chapters on Barth will be a stretch intellectually and likely will run into the most resistance because of Barth's objective soteriology. However, his view of justification by grace through faith is directly descended from the thought of Luther and Paul the apostle. Luther's interpretation of Paul has been subjected to critical scrutiny in recent years; in the footnotes where Paul's theology of justification is discussed, I point to

29. Osmer and Douglass, *Cultivating Teen Faith*, 133.

some of Luther's critics and those responding on his behalf. Barth's extension of the theme, Christ in our place, to include sanctification and vocation is his own innovation in the tradition of Christian theology. I believe it is solidly grounded in Scripture. Barth's doctrine of election also represents a major innovation in the Christian tradition and generally is acknowledged to be one of the most brilliant parts of his theology. Remember, evangelization as discussed in this book represents an understanding of this ministry based on the theology of the Reformers as mediated through Karl Barth. The Reformers did not develop a theology of mission or evangelization. It is to be expected that the view will be different from that of Baptists and Methodists.

2. Use the guidelines provided above as a starting point to develop your own guidelines for evangelization. I have barely scratched the surface of my exploration of Paul, Mark, and John as dialogue partners for new thinking about evangelization. Go beyond what I have done.

3. Of all the things you might do, try to focus on one concrete change and the kind of organizational structure you might adopt to support this change. For example, if you do not have an evangelization committee, creating one may be the place to start.

4. In the third part of the book I began to emphasize the relationship between the ministry of evangelization and the shift to a missional ecclesiology. This is not a book on missional theology. It focuses on only one ministry of the church, but it develops an understanding of this ministry in part on the basis of a dialogue with a theologian who is generally considered to be one of the most important influences on the missional church discussion, especially through the influence of Darrell Guder. To learn more about this discussion consider reading one of the books he has edited on this topic.

For Further Reading

Barrett, Lois, et al. *Treasure in Clay Jars: Patterns in Missional Faithfulness*. Grand Rapids: Eerdmans, 2004. Drawing on observational research, offers a depiction of missional congregations.
Guder, Darrell. *Be My Witnesses: The Church's Mission, Message, and Messengers*. Grand Rapids: Eerdmans, 1985. Remains the single best book on evangelism written after 1975.
———. *Called to Witness: Doing Missional Theology*. Grand Rapids: Eerdmans, 2015. Examines fundamental issues in the missional theology discus-

sion. Of interest regarding practical and dogmatic theology as well as missiology.

——. *The Incarnation of the Church's Witness.* Harrisburg, PA: Trinity Press International, 1999. The theological basis of the importance of embodying the gospel as well as saying the gospel.

Hunsberger, George. *Bearing the Witness of the Spirit: Lesslie Newbigin's Theology of Cultural Plurality.* Grand Rapids: Eerdmans, 1998. Very timely exploration of a theological understanding of cultural plurality in our pluralistic global and national context.

Newbigin, Lesslie. *The Open Secret: An Introduction to the Theology of Mission.* Rev. ed. Grand Rapids: Eerdmans, 1978. The single best introduction to the foundations of missional theology.

Paas, Stefan. *Church Planting in the Secular West: Learning from the European Experience.* Grand Rapids: Eerdmans, 2016. Excellent examination of church planting in Europe, drawing on empirical studies, theology, and history.

Roxburgh, Alan J., and Fred Romanuk. *The Missional Leader: Equipping Your Church to Reach a Changing World.* San Francisco: Jossey-Bass, 2006. An excellent and practical framework for understanding and implementing missional leadership in a congregation.

Van Gelder, Craig, ed. *The Missional Church in Context: Helping Congregations Develop Contextual Ministry.* Grand Rapids: Eerdmans, 2007. Collection of essays that explore issues important to the life of the church and missional theology.

Woodward, J. R. *Creating a Missional Culture: Equipping the Church for the Sake of the World.* Downers Grove, IL: InterVarsity, 2012. A leading figure in the missional theology discussion offers practical and incisive guidance in creating a missional culture in a congregation.

CHAPTER 7

Teaching Evangelization as Practical Theology

Throughout this book, I have examined evangelization through the lens of practical theology. In this chapter, I explain what this means. I have given much more attention to Scripture and dogmatic theology than is normally the case in this field. I want to explain why I have done this and deal with a few questions that were raised along the way. I also want to describe why I have included case study material in most chapters. These were taken from the beginning of a longer series of cases written for my evangelism classes at Princeton Theological Seminary. In these classes both the pedagogy and subject matter were influenced by my commitment to teach evangelism from the perspective of practical theology. I will begin with the case study method and an explanation of why this is frequently used in courses on practical theology. I then will move to the understanding of practical theology that informs this book.

Case Studies and Evangelism as Practical Theology

Case studies have long been used in schools of business, law, social work, theology, medicine, and the helping professions. In theological education they have played a particularly important role in clinical pastoral education, doctor of ministry programs, and classes in practical theology. Studying cases has proved important for many reasons, and here I lift up three.

First, studying case material offers students who are new to a field the chance to encounter the kinds of situations they will face once they begin working. In chapter 3, for example, we encounter a case that raises questions that pastors are likely to face at some point: Should you baptize an adult if he or she is not joining your church at that time, or any church for that matter? The case also raises other questions: Why is listening so important in relational evangelism? Is it appropriate to share your faith with people at work? How should you respond to someone who reveals traumatic memories from childhood? When should you refer them to a therapist? What if no therapist is available or affordable?

Case studies are a wonderful way to give students the opportunity to think about issues they may face when they start working in the future. For a similar reason, it also can be helpful in courses on evangelism in both seminaries and congregations. The very idea of evangelizing another person is daunting to many; they feel totally at a loss about what to say and do. By reading and talking about cases, both seminary students and laypeople develop a sense of confidence about sharing the gospel with others. Sometimes they role-play situations that are similar to the case. They develop skills and verbal scripts that they can use as they learn to evangelize. As they gain more experience, they will leave these behind.[1]

A second reason case studies are often used in professional education is the way they help students learn the importance of attending to the particularities of each case. Even very similar cases are different in certain ways. Leaders must take these particularities into account if they are to exercise good judgment. This is especially important in evangelism, which often is formulaic in its message and programs.

In chapter 4, we explored a case in which the writer is so locked into thinking about evangelism in a particular way—sharing the "message of salvation" through preaching—that he misses opportunities for evangelism in the situation he faces. Learning to pay attention to the particularities of people and situations is very important in evangelism. One way of presenting the gospel will not reach all people. The message and approach need to be sensitive to the particular person. Moreover, programs working well in one context will fail miserably in another. This is especially true when an approach to evangelism is taken from one culture to another. The case study method helps people attend to the particularities of persons and contexts. It helps us move beyond a one-size-fits-all approach to evangelism.

This leads to a third reason case studies are useful in learning evangelism. Students can learn a lot about themselves, especially if they write up cases in which they are personally involved. I always required this in my courses. I believe that we can only know God through God, through God giving himself to us in his Word, Jesus Christ, and the Holy Spirit. But it also is true that God

---

1. Hubert Dreyfus and Stuart Dreyfus, *Mind over Machine: The Power of Human Intuition and Expertise in the Era of the Computer* (New York: Free Press, 1986).

uses people to reach other people. Evangelism involves us becoming God's instruments in sharing the gospel with others. It is easy to get in the way. We may come across as judgmental or manipulative without even realizing that we are doing so. Some of us may have grown up in the South and rely on scripts learned in high school that come across as naive when used at a college on the West Coast.

Knowing ourselves is important in evangelism—knowing our personality, our personal history of evangelism, and our gifts. In my teaching I discovered that many students brought to class unresolved feelings about evangelism from their past—both positive and negative. Case studies in which they were involved helped them gain a deeper understanding of themselves in ministry, especially in a ministry as personal as evangelism.

In short, by giving people chances to reflect on the kinds of issues they will face when they start working, to pay attention to the particularities of different cases, and to learn about themselves in ministry, the case study method builds on students' ability to learn from experience, especially experiences related to practice. If they continue to reflect on their experience of evangelism over the years, they will develop expertise and perhaps even wisdom.

In this book we have thus drawn on an opening vignette of case material in most chapters. We think about theological issues in relation to concrete cases. This is one of our direct links with evangelistic practice. In a seminary course on the Bible we might study the historical and cultural background, genre, and literary features of a passage or book of Scripture. It is very rare to study the Bible while also engaging present practice at the same time. In contrast, this is crucial in practical theology, where we think about theology and Scripture as we also reflect on practice. This can be done in many different ways. In contrast to case studies, for example, present practice might be engaged in the form of research into a practice of the church. This is what we did in the Confirmation Project. We studied confirmation through survey research and an ethnographic method called portraiture. Case studies are up close and personal. Quantitative research on practice is at the opposite end of the spectrum. Qualitative studies allow readers to gain a firsthand impression of practice, but they lack the self-involvement of a person involved in a form of ministry writing it up.[2] All study types have their advantages.

---

2. It is true that ethnographic research like portraiture encourages researchers to write themselves into the report, sharing what they are experiencing personally as well as what they are observing. Even so, it is highly unusual for the observer to be the leader at some point.

The important point is that practical theology engages present practice while carrying out biblical or theological reflection. In this book we have adopted an approach I used frequently in my courses on evangelism.

In addition to case studies, we also have reflected on traditions of evangelism that shape our understanding of this ministry today. Starting with present practice is central to practical theology. If the Bible is the subject matter of biblical studies and church doctrine of dogmatic theology, then present practice is the subject matter of practical theology. In this particular book, I have focused primarily on the present practice of one of the ministries of the church. I have not looked at parachurch groups, televangelism, or solo evangelists. I have argued that the dominant traditions of evangelistic practice are influenced by a model I have called evangelism as conversionism. Once we become aware of this, we begin to understand why many denominations are wary of evangelism.

Evangelism as conversionism grew out of the renewal movements that emerged after the Reformation. They worked with a different understanding of salvation than that of the Reformers. In these renewal movements and the traditions that grew out of them, Christ is portrayed as accomplishing salvation objectively on the cross, but this does not become real and effective in the lives of individuals until they place their faith in Christ as their Lord and Savior. It is only then that they are saved. I offered a hypothesis in the introduction that explains the domination of evangelism as conversionism across the modern period by viewing it along the lines of a cultural toolkit that is flexible and transportable. Its emphasis on freedom and conversion at a single point in time had great plausibility in an American frontier culture spreading westward for decades. This hypothesis is not proved, only suggested.

By reflecting on the contemporary practice of evangelism, I attempted to clear space for an alternative, especially in the face of dissatisfaction with this model across a wide range of Christian traditions, including evangelical churches. Revivals, altar calls, cold call evangelism, and door-to-door evangelism do not work today as they did in past decades. This set in motion my dialogue with Scripture and the dogmatic theology of Karl Barth. This brings me to the question of what practical theology might look like when it draws on Barth.

Before taking up this question in the second half of this chapter, I want to share some of the materials I have used in the past to teach students how to write good case studies and how to discuss them in precept groups. During each first session, I run off handout copies of the following points and discuss them in class. I also post the material on Blackboard, the online platform used by our seminary. Along with this, I would post several complete case studies from past classes (after obtaining students' permission and changing names). Some were A quality, but others were not. For some students, my class presents them with their first experience writing up a case, and they find it helpful to see examples of varying quality.

HOW TO WRITE A GOOD CASE STUDY

Preliminary Considerations:

Several questions will be important in this course.

1. *What counts as evangelism?*
   a. Most of the time, we think of evangelism as communication of the gospel to people who have never been Christians or do not believe in God. It is the church's mission to nonbelievers. But some theologians and church leaders argue that in our American, post-Christendom context, evangelism should be more expansive. It should include the communication of the gospel to (1) people who grew up in the church but no longer participate; (2) people who are nominal Christians, people who only show up at Christmas and Easter and don't participate in programs or ministries. Should we think of evangelism as directed to nominal Christians, as well as to nonbelievers and nonparticipants in the church?
   b. In this course, we do not presuppose one, normative definition of evangelism, which all students are expected to hold. We affirm a range of understandings of evangelism as legitimate. *For the purposes of your critical incident report, however, you will need to decide what counts as evangelism in your own theology.* This will be important in the kind of critical incident you choose to focus on. Do you believe evangelism only focuses on non-Christians or drop-outs? What about nominal Christians? The important thing is to be able to explain why you view evangelism in a particular way on biblical, theological, and contextual grounds.

2. *What is meant by conversion and what is its relationship to salvation?*
   a. Many people think of conversion along the lines of Paul's experience on the road to Damascus. Here, conversion is a sudden event, a crisis that leads people to turn away from their former life (repentance) and turn toward a trusting relationship with Jesus Christ (faith).
   b. Other people believe that conversion can take place over time. They point to Jesus's relationship with his disciples. Conversion was not a sudden event; it was a process unfolding over time. Only gradually did they come to see Jesus as Lord and Savior and why he must suffer and die.
   c. Not only are you asked to think about these patterns of conversion, but also, about the relationship between conversion and salvation. You are expected to address this issue as well.

3. *What is the role of the church or Christian community in evangelism?*
   a. Mass evangelism in revivals and televangelism has a poor record of leading people to join a community of disciples. They focus on individuals. Others critique them as making converts but not disciples.
   b. In contrast, Lesslie Newbigin once wrote that the congregation is the first hermeneutic of the gospel. If so, then evangelism requires a community that embodies the gospel in certain ways. In your critical incident report and your case study, you will do well to consider the contribution of the Christian community to evangelism.

We will explore these questions over the course of the semester. When you present your critical incident in your peer group, you will have to make certain preliminary judgments about how you understand what counts as evangelism, your understanding of conversion and its relationship to salvation, and your view of the role of Christian community in evangelism. In your final project, these should be fully discussed in the section called Normative Theological Reflection. You should draw on assigned reading (using footnotes) and class discussion.

The Basic Structure of the Case Study

Opening Vignette (1–4 pages)

Begin with a critical incident that describes a conversation in which you engaged in evangelism. Help us see, hear, and feel what is going on in the incident. It is often helpful to provide verbatim material: a recollection of the actual conversation as best you can remember it. It is helpful to provide an initial sense of who is involved, your relationship, the setting, and the larger context.

Rationale (1–1.5 pages)

This section should give readers a sense of why this critical incident was chosen to be the center of the case study. Give a preliminary description of your understanding of the parameters of evangelism, as noted above. You can explain and justify this under Normative Reflection when you write up your case study. At this point, simply describe your understanding of what counts as evangelism and then focus on questions like these: What are some of the questions related to evangelism that are at stake in this incident? How are you personally implicated in this incident, that is, why did you choose this incident of all those you might have focused on? What do you have at stake personally? Professionally? What is at stake for your church or ministry in carrying out evangelism with people like the one who is the focus of your Opening Vignette?

Contextual Analysis (5–8 pages)

Analyze the setting and context in which this incident occurred. Think of this as concentric circles, moving from the particular persons and the events surrounding your critical incident, to your relationship with this person(s), to the congregation/parachurch ministry, to the broader local context, to the social context. Here is an example. While this example is set in a congregation, your critical incident can be located in a parachurch organization, a family (even your own), or a chance conversation. In all cases, this section of your case study places the incident in context.

1. Critical Incident: Conversation with an adult member who has not been involved in the church for seven years. The conversation occurred after this person was recently divorced by her husband, who left her for a younger woman.

2. Relationship: Description of your relationship with this couple (and their children) prior to the divorce and recent conversation. Description of the family's involvement in the congregation—in this case their total lack of involvement.

3. Description of the congregation as it is relevant to this case. Are there other couples their age? Are there single persons, especially divorced persons, in the congregation? How does the congregation respond to people who have divorced? What sort of ministries does it offer? Is it a poor working-class church, middle class, etc.? What about the racial composition? You can't describe everything. Select those features that are relevant to the case.

4. Description of the community in which the congregation is located and the congregation's profile in this community. In this case, the family lives in one of the northern suburbs of Atlanta, composed of professionals who commute to work. The church's profile is a "program church," which offers quality Sunday school, youth groups, fellowship, etc. to those who choose to attend.

5. Discussion of trends related to divorce in the U.S.

To do contextual analysis well, you may need to draw on theories you've learned in other courses or do additional reading about issues pertinent to your particular case. There is excellent literature on divorce, for example. This may be relevant to how you share the gospel with this woman. Feel free to draw on the social sciences to make sense of the context of your case.

Normative Theological Reflection (5–8 pages)

This section is theological. Here you describe your theology of evangelism and draw on this theology to interpret what is going on in your case and the adequacy of your evangelistic efforts to this point. Cover the following:

1. What is your theology of evangelism? Point to biblical and theological foundations. Be sure to include some discussion of the three issues highlighted under Preliminary Considerations: What counts as evangelism? What is the relationship between conversion and salvation? What role does the church or some form of Christian community play in evangelism?

2. What might the social sciences contribute to your understanding of the goals and methods of evangelism in this particular case?

3. Bring your theological perspective and your dialogue with the social sciences to bear on the particular incident that is the focus of your case. Take into account the particularities of this incident, as well as the context in which it occurs. What are the goals and methods of evangelism that might be most helpful in this particular case?

Moving Forward (1-3 pages)

This section involves two things. You can outline both of them in bullet points, being brief.

1. Imagine the critical incident as a relationship in which you are still involved. In light of your reflections in this paper, what might your next moves be? Do they involve others as well as you?

2. State what you have learned from this paper that will help you equip members of your church or parachurch organization to practice evangelism in the future. How will you equip the saints for this ministry? State only key insights. You can be brief and suggestive.

I have found students to be appreciative of these handouts and discussion in class at the very beginning of the course. They also appreciate seeing examples of good and mediocre cases. Typically, students do very well on writing up their theology of evangelism, its relationship to the church, and the relationship between conversion and salvation. The latter commonly evokes some the best class discussion. Evangelical students pointed to the many places in the New Testament where it seems to imply that people must convert in order to be saved. Their interlocutors typically turned to Paul for help, and of course Barth.

The weakest part of their papers was usually their use of the social sciences for contextual analysis or for understanding the people they were trying to evangelize. I finally started adding some books along these lines. For example, Erin Dufault-Hunter's *The Transformative Power of Faith: A Narrative Approach to Conversion* proved very helpful. I also started to leave a week without any assigned reading so each of them could choose a book from the social sciences that was relevant to their case. They had to submit the name of the book two weeks before they were supposed to read it.

Since my background also is in Christian education, I also require students or teams to teach at some point in my courses. I try to teach them ways of doing this and offer feedback after they teach. For example, leading a discussion in a small group is an extremely important skill for pastors. It is hard to believe that many students graduate from seminary with no formal instruction or practice in leading a discussion.

In this course, the precept is structured in a way that allows each student to have one experience leading a discussion. Usually, the class is large enough to have a PhD student in practical theology serve as my teaching assistant. That allows one of us to be in every precept, and we typically provide feedback immediately after class. I usually begin this time by asking the person who just taught what he or she would like to learn from the experience. We'd start there and move to other matters. Here is the handout I would provide to students and also post on Blackboard:

PRECEPT DISCUSSION

Email your critical incident report to the members of your precept, twenty-four hours prior to the class in which you are presenting. We are assuming that all members of the peer group have read the report prior to class.

Roles in Group

Each week, four people in your group will fulfill four roles: **facilitator, presenter, initial respondent,** and **insight catcher.**

- The "**facilitator**" is responsible for leading the group using the discussion guidelines given below.
- The "**presenter**" writes up a critical incident and presents it to the group.
- The "**initial respondent**" provides a verbal response to the presenter.
- The "**insight catcher**" writes down insights from the group's conversation and adds them to the end of the case in electronic form. He or she then sends the case, with comments, to the presenter, professor, and teaching assistant.

Discussion Format

Task 1: Quick Review of the Incident

The members of the peer group look over the report, which they have already read, as a way of reminding themselves of key information and questions.

Task 2: The Presenter Shares "Further Thoughts" (5 minutes)

The presenter shares why he or she focused on this particular incident.

- Does it bring into focus personal issues related to evangelism? For example: This sort of conversation really makes me anxious. Or I've been wanting to talk to my brother about my faith for a long time.
- Does it reveal anything about the setting in which you are working? For example: We have many young people in our church who know almost nothing about the gospel and have never been invited to talk about what it might mean to be a disciple of Jesus. Or this was a chance encounter with a person at Starbucks. Etc.

The presenter also shares additional details about the incident that he or she may have thought of after the report was written.

Task 3: Clarification of Information (5 minutes)

After the presenter adds this additional information about the critical incident, the group may ask the presenter questions of information and clarification. The facilitator steers the group away from analysis or evaluation at this point. The facilitator stops the questioning after five minutes and guides the group to its next task.

Task 4: Analysis of dynamics in the critical incident (15 minutes)
Why Is This Going On?

The presenter does not participate actively in this part of the discussion. First, the initial respondent offers a response to the critical incident. Then, the group begins discussion. In this part of the discussion, the group will analyze the incident using the readings and insights from class. The group will pay attention to clarifying the issues involved and identifying the critical factors and turning points. The main function of the facilitator is to guide the discussion, keeping the group from jumping too quickly to evaluation, and inviting them to clarify their understanding of the dynamics of the event. During this task, it is appropriate to draw on learnings from psychology, sociology, mental health professions and other fields. How might we interpret what is going on in the incident? How does this help us think about how to approach the task of evangelism in this particular case? The insight catcher takes careful notes. At the end of twenty-five minutes the leader turns the group to evaluation.

Task 5: Evaluation of performance (10 minutes)
What Ought to Be Going On?

The group now assesses what occurred in the critical incident. This evaluation has two parts: evaluation of the critical incident and assessment of theological adequacy.

· The **first task**, evaluation of the incident, considers these questions: Did this person do what he or she set out to do? How well was it done? What, if anything, might have been done differently? If the presenter offered any self-evaluation in the written case, the group can begin with the personal evaluation. This helps the presenter to clarify his or her objectives and the intended outcome.

- The **second task**, assessment of theological adequacy, addresses the following questions: In what ways does this incident embody evangelism? What did this involve in this particular incident? What might have been done differently? Is there an implicit theology of evangelism that is informing this incident? If so, what is it? How adequate is this understanding of evangelism in light of Scripture, tradition, and issues raised in the course? It is not assumed that everyone in the peer group will think about evangelism in exactly the same way. The facilitator works to draw out these different perspectives and to make sure that people engage one another in a constructive, not negative, manner. Differences can be helpful, but not if they are used to shame people or put them down. Members of the peer group might say things like: "From my perspective, I think X, Y, or Z." They also should try to get outside their own perspective and see things from the point of view of the presenter, especially when assessing theological adequacy. The insight catcher continues to take careful notes.

Task 6: Reflection and reaction by presenter (10 minutes)
What might take place next?

The presenter now has opportunity to respond to the discussion. Some questions the presenter can address include: At what points was the analysis and evaluation of the group most helpful? What has the group failed to see and understand? Finally, in light of the discussion, what might the presenter project as the next steps in relation to this incident?

Before a first plenary class meeting, I would send out an example of the sort of partial case they would present in future classes. Several times, the PhD student who was my teaching assistant would write this up and serve as the presenter. I would organize the class into a fishbowl seating arrangement with ten chairs in a circle for eight students, the presenter, and me as the facilitator. I would then facilitate an abbreviated discussion in a kind of role-play. I would look over the list of class participants in advance and would ask a student I knew to be a good fit to play the role of the initial respondent.

I believe courses in practical theology ought to bring practice into the classroom as much as possible. Here, students had the opportunity to practice leading a discussion and to receive direct feedback. I try to include input at some point in the class on the art of asking good questions, how to create a discussion thread by guiding people to build on one another's comments, and how to handle people who talk too much or not at all. In addition, students bring their own experiences of evangelism into the course and reflect theologically on this ministry in relation to concrete instances of practice. Trying to teach courses in practical theology solely by lecturing excludes the kind of knowing in relation to doing that Rod Hunter and Bonnie Miller-McLemore describe as central to practical theological reflection. I noted their writings at the beginning of a previous chapter and have offered here one example of the pedagogical implications of their perspective for seminary education.

Is there a way that the case study approach to teaching evangelism could be adapted for a church context? I think so. After all, the Harvard Business School was a pioneer in the use of the case study method and continues to make it a central part of its MBA and continuing education. I have included several cases in Appendix 2 that might be used as a way of getting started. As soon as possible, however, people should begin writing their own cases. The format I have provided could easily be adapted for people who are not spending a lot of their time reading theology. The more difficult question is which venue is best for this kind of education. A church school class? A training course for an evangelization committee comparable to deacon training?

What is really needed is a program like the Stephen Ministries for evangelization. My wife went through this training and is actively involved in our congregation as a caregiver. She already had a master of divinity degree from Yale and a master of social work from Virginia Commonwealth University. To say the least, she was highly educated in pastoral care and therapy. But Stephen Ministries offers the possibility of being part of program of caregiving that is supported by her congregation and provides training that pulls together theology, a repertoire of skills and practices essential for a caregiving ministry, and ongoing peer supervision and support. Stephen Ministers are matched with care receivers by a pastor, and they meet weekly in person, by phone, by text, or by other means. It is a ministry of listening, prayer, and witness to God's love. Typical issues that care receivers have are grief after a death or major loss, loneliness and isolation in older age, family stress due to conflict, divorce, parenting difficulty, or job loss. My wife receives from the program as much as she gives as she gets to know other people deeply, to anticipate their needs and tailor prayerful responses, and to delve into the resources of Scripture and prayer to address immediate concerns. It has been both a spiritual challenge and a gift for her to serve as a Stephen Minister.

The church needs a program that is the equivalent of this to teach evangelization. I have argued that we can begin thinking about this ministry in new ways on the basis of a fresh encounter with Scripture and with Karl Barth's constructive retrieval of the theology of the Reformation. The next step is innovation at the level of congregations and perhaps even a program like Stephen Ministries that could help a cadre of new evangelists emerge in congregations across the country. Stephen Ministries began with one person, the Rev. Kenneth C. Haugk, a pastor and clinical psychologist, and nine people who asked to receive training in caregiving for their congregation. Today more than 13,000 congregations participate in this program.

Roman Catholics already use the term "the new evangelization." It is the right term. Protestant congregations that wish to reclaim and innovate in their own Reformation tradition need their own version of this. We can only pray that it will come to be.

Practical Theology and Karl Barth

My best friends and colleagues in Europe are all theological liberals in the tradition of Friedrich Schleiermacher. I cannot tell you how many times they have told me that Karl Barth almost killed practical theology in Europe. I keep telling them that the only ones keeping the idea of practical theology alive in the United States were Barthians like James Smart, who studied with Barth at Basel and was exposed to the European tradition of practical theology. The rare non-Barthian exception to this was Seward Hiltner, whose *Preface to Pastoral Theology* is aware of the field of practical theology.

Practical theology has long held a slot in the curriculums of American seminaries and divinity schools through the influence of American scholars who studied in Europe during the nineteenth century and were exposed to the organization of theological education along the lines of the theological encyclopedia.[3] But it is virtually impossible to find examples of Americans

---

3. For an overview and a detailed account of the history of practical theology at Princeton Theological Seminary, see Gordon S. Mikoski and Richard R. Osmer, *With*

who reflected explicitly on practical theology as a field. The dominant alternatives were the "new" fields closely related to psychology, education, and sociology: religious education, pastoral psychology, and the psychology of religion. In their view, practical theology represented applied theology, which lacked any research agenda of its own.

Even as a PhD student at Emory, I had serious doubts about these new fields. It seemed to me that the tail was wagging the dog. Cognate fields like psychology, psychotherapy, sociology, or education were defining the terms and setting the agenda for the ministries of the church. Should not such ministries be defined on theological grounds and develop their own methods and practices?

I have come to believe that Barth is a very helpful resource for practical theology precisely because he insists that the church should take seriously God's self-revelation in Jesus Christ. We learn of God through God, and Christ holds a special place in the knowledge given to faith. Turning to other professions or to the social sciences to discover the nature and purpose of the church is to import the "alien framework" of another field instead of starting with the primary source of our knowledge of God.

Contemporary practical theology, however, generally criticizes or ignores Barth as a resource for its work. Don Browning, for example, characterizes Barth in the following way:

A theologian as recent as Karl Barth saw theology as the systematic interpretation of God's self-disclosure to the Christian church. There was no role for human understanding, action, or practice in the construal of God's self-disclosure. In this view, theology is practical only by applying God's revelation as directly and purely as possible to the concrete situations of life. The theologian moves from revelation to the human, from theory to practice, and from revealed knowledge to application.[4]

As I have engaged Barth more intensively, I have come to believe that this characterization of Barth is completely misleading, showing very little understanding of his theology and its possible contribution to the field of practical theology. Yet these kinds of caricatures of Barth have been offered and

Piety and Learning: The History of Practical Theology at Princeton Theological Seminary, 1812-2012, International Practical Theology, vol. 11 (Berlin: Lit Verlag, 2011).

4. Don S. Browning, *A Fundamental Practical Theology: Descriptive and Strategic Proposals* (Minneapolis: Augsburg, 1991), 5.

repeated uncritically by practical theologians again and again. Most of the time, I think they come from people who have not really studied Barth in any depth.[5]

Only recently has a more serious engagement of Barth by practical theologians begun to appear as part of a broader revival of interest in Barth in Great Britain and the United States. Darrell Guder, Deborah van Deusen Hunsinger, Gary Deddo, Theresa Latini, Angela Dienhart Hancock, Nathan Stucky, Blair Bertrand, and Patrick Johnson are representative of the renewed interest in Barth's work as a resource for practical theology.

Barth sometimes characterizes his theological posture and the stance of the church as swimming against the stream.[6] This is a fitting image of those practical theologians who are in dialogue with Karl Barth. They are swimming against the stream of contemporary practical theology in its modern and postmodern forms. Here we explain why engagement of Barth's theology represents an alternative to the mainstream of practical theology as currently practiced. We highlight methodological issues, which of course always are rooted in substantive claims.

The Priority of Revelation and Reconciliation in Practical Theology

Across the twentieth century and into the twenty-first, the field of practical theology has been dominated by correlational approaches to theology under the influence of Paul Tillich, David Tracy, Rebecca Chopp, and, more recently, postmodern and postcolonial philosophers. Correlational approaches focus on bringing theology and other forms of human knowledge into a mutually influential relationship. Especially important dialogue partners in correlational practical theology are the human sciences, philosophy, feminism, critical social theory, empirical research methodology, and various forms of emancipatory praxis. Practical theology in its correlational modes constructs knowledge out of the dialogue and interaction of these resources.

Barth rejects correlational approaches to theology and affirms the absolute centrality of God's self-revelation and self-giving in Jesus Christ. He

5. In the final part of this chapter, I draw on insights I have developed further in "Barth and Practical Theology," *Wiley Blackwell Companion to Karl Barth*, ed. George Hunsinger (Hoboken, NJ: Wiley Blackwell, 2020), ch. 64.

6. Karl Barth, *Church Dogmatics*, ed. Geoffrey W. Bromiley and T. F. Torrance (Edinburgh: T. & T. Clark, 1956–75), IV/3, second half, 528.

focuses on revelation and reconciliation in a way that is almost nonexistent in practical theology today. This leads him to emphasize the dialogue between practical theology and the other theological disciplines—dogmatic, historical, and biblical theology—over its dialogue with the social sciences, philosophy, and other fields. This is what I have done in this book. I have privileged the dialogue with Scripture and dogmatic theology. I could have spent a great deal of time drawing on the social sciences to describe the contemporary context and the "needs" of people living during a pandemic in an age of skepticism. This is the approach of theological liberalism that seeks to reinterpret Christianity in relation to the present context. This is not the position I have taken in this book, though it is the dominant position in contemporary practical theology.

Barth's theology affirms the absolute uniqueness of Jesus Christ as the source of knowledge of God. Jesus Christ is Emmanuel: God with us. When we look at Jesus, we do not merely see what God is like. We encounter the mystery of God in human flesh. Barth's theology is Christocentric. This means that any formal definition of theology, including practical theology, must be grounded in material claims about God derived from God's self-giving in Christ. Other starting points, inevitably, define the nature and purpose of theology in terms of an "alien" framework derived from philosophy, the social sciences, history, general hermeneutics, critical social theory, and so forth. Barth's approach rules out some of the most influential ways of defining practical theology: as a hermeneutical discipline, action science, empirical-practical discipline, or accrued wisdom of a way of life.

In Barth's view, the subject matter of theology must determine the methods appropriate to its investigation. He argues that the appropriate subject matter for Christian theology is the God revealed in Jesus Christ through whom we encounter the one true living God and learn of the world in relation to God. Other fields have their own subject matters and methods of investigation, and their findings should be respected on these matters. Moreover, Barth affirms that theology as a form of "science" develops positions that are tentative, subject to criticism, and historically situated. He makes this point forcefully when describing Christian theology as it listens to and follows after God's Word.

In the first volumes of the *Church Dogmatics*, Barth develops his understanding of revelation through a critical appropriation of the Reformed tradition's doctrine of the threefold form of the Word of God: God revealed through Jesus Christ, Scripture, and the proclamation of the church. He develops a dynamic understanding of revelation that portrays knowledge of God as an "object" or subject matter that never comes under human control. His theology is highly dialectical, both affirming and negating what is known of God.

Christian theology, thus, never brings God's Word under control, though various efforts have been made throughout Christian history to treat God as a subject matter that can be systematized in terms of particular patterns of rationality or interpretation. Barth rejects such efforts as dangerous, as comparable to the many ways religion has attempted to bring God under control in order to make the divine serve human interests. Barth remained remarkably free in his methodological commitments over the years. He encouraged theologians to maintain a stance of humility and openness as they pursue the task of critiquing the speech and action of the church in light of God's Word. When Don Browning and others portray Barth as offering a timeless dogmatic system or a theory which is subsequently applied to practice, they not only are wrong but misleading.

The Differentiated Unity of Theology: Dialectical Inclusion

Along with David Tracy, Barth is one of the few major theologians to take practical theology as a field seriously. He argues that practical theology, biblical theology, and dogmatic theology need each other. They cannot do their work well without taking each other's work seriously. He describes the relationship between these forms of theology with the image of three circles "which intersect in such a way that the center of each is also within the circumference of the other two."[7] The image implies considerable overlap, mutual dependence, and interpenetration. Barth describes dogmatic theology in just this way:

How, then, can there be dogmatics unless exegesis not only precedes but is included in it? . . . How, then, can there be dogmatics unless practical theology, too, not only follows but is already included in it?[8]

This depiction of the close relationship between various forms of theology represents a real alternative to the way the unity of theology has been conceptualized since the rise of the modern research university and its em-

7. Barth, *CD* I/1, 4.
8. Barth, *CD* I/2, 767.

phasis on the specialized research of separate fields. In that context, the relationship between the specialized theological disciplines is like a relay race in which each field runs its own leg and then hands off the baton to the next discipline. Each has its own specialized task, methodology, and subject matter. Typically, practical theology is portrayed as running the last leg and bringing the baton across the finish line to the church in the form of practical application.

In contrast, the differentiated unity of theology as described by Barth is closer to the collaboration and mutual assistance of a medical team working to save a person's life. The expertise and ongoing cooperation of each member is essential to a successful outcome. This means that practical theology must engage biblical and dogmatic theology as it carries out its own constructive work. It also means that the converse is true. Biblical studies and dogmatic theology must engage practical theology in their commitments to the critical examination and strengthening of the proclamation of the church. Theology is a differentiated unity in which each part contributes to and receives from the larger whole.

Indeed, Barth takes this a step further. Not only is each part of the theological enterprise a contributing member to the larger whole, but the whole is reiterated within each part. This way of conceptualizing the differentiated unity of theology reflects a pattern that appears throughout the *Church Dogmatics*, a pattern that George Hunsinger calls dialectical inclusion. He describes it in the following way: "Each part is thought to contain, from a certain vantage point, the entire structure. The part includes within itself the entire pattern and way of functioning of the whole. The part is not just a division of the whole but a reiteration of it."[9]

The best example of dialectical inclusion in the theological disciplines is the way Barth himself works as a dogmatic theologian. Not only does he draw on the biblical scholarship of others, but he also undertakes his own explication of Scripture again and again in the small print sections of the *Church Dogmatics*. Moreover, he repeatedly addresses matters of practice that are important to practical theology, like sermon preparation, catechetical instruction, baptism, and Christian vocation. These are not afterthoughts tacked on to the "real" work of dogmatics. They are part of the very fabric of dogmatics as Barth pursues it. The construction of church doctrine cannot take place without engaging Scripture, the history of the church's prior con-

---

9. George Hunsinger, *How to Read Karl Barth: The Shape of His Theology* (New York: Oxford University Press, 1991), 58.

fession and action, and the challenge of proclaiming the gospel in the contemporary church. As Hunsinger's definition of dialectical inclusion helps us see, the theological whole is reiterated *within* dogmatic theology, even as this particular part of theology carries out its own distinctive task. In Barth's view, the same should be true of the other theological disciplines as well.

Perhaps the clearest example of this pattern in Barth's work in practical theology is his *Übungen in der Predigtvorbereitung* (*Exercises in Sermon Preparation*), examined in depth by Angela Dienhart Hancock.[10] Originally, these were classroom lectures and exercises offered by Barth while teaching at the University of Bonn in 1932–33 as Hitler was coming to power. They later were published in several versions on the basis of notes by students and Charlotte von Kirschbaum. We now will lift up four dimensions of the *Exercises* that provide insight into Barth's approach to practical theology and the importance of its dialogue with other forms of theology. It is no accident that Barth lifts up the importance of this dialogue in his opening lecture.

Contextual and Public

In his lectures, Barth offers a theory of preaching and practical guidelines that might help students who are just learning how to preach. Both are developed with an eye to the political, cultural, and religious context that preachers faced at the dawn of the Third Reich. The preaching classroom, in effect, became a place of resistance in Germany, directly challenging scholars, denominational leaders, pastors, and politicians who were championing Hitler's rise to power as God's work through the history and culture of the German people. Barth encouraged his students to recognize that preaching the gospel demanded resistance to the easy identification of God with popular movements and dominant ideologies in contemporary culture.

Barth was prompted to teach this course on practical theology by students taking his classes in dogmatics and his personal reservations about the professor of practical theology currently teaching classes on preaching, Emil Pfennigsdorf. Pfennigsdorf had joined the first pro-Nazi group to appear in Bonn in 1929 and was sympathetic to theological currents lending support to the extreme nationalism and *völkisch* antisemitism of the National Socialist movement. Barth was determined to offer his students an alternative that

---

10. Angela Hancock, *Karl Barth's Emergency Homiletic, 1932–1933: A Summons to Prophetic Witness at the Dawn of the Third Reich* (Grand Rapids: Eerdmans, 2013).

would prepare them to preach the gospel in the crisis situation they would soon face as pastors of congregations.

Barth had this concrete context in mind as he developed his theory and practice of preaching. He did not see himself as developing a model of preaching relevant to all times and places, a key insight into his understanding of practical theology. This is readily apparent in his response to a request by a Scottish pastor, John McConnachie. McConnachie asked Barth to write an introduction to a book he was writing, *Karl Barth and the Preacher*, which would address practical questions and demonstrate that Barth's theology was preachable. Barth refused, writing to McConnachie that it would be better if preachers and theologians would become "thoroughly disturbed and unsettled in their praxis instead of moving swiftly from one magnificent and lively praxis to another." What is needed is a "new questioning and seeking," rather than turning to practical matters as quickly as possible. He adds, "I have much too much respect for the peculiarity of the spiritual situation in another country to judge offhand if another way is pursued there than in my own."[11]

Barth's understanding of practical theology—much like his ethics—is deeply contextual. Models appropriate to one context can never be directly transferred to another, evoking the need to ask anew how best to preach the gospel in a particular time and place. Moreover, Barth's preaching lectures represent a form of public theology quite different from its typical conceptualization in contemporary practical theology, one that often relies on a *tertium quid* (typically philosophy or ethics) to mediate Christianity and particular social contexts.

In Barth's teaching of preaching, the classroom becomes a site of Christian resistance to the idolatry of Nazism, a witness rendered in obedience to God before the watching world. Throughout his writings and church leadership, Barth consistently called the church and individual Christians to resist the disorder of life flowing from the world's rebellion against God. He was not just thinking of extreme situations like Germany under the rule of the Nazi party. He was thinking of institutions and everyday practices we take for granted, like global capitalism, racism, inequitable tax codes, and so forth. His politics were quite radical, for he believed the church should publicly proclaim and embody, at least provisionally, the liberty of the children of God who live in the light of Christ's victory over sin and death in anticipation of his *parousia*. This is practical theology in the service of the church's public witness. It is readily apparent in the *Exercises in Sermon Preparation*.

11. All of these quotations come from Hancock, *Emergency Homiletic*, 189–91.

Reflection on the Theology of Preaching

The need to rethink the why and how of preaching anew, however, is grounded in something deeper than an awareness of context. It is rooted in Barth's theology of preaching as proclamation of the Word of God, which resists all forms of systemization, including the formulation of a practical program. Barth offers his own dogmatic reflections on preaching and its relationship to revelation only after he examines eight theologians who have defined the theory and practice of preaching in the recent past. He covers a broad spectrum, from the orthodox theologian David Holaz to the father of modern liberalism Friedrich Schleiermacher. He concludes that each of these figures addresses nine elements that are constitutive of a theology of preaching: revelation and the Word of God, the church, the divine command, the office of the preacher, the nature of preaching as an attempt, Scripture, preaching as the preacher's own speech, the church as a community, and the Holy Spirit. He offers his own definition of preaching and then unpacks the constitutive elements in detail.

Those familiar with the *Church Dogmatics* will have little difficulty recognizing the way Barth draws on his own work as a dogmatic theologian to set forth a theology of the nature and purpose of preaching as he addresses these topics, giving special attention to divine and human action in preaching and the all-important context of the church as a community of witness to the gospel.

This sort of dialogue between dogmatic theology and practical theology is necessary whenever the latter reflects on any form of ministry or Christian witness. It is impossible to describe, much less evaluate, Christian speech and action without a theological understanding of what this practice is and what it ought to be normatively. Preaching in theory and practice implies some sort of view of revelation, the nature of the church, the work of the Holy Spirit, and so forth—as Barth points out. Practical theology is not dogmatic theology, and it need not develop a full-scale treatment of doctrine in the context of its work. But it does need to point to the dogmatic framework on which it draws or else its use of theological concepts will be haphazard. Even worse, it will adopt the implicit values and beliefs of a community or guild and never examine them critically.

The Special Importance of Scripture

One of the central tasks of Barth's lectures on sermon preparation is to help students learn an alternative to modern "theme" preaching which was being co-opted for propagandistic purposes. The preacher, Barth argues, should not come to the task of sermon preparation with a preexistent theme in hand, based on the needs of the local community or the German people. Rather, the sermon must grow out of the preacher's encounter with a particular biblical text. Here, Barth explores practical theology's dialogue with biblical theology, which is portrayed as making an important contribution to sermon preparation.

The preacher should begin with a close reading of the text, attending to what is said. This should involve reading the text in its original language, for every translation is an interpretation. This passes to grappling with the content of the text, as well as its context and background. Only after preachers have wrestled with these matters themselves should they should turn to commentaries. Barth believes these should include commentaries based on modern historical criticism as well as older, premodern commentaries that explore the theological significance of biblical texts as they point to God.

Barth then explores how particular texts attest to God's revelation with his explication of two themes: "the peculiar way of witness" of a text and the "present situation" of this "peculiar way of witness."[12] He argues that biblical texts not only are "historical monuments" embedded in a particular time and place, but also "living documents" whose ultimate theme is none other than Jesus Christ. He explores how to take seriously the witness of a text to God's Word as it was spoken into a particular situation and to seek a "repetition" of its way now in the act of preaching. As Scripture, it "speaks to none other than precisely us at this particular moment and does so as the one and only witness to the revelation of God, a Word which God has spoken to this age."

Barth provides concrete guidance on how preachers might approach texts in this way and offers sermon sketches focusing on Psalm 121, John 13:33–35, and Ephesians 2:1–10. He concludes the lectures with sessions offering guidelines for the actual writing of sermons and invites the class to reflect with him on two sample sermons. It is noteworthy that Barth's reflection on and practice of biblical theology have given rise to new developments in the theological interpretation of Scripture.

The dialogue between practical and biblical theology is important in the *Exercises in Sermon Preparation* for two reasons. First and most importantly,

12. The quotations in this paragraph come from Barth, *The Christian Life: Church Dogmatics, IV, Part 4, Lecture Fragments*, trans. Geoffrey Bromiley (Grand Rapids: Eerdmans, 1991), 102.

Scripture is the second form of the Word attesting to Jesus Christ in ways that are unique. The church must turn to and rely on its encounter with Scripture if it is to hear God in the present and respond in faith, love, and hope. In the end this is not a matter of mastering certain methods of study or interpretation but adopting a stance of openness to the text itself. The interpreter becomes the one interpreted.

Second, the uniquely authoritative status of Scripture in the church has implications for all forms of Christian practice, which are exemplified paradigmatically in preaching. Preachers must learn how to interpret and proclaim Scripture as God's Word. So too must Christian teachers, caregivers, leaders, and evangelists, for it is here that the church learns who it is as God's people and nurtures a living relationship with its Lord. The absence of attention to the dialogue with Scripture in contemporary practical theology signals reliance on other sources of authority, especially philosophical and social scientific interpretations of human life.

The Expectation of a Human Response

Barth pays less attention in the *Exercises* to human freedom and action than he does in other writings, particularly in the ethical portions of the *Church Dogmatics*. But these themes do come to expression in his discussion of listeners and hearers of the Word and the way preaching is rooted in the life of the church community. Preachers must first listen to texts in prayer and study if they are to have anything to offer. They are like heralds who must listen first and then speak after. Moreover, they must listen as persons who belong to a particular church community, not as persons who stand over against the persons to whom they preach. Explication of the Bible must become a form of address for a particular community that challenges them to respond to its claims in their inward and outward relations.

Since Barth is so often accused of overemphasizing the Godness of God to the exclusion of human action, it is worth spending a bit more time on the human response to God's word, drawing on recent scholarship that explores his ethics. We have explored some of his thoughts about human agency under the themes of Christ in our place and the Holy Spirit as the mediator of communion. As we have noted, Barth is deeply critical of the modern affirmation of human autonomy in which human beings view themselves as the masters of nature and history. Having lived through the inhumanity of two world wars, the rise of weapons of mass destruction, and the devastating economic inequalities of the new world order following World War II, Barth viewed modernity's quest for autonomy as one more example of human pride and folly masquerading under the illusion of human progress. He took very seriously the realities of sin and evil, which hold human beings in their grip. The coming of Christ is required to set human beings free.

Yet it is also the case that Barth drew on theological themes like covenant to portray the reciprocity of divine and human action empowered by the reality of God's grace. Preaching, like all forms of proclamation, expects, enables, and even requires a human response. God's action on humanity's behalf in Christ as it is announced in the witness of the church calls for a free response by humans as hearers of the Word through the power of the Holy Spirit. Barth uses a variety of terms to describe this response, like correspondence, analogy, and (nonidentical) repetition.

Barth's understanding of human freedom and action in correspondence to the action of God has many important implications for practical theology. Most importantly, it decenters human agency as the means of saving, liberating, and transforming human beings. God alone does this in Christ and through the continuing action of the Holy Spirit. Preachers do not control how their hearers receive the Word. Nor do teachers, evangelists, caregivers, and other witnesses to the gospel. It is not a matter of the right sermon technique, educational program, or evangelistic method. Reflection on these matters is not ruled out, as we have seen in the reflection Barth himself provides in the *Exercises in Sermon Preparation*. But such offerings remain contextually specific and are provisional models and guidelines that seek to serve the communication of God's Word in a particular time and place.

By way of summary, practical theologians in dialogue with Karl Barth swim against the stream of modern and postmodern practical theology for two fundamental reasons. They take seriously God's revelation and reconciliation of the world in Jesus Christ as the grounding point of Christian practical theology. And they prioritize the dialogue of practical theology with other forms of theology, which are viewed as contributing knowledge that is more important to their work than philosophy, the human sciences, and other nontheological disciplines. I have attempted to embody these methodological commitments in this book in order to make a constructive contribution to the field of evangelism.

For Further Reading

Barth, Karl. *Homiletics.* Trans. Geoffrey Bromiley and Donald Daniels. Louis-ville: Westminster John Knox, 1991. One of several books in which Barth offers his approach to preaching.

Haddorff, D. *Christian Ethics as Witness: Barth's Ethics for a World at Risk.* Eugene, OR: Cascade Books, 2011. A timely exploration of the contextual nature of Barth's ethics with an eye to the contemporary world.

Hancock, Angela. *Karl Barth's Emergency Homiletic, 1932–1933: A Summons to Prophetic Witness at the Dawn of the Third Reich.* Grand Rapids: Eerdmans, 2013. A brilliant overview of Barth's *Exercises in Sermon Preparation,* which places it in context and illuminates the way Barth carries out practical theology.

Hunsinger, Deborah. *Bearing the Unbearable: Trauma, Gospel, and Pastoral Care.* Grand Rapids: Eerdmans, 2005. A brilliant theological exploration of trauma informed by Barth and also engaging the contemporary psychological literature on trauma.

———. *Theology and Pastoral Counseling: A New Interdisciplinary Approach.* Grand Rapids: Eerdmans, 1995. One of Barth's most able interpreters in practical theology rethinks pastoral counseling in light of his theology. An especially important contribution to interdisciplinary method.

Johnson, P. *The Mission of Preaching: Equipping the Community for Faithful Witness.* Downers Grove, IL: InterVarsity, 2015. One of the best books on preaching in congregations that seek to be missional in ways informed by Barth's theology.

Latini, T. *The Church and the Crisis of Community: A Practical Theology of Small Group Ministry.* Grand Rapids: Eerdmans, 2011. Bringing together empirical research on small groups and Barth's theology of *koinōnia,* this book represents an excellent example of practical theology in the spirit of Barth.

Loder, James. *The Logic of the Spirit.* San Francisco: Jossey-Bass, 1998. Perhaps the greatest American practical theologian of the second half of the twentieth century draws on Barth's understanding of the Chalcedonian paradigm and his own work in the logic of transformation to construct a new basis for practical theology and interdisciplinary work.

Smart, J. *The Teaching Ministry of the Church.* Philadelphia: Westminster, 1954. One of the earliest and most influential students of Barth's thought offers an understanding of the teaching ministry that reflects Barth's commitments. Shows the limitations of early practical theologians who drew on Barth and failed to develop an understanding of the contribution of practice to the constructive work of practical theology.

Stucky, Nathan. *Wrestling with Rest: Inviting Youth to Discover the Gift of Sabbath.* Grand Rapids: Eerdmans, 1995. A very timely study of the theology of Sabbath informed by Barth, which guides the church's response to young people who are connected to social media 24/7.

Thurneysen, Eduard. *A Theology of Pastoral Care.* Trans. Jack Worthington and Thomas Wieser. Richmond: John Knox, 1962. Barth's friend and collaborator in the theological revolution that Barth championed offers an approach to practical and pastoral theology informed by their work.

The Motif of "The Jews" and the Theme of Conflict in John

In recent decades, many scholars have come to believe John was originally written for Christian communities maintaining close ties with Judaism. Perhaps they were even viewed as a Jewish messianic sect. This changed after the Jewish rebellion against Rome in AD 66–70, which resulted in the destruction of the temple in Jerusalem. After this terrible event, the center of Jewish life began to shift to synagogues under the leadership of rabbis descended from the Pharisees. This made it impossible to tolerate Jewish Christians who believed that Jesus was the Messiah. At three points, John uses a technical term for exclusion from the synagogue (*aposynagōgos*) to refer to events in his narrative (John 9:22; 12:42; 16:2).[1]

One story using this term is about a man born blind who is healed by Jesus on the Sabbath (John 9:1–34). Like many of the stories in John, readers are invited to engage his story on several levels: (1) the events of the story as it is told, (2) the symbolism of blindness and seeing as it relates to faith in Jesus and the Pharisees' lack of faith, (3) Jesus's authority to heal on the Sabbath, (4) the resonance of water-washing and Christian baptism, and (5) the exclusion of those who believe in Jesus from the synagogue.

During the story, the healed man's parents are questioned by the Pharisees. They affirm that their son was born blind and now can see. But they refuse to answer the Pharisees' question about how this happened. The narrator adds: "His parents said this because they were afraid of the Jewish leaders, who already had decided that anyone who acknowledged that Jesus was the Messiah would be put out of the synagogue" (John 9:22). When the

---

1. Francis J. Moloney, *The Gospel of John*, Sacra Pagina (Collegeville, MN: Liturgical, 1998), Kindle edition, loc. 528. For a slightly different interpretation, see Craig S. Keener, *The Gospel of John: A Commentary*, vol. 1 (Grand Rapids: Baker Academic, 2003), 194–214.

healed man is questioned a second time by the Pharisees, he tells them "I was blind, but now I see" and Jesus is "from God" (9:25, 33). The leaders, then, "threw him out" (9:34).

This story and others in John appear to reflect a context in which there is sharp and painful conflict between the Johannine community and Jewish leaders emerging after the destruction of the temple. Frequently in John's Gospel, these leaders are simply called "the Jews." This term appears seventy times in John, compared with five or six in each of the Synoptics. While the term, "the Jews," has different shades of meaning in John, it primarily refers to the Jewish authorities, especially those in Jerusalem.[2] They are presented as hostile to Jesus and anyone who confesses him as the Messiah (for example, John 9:22; 12:42; 16:2). They plot against him and encourage Pilate to crucify him. After Jesus's death, his disciples hid behind closed doors "for fear of the Jews" (20:19).

Conflict between Jesus and Jewish leaders is not found in John alone. Nor is conflict between the early church and the Jewish community found only in this Gospel. But the level of vitriol and the numerous times John refers to Jewish authorities with the catchphrase "the Jews" brings us up short. We start here, for it is important to think about how to interpret this motif in John's Gospel.

John's highly polemical tone, when taken out of context, has been used to justify a long history of antisemitism throughout Western history, beginning during the Roman Empire and continuing into the modern period. Even Martin Luther, the great leader of the Protestant Reformation, made horrific charges against the Jewish community based on John and other parts of the New Testament. In *On the Jews and Their Lies*, for example, he wrote: "And Christ himself declares in John 4:22, 'Salvation is of the Jews.' Therefore they boast of being the noblest, yes, the only noble people on earth. In comparison with them and in their eyes we Gentiles (*Goyim*) are not human; in fact we hardly deserve to be considered poor worms by them."[3]

Luther grew increasingly frustrated when the Jewish community did not convert to the Protestant cause. He was not alone among Protestant, Roman Catholic, and Orthodox leaders in expressing antisemitic sentiments. These contributed to legalized forms of discrimination, cultural prejudice, and acts

---

2. See Raymond E. Brown, SS, for a discussion of the different ways this term is used. See *The Gospel according to John*, vol. 1, *I-XII*, The Anchor Bible Series, vol. 29 (Garden City, NY: Doubleday, 2003), lxx–lxxvi.

3. Martin Luther, *On the Jews and Their Lies* (Austin: Rivercrest, 2014), 224.

of violence. Antisemitism is once more on the rise in Europe and the United States, going well beyond criticism of the state of Israel's current policies.

Those of us who are Christians must keep in mind both the original historical context of John and the later history of antisemitism after Christianity became the dominant religion in the West. This has implications for how we draw on John in evangelism.

First, we must be aware that John's portrayal of "the Jews" is the result of a period of separation between Jewish and Christian communities. The divorce was acrimonious. But there is absolutely no justification for moving from the historical context of John to scapegoat, vilify, or discriminate against the Jewish community in later contexts (as Christ-killers, for example). Second, we must interpret Scripture in light of Scripture. We must look to the larger story of John and interpret the parts and the whole together. This story focuses on the mutual love of the Father, Son, and Holy Spirit. This is the source of Jesus's mission to the world. Christians who believe in Jesus begin to participate in the divine life of mutual love. They are to love the world as God loves it in Christ. This is the primary motivation for all forms of ministry, including evangelism. Verses from John thus cannot be used to justify demonizing "the Jews" with any integrity.

Sample Cases

I n the following cases, names have been changed to protect the anonymity of the participants. The four cases—each written in first person by a different student and lightly edited—appear in different formats I have used over the years. Like the cases used earlier in this book, these represent the first write-ups of the initial stage of the case project for discussion in precept. Students would revise them later in light of feedback and submit much longer cases for their final projects.

Case 1: A Spiritual Conversation in Brooklyn

Background

This incident happened while I was working at a church-owned coffee house in Brooklyn, NY. The church was nondenominational and rented a building on Sundays, so it used the coffee shop as its office space as well as a place for church members to mingle with members of the community. The purpose of the café was not evangelism, per se, but mainly a way for the church to have a presence in the community. Various local freelancers and community members came to the coffee shop to work on their projects; most came in and out and did not know that a church owned and ran the café. I was hired to be the manager of the coffee shop, and since it was a nonprofit with limited funds, I also happened to be the main person behind the bar, serving coffee. I got to know several coffee shop regulars and often had informal conversations with them in the afternoons when not many people were coming in for coffee.

Sample Cases

The Incident

Sharmila, a professional woman in her late twenties, was one coffee shop regular who came in on Tuesdays and Thursdays to do some freelance work for art magazines. Her parents had emigrated from India, and she was born and raised in the United States. Now, she lived right beside the coffee shop. When she would get her tea, a strong Earl Grey with a touch of milk, she would tell me about her horrible roommate situation and the mouse problems in her apartment. The roommate also came into the coffee shop at separate times, so I knew her as well. She also complained about mice and her roommate. Once, when Sharmila had the flu, she came in to have me make her dinner—grilled cheese and Ramen noodles—and she kept her physical distance but told me how horrible it was to have the flu. I could tell she just needed to have someone know that she was sick, someone to commiserate with her. In these ways I became a part of Sharmila's life.

One week, several months after I had become the café manager, I was invited to preach at our church. So I spent the week preparing a sermon. I sat in the café in the afternoons at my own table with my laptop to write the sermon, and I would get up when a customer came in. Sharmila was working at her own table. She got up to take a break from her work and came to sit with me at my table. She asked me what I was working on, and I told her how I was preaching on Sunday. She became immediately intrigued that I was going to preach a sermon—she had never known a young woman who preached—and she said she wanted to come hear me. So I told her where the church met and what time. She asked me several questions about the service: what she should wear, what typically happened at a church service. It became clear to me that she had never gone to church. I explained to her how it began with some worship songs, and I told her what worship songs did—expressed love to God. I told her that after the songs we had a sermon and then we ended with communion. I explained what communion was and then assured her that she did not need to feel pressured to participate in anything she did not want to do.

"Will people stare at me?" she asked. "They'll know I've never been there before."

I explained to her that many of the people she knew from the café already went to the church, so she would know several people when she came. That calmed her down, and she told me how excited she was to come.

I prepared the sermon on Colossians 2–3, which emphasized freedom in Christ from strict religious rules and rituals. I tried to avoid Christian lingo and to explain anything that would seem odd to a non-Christian. Sunday came, Sharmila showed up, and I greeted her, and she began talking with people she knew from the coffee shop and found a seat with them. After the service, I went up to her to get her reactions to the service. "There were a lot of songs," she said. "I thought that went on a little too long. But I thought your talk was great. I'd actually love to talk with you more about it. Would you have coffee with me sometime this week?" We set up a time to have coffee, at a different coffee shop, in the evening during the week.

When we met at the coffee shop, I was feeling a bit nervous about having a possible evangelical conversation, as though her salvation depended on this. I decided that I would just remain relaxed, not put that kind of pressure on myself, and let her direct the conversation. I told myself that God was already a part of this encounter and that I just had to be myself. We ordered some sandwiches and tea and we talked about how our day was. Then Sharmila began telling me about her past. She told me how she had grown up Hindu, how her parents were leaders in the temple, but now she no longer attended services. Since she moved to Brooklyn, she didn't really think about religion, she said. She told me how strict everything was when she was a Hindu, how many rituals there were. That was why the sermon had impacted her, she said. "They were just human rituals, like what you were talking about on Sunday," she said. "Does Christ really set us free from all of that?"

"Yes," I said. "A lot of times, human rituals are ways we try to please God or get right with God, but Christ came to show us that God already loves us and that we don't need to do all this extra stuff. Because of Christ we can have direct access to God because we know that God loves us already."

"I had never heard that before," she said and took a bite of her sandwich, and I took a moment to eat a little more, as well. "Sometimes I feel that I really need freedom," she continued. "Like I feel so trapped all the time by my cell phone and email. I can't go two minutes without checking my phone. I feel so anxious all of the time, like the world will fall apart if I don't check my email. And I really want to be free from all of that."

I did not know immediately how to respond to what she said, since she was taking the conversation in a new direction. But I remembered some spiritual direction training I had received in seminary, about listening for the Holy Spirit's guidance in spiritual conversations. So I took a moment to pause and say a mental prayer, and I decided that I should prompt her to continue talking. "I know a lot of people struggle with feeling trapped in that way," I said.

"It's like I'm addicted," she continued. "Is it possible to be addicted to your cell phone?"

"Maybe," I said. "If you feel like it's something you can't really control."

"I just want freedom," she continued. "I want to feel peace. Maybe I should try to just check my email only at certain times. Do you think that would work?"

"Yes, that would probably help," I said. I wanted to find a way to bring the conversation back to Christianity, but when I said another prayer for guidance, I felt that I should just listen to her and her cell phone addiction problem and not push anything. So we spent the rest of the time talking about her cell phone addiction and methods that might help her break free.

When we finished eating, we walked back to the church's coffee shop, now talking about various other things—more about her roommate problems and work. When we reached the café, she gave me a hug and told me how much she needed just to talk like this. Then she went up to her apartment and I went home.

After that encounter, Sharmila did not return to church, but she did continue coming to me with various problems, including her feeling of attraction to a married man who was pursuing her. We had a long conversation about that, and I encouraged her to find a community, perhaps even church, so she wouldn't feel so lonely, which could help ease unwanted attraction. I never knew what happened, because she moved out of her apartment the next week to another neighborhood due to roommate problems, and she never came back to the coffee shop.

Rationale

Since I grew up in the evangelical tradition, for many years I had a narrow understanding of evangelism—that it consisted of initiating conversations with non-Christians, telling them the Romans road of salvation, and then urging them to make a decision to follow Christ. This conversation had virtually none of those characteristics. Sharmila initiated the conversation; I did not tell her the Romans road of salvation (although discussing God's love is a part of the Romans road), and I certainly did not push her to make a decision. I was hesitant to talk with her because I do not like this idea of evangelism, and yet it still hangs over my head.

I chose this incident because it shows my actual approach to evangelism. I like to think of evangelism in terms of spiritual conversations with people, usually people who aren't Christians. I like to form relationships naturally, to be a friend with no ulterior motives such as conversion. If a spiritual conversation arises naturally within the relationship, then I will engage in that conversation and say what I believe. Often spiritual conversations arise simply because of my education and career aspirations; when people ask about my education (an Mdiv from Princeton Theological Seminary) and what it is I do, then they know that I am someone they can talk to about their spiritual questions. In this incident, the conversation came about from writing and preaching a sermon.

Some questions that arise for me from this incident include: How much should the other person direct the spiritual conversation, and how much should we? I could have directed the conversation back to Jesus instead of cell phones, but I chose not to, deciding to focus on her perceived needs. Also, what is the role of the Holy Spirit in these conversations? How can we really know how the Holy Spirit is directing a conversation? And should principles of spiritual direction apply in "evangelical" conversations?

What was at stake for me in this incident was a desire to have a spiritual conversation with Sharmila, without pushing her too far and losing our friendship. I do feel a sense of mission, of telling others about Jesus, since I am a Christian, but it is not an urgent feeling. I also resist my old understanding of evangelism, which frightens me in many ways—approaching strangers frightens me, telling them about sin and hell is abhorrent to me, and pushing them to make a decision terrifies me. So I draw on principles of spiritual direction to help me out, and I try to push away my old understanding of evangelism, although it still hangs over my head.

What is at stake for the church is being able to draw in people who have not "thought about religion" for a while. It is important for the church to make religion relevant to their lives and to not obscure the Bible and Christianity with religious lingo. It is important for the church to find ways to develop relationships with these people, who are often found in coffee shops or other public settings. The Brooklyn church's approach was positive, opening a coffee shop so that it could form these relationships with members of the community. In other churches, lay members already have these relationships in their places of work or other locations. The church can help them be open to having spiritual conversations in these everyday relationships.

Contextual Analysis

One thing that was important to Sharmila in coming to church for the first time was knowing people who went there. She knew some church members from the coffee shop, which made her feel comfortable and not too out of place. The church consisted of young professionals like herself, some single, some married, and so she found some people to sit with and relate to. Without those other relationships, this incident may have occurred differently; she may have been too nervous to come to the church or felt too uncomfortable in the church. The coffee shop culture of Brooklyn was also important. The coffee shop was a way for people in the community to form community—to get to know their neighbors and to get work done. It was not odd for Sharmila and I to go and get some coffee together. So the larger context contributed to this incident occurring as it did.

Case 2: Evangelizing a Family Member

Section 1: Opening Vignette

In January, my wife Jane, our 16-month-old daughter, and I drove from Princeton to Springfield, Illinois, for the memorial service of her grandmother, who had passed away peacefully in November at 95 years old. "Grammy" was the family matriarch. She and her husband (who had passed ten years earlier) were all about family. They were intentional in bringing together their adult children and their families for regular family vacations and reunions. Aunts, uncles, cousins, and now many second cousins and cousins once removed are all growing into the mix. I quickly grasped the impact and legacy of Grammy as I got to know my wife's family, and without hesitation I too became a "member" of this family after we were married. I always received a birthday card from my grandmother-in-law, which included a check for $50 just like every other grandchild received. Grammy's two daughters live and raised their families in Springfield, but Grammy's son lives in St. Louis with his family. The memorial service was truly a celebration of life. Delaying the service for two months was primarily to ensure that all the grandchildren (and families) could attend, but also to allow for the service weekend to be another family-filled gathering, which Grammy was central in creating throughout her life.

The critical incident focuses on a brief conversation I had with Devin, my wife's cousin, in the evening after Grammy's memorial service. Our conversation took place with wine in hand and stomachs well fed at the large and beautiful home of Uncle Sebastian (Grammy's son, whose house many of us stayed in for the weekend). Devin works for a large, international consulting firm and travels all over the world for work, probably spending three quarters of every month away from home. Devin is a very gifted and successful individual professionally and personally. He is also extremely fit and an ultra-distance runner. He and his wife, Sarah, have a three-year-old son and a daughter who is one month younger than our daughter. Jane and I have enjoyed connecting with Devin and Sarah as we watch our daughters interact and grow in the recent family events over the past few years.

Devin is not religious and from what I can tell is either an atheist or agnostic. I had a brief conversation with Sarah at the memorial service reception about her Catholic faith and how much she values it, but she said that Devin wants nothing to do with it. I actually did not know Sarah grew up Catholic until this conversation. Sarah has also been outspoken with Jane and me about her desire for more children, but she said that if she pushed that with Devin, it would lead to divorce. There are clearly places of tension and issues in Devin and Sarah's marriage. I have not observed it directly, but my wife has shared how Devin can be noticeably rude towards Sarah and does not treat her very kindly. Success, appearance, prestige, and money appear as core values for Devin. He has everything you could ask for in life, but there does seem to be a hint of unhappiness in him, or at least grumpiness. The dynamics of Devin's marriage reveal enough that there is some brokenness in his life in need of healing. Additionally, the obsession with financial and physical accomplishment also echoes some type of search for meaning.

All of my wife's family show some kind of courteous interest in my education at seminary and my plans to be a pastor. Most of her family is unchurched, or the "spiritual, but not religious" type, with the exception of her parents and one other couple. I feel that Devin and Sarah have shown more intentionality toward my education and the process moving forward for me in family gatherings over the years. Although the conversation with Devin was brief, it reflects well the kinds of conversations I have with Devin.

Verbatim

The following conversation happens in a house with adults and children all moving about. It is a big family house party. Some conversations last longer than others, but due to the context, people catch up, talk for a while, and then move on to get more food or wine.

Devin: Michael, so how is Princeton going?

Michael: It is going well. It is hard to believe that three years is almost over and I'll be graduating soon.

Devin: Wow, that was quick. Now, how does searching for a job go at a seminary? Are you placed or are there recruiters that come to the school?

Michael: The seminary does help with preparing your resume, highlighting opportunities, and there is a job board. To find a "call," as it is termed, is determined by the denominational tradition you belong to. As a Presbyterian, I will seek employment on my own by talking and applying to jobs at individual churches.

Devin: How is that process going?

Michael: We are looking all over the country and willing to go where there is a good position that is a good fit. It could be a long process, but we'll have to just wait and see. I've been devoting a lot of time over my Christmas break getting ready and applying for church positions.

Devin: Well, you know, with Jane's music ability, you guys could always go down the religious programming route—start something for TV. Those guys always seem to have a lot of success.

Michael: (Laughing at the comment) Yes, those folks seem to have quite a ministry going. I can say confidently that that is not the kind of path I am moving toward. My theology does not quite match up with most of the individuals I have observed on TV. If anything, there might be a lot of ministry work needing to be done with people to correct what is broadcast over TV.

Devin: Interesting. So have you and Jane formed close friends and a good community out there? I remember when Sarah and I were at Yale how we made some really good friends.

Michael: Yes, we live in a great complex, and have made some close friends with other couples. A lot of our friends are in the same stage of life, starting their families and trying to juggle all of that while in school. It's been a good bonding experience.

Devin: That's great. I am sure you will miss those friendships as everyone disperses.

Michael: Yes, we definitely will, but it will be exciting to see where everyone ends up after graduation.

Michael: How has it been living in St. Louis? Are you feeling settled now?

Devin: Yes, it has taken a lot of time to get the house in the shape we want it to be. I also still travel a lot, and it is getting more difficult with the kids, especially Parker. He is already meeting with a therapist to help him understand why I am away so much.

Michael: Wow, it's good that he is already able to speak with someone about how he is feeling.

Devin: Yeah, it is.

The conversation fades off. Another family member comes to join us and we move on to discussing something different.

Section 2: Rationale

I am working with the understanding that evangelism is sharing your walk of faith with others in an authentic way. Also, this includes sharing what you believe. I selected this incident because I foresee many future conversations with Devin (and other family members) about the vocation I will be in as an opportunity for evangelism. I want to reflect upon ways to better represent my faith and find pathways to share the gospel well, with authenticity and boldness. Furthermore, as a highly accomplished business professional, Devin represents many people in the world who I will meet in airports, school events, youth athletics, community spaces, and so on. My identity as a pastor will make an impression, positive or negative, as I meet people. I think many individuals with such material and visible success have a hard time understanding the purpose of faith—let alone someone like me, who will devote his life to the care and nurture of others. I do not know any statistics on how many upper-class professionals attend or do not attend church, but it is clear from Devin's own lifestyle that regularly attending a traditional church on Sunday morning would not even fit into his family's schedule with the amount of time he is away. This is a significant challenge for evangelism and inviting people to be a part of a church community. How is it logistically possible for someone like Devin to join a church if he were ever to believe in Christ or see the importance of belonging to a religious body?

In addition, I believe Devin needs Jesus. Devin needs a transformation in how to view work, treat his family, and see his own life. Devin is a difficult case because I do not think he outwardly displays any needs or areas for healing. Everything is put together very nicely on the outside—a big beautiful home in St. Louis, healthy children, personal and family success, impressive job and education. Why would a person who has achieved so much on his own see the need for faith? What is the good news for someone in Devin's situation? The hint of a rocky marriage is one potential area of need, along with his drive to overwork. But Devin does not seem to see either as an area of brokenness or struggle in his life. It seems some pre-evangelism work needs to be done before simply telling Devin the good news or sharing about the gospel of Jesus Christ.

Case 3: Rainbow-Sensitive Evangelism

The Incident

I was sitting in Starbucks writing a sermon when Mike arrived, waved, and walked over with his coffee in hand. Mike is the gay best friend of one of my youth group members. Mike is not a member of the congregation, but had interacted with me on our church mission trip, which he attended. He wanted to touch base with me and chat about some things he noticed on the mission trip, so we arranged for this meeting about a month after the trip.

Verbatim

The following conversation began with us shooting the breeze: How has your summer been? Where did you vacation? Did you see [landmark] while you were in [country]? After a bit of that, the conversation turned back toward the mission trip.

Joshua: The mission trip was a while ago, but how does that play into your report on your summer? Was it a highlight? A lowlight?
Mike: It was interesting. I mean, it wasn't a trip to Europe or anything, but it was definitely highlight material.
Joshua: What makes you say that? What was a highlight of the trip?
Mike: Well, it was really fun to be with Sara and Jenny all week. And it was actually fun to get to work with them—and Momma Jean too. We made the work a fun time, all while helping people too.
Joshua: So, I'm gonna call it like it is and I want you to tell me what you think: This was a church trip. I get the feeling you don't have too much experience with the church. How did that work out?
Mike: Ha ha, I was surprised. Sara told me that the trip wasn't going to be all about Jesus and God and stuff, but there was still a lot of it there.

Joshua: Was that a good or a bad thing?

Mike: Not bad, that's for sure. It's not my thing, so it wasn't good for me, but it wasn't bad either. You guys did a good job balancing the God stuff for us guys that don't usually do that stuff.

Joshua: So what is your experience with the church?

[Mike shared his experience with and impression of the church. He shared his minimal experiences with the local Roman Catholic Church as a child and his experiences of being discouraged by displays of hypocrisy in Christianity in general. He shared that he identified as atheist though his description of his beliefs would indicate more apathy and a tendency toward agnosticism.]

Joshua: I simply accepted what my parents taught me until I was a senior!

Mike: Yeah, so how did you get here? A Canadian pastor in this town? And you're . . . well . . .

Joshua: . . . gay?

Mike: (Visibly relieved) Okay, yeah, how did being gay play into that? What's your story?

Joshua: Ha ha. That is a long, long story, but I think you'll appreciate it more than most.

Mike: Ha ha. Probably.

(I shared my personal faith journey, including experiences that helped me identify my sexual orientation, personal faith, denominational affiliation, and calling to ministry.)

Joshua: And so you know, most people haven't heard that entire story—at least not the part about my dating preferences and how that plays into my journey.

Mike: Huh. Wow. That is interesting, but why would you stay? I just don't get that! Why would you stay in a community that doesn't accept you for who you are, but only who they think you are? What about the thousands of years of hate toward people like us? Why would you work for the church when you could get a job doing something that makes more money or something?

Joshua: It's kind of complicated. It's a calling, if that makes sense. I was going to be an accountant or a teacher, but it just didn't feel right. I just knew what I needed to do. I had spent most of my life in the church and was really sensitive to God in my life. I also knew that God loved me just the way God made me. I knew that my life's calling and who I was couldn't be completely at odds with each other. I guess that's when I figured out what was wrong with the world: the church is the one that's wrong, not God, not my faith. The church has a few things it needs to get figured out—like how to love people that are different from who they are and how to see the Bible as a tool to affirm that love instead of a tool to hurt people.

Mike: It's cool that that's how you got here, I guess. People have great stories, and I always wondered how you got here, of all places.

Joshua: Yup. Any idea where you'll end up?

Mike: Naw. I have a year before I have to figure that out. I don't have great grades, but I have a year to get that lined up before college becomes a major problem. I kind of want to take a year off to work and figure out what I really want.

(The conversation continued about college plans and school.)

Joshua: Well, Mike, I have to get back to work. I really enjoyed talking with you and catching up. I know you're not really a churchgoing guy, but I see you as one of my youth—like Sara and Jenny. If you ever need to talk, let me know. I'm always down for an excuse to drink coffee and chat. We've got some stuff in common, and hopefully I can be a helpful resource for you.

Mike: Yeah, that sounds good. Thanks, Joshua.

Joshua: And be good, Mike. Be safe and stay away from things that you shouldn't be doing. You know what I'm talking about!

Mike: I know. I will, Joshua.

Rationale

This interaction is pretty indicative of my perception of evangelism, but it has brought a twist that really caught me off guard, namely the tie toward such sensitive material in my own journey and the vulnerable place in which this experience of evangelism left me. In general, I understand evangelism to most often be a series of interactions that requires time and impact in order to make a long-term change. When I consider evangelism for Mike, I believe that this will be a long-term experience of building trust and relationship. Mike has made a decision regarding religion, but I believe that by seeing my faith at work in my life and actions he might be swayed to consider the good news in a new and personal way.

The primary questions that arise out of this interaction revolve around conversion for the LGBTQ community and those who stand in solidarity with that community. What can evangelism look like for the LGBTQ community and, in particular, for the youth that have found themselves in a situation where they want to support the LGBTQ community but to do so would apparently leave them at odds with the church? And in response to this particular scenario, where does a personal experience cross a line into something that is too personal? I came out to a person when no one else in that ministry setting is officially aware of my sexual orientation.

Contextual Analysis

This conversation was with Mike, a junior at the local high school in the town where I currently work. I was first introduced to Mike during one of my first weeks at the church during a concert his choir did in our sanctuary. Mike is one of the only openly gay students at his school, but he claims that this fact has not weighed too heavily on him since coming out three or four years ago. Mike is an only child, and his parents are high-ranking professionals in Fortune 500 companies, making him an only child with a lot of financial resources and a lot of time alone at home. Mike has been in trouble with the law a couple of times (for example, disturbing the peace, mischief, possession of marijuana), but those incidents were nothing that has completely damaged his reputation or significantly impacted his criminal record (he is still a minor). Mike ended up joining our mission trip team for the summer of 2013, but not without some concern from a few parents first. The trip ended up going just fine, with only one or two experiences of Mike being ignored by a few of the "jocks" in the group—a problem I was sure to address through a discussion of inclusion and emphasis of our theme ("One Body, Many Parts"). Mike was actually one of the most well-behaved participants and did anything I asked of him throughout the trip.

On the last day of the trip, everyone was given an opportunity to write notes to all the other trip participants. Upon returning home and opening my notes, I found one from Mike. On it he had written, "Thanks for this week. It was great getting to be a part of this! Maybe I'll see you around on [gay dating site]! ;)" While I was indeed dabbling in the online dating world, I had not consciously come across Mike, nor had we communicated. After getting over the shock of being privately "outed" as gay and also for being on a gay dating website, I decided that I needed to discuss this with him. Because of my summer mission trip and travel plans and his own family's vacation schedule, we were not in town again at the same time until approximately four weeks later when I texted him (I had everyone's cell numbers on the mission trip in case of an emergency), and we arranged an opportunity to grab coffee at the local Starbucks "to debrief the mission trip."

Mike and his family identify as Catholic, though I get the impression that he hasn't been to mass more than a dozen times in the last decade. As such, Mike doesn't have a strong religious background and tends to think of church as a social activity with strange traditions tied to it. This came across clearly when we were conversing about how I stayed in the church despite its generally nonwelcoming stance. While I am not convinced that this conversation changed his view completely on this subject, it does plant a seed of hope.

Case 4: Can You Evangelize a Friend?

Background

Chas is one of my oldest friends. We first met in middle school and have always had common interests. We've remained close for a long time now and still talk to each other fairly regularly. Both as youth and adults we have always enjoyed talking about science, religion, sports, art, culture, and we have generally had commonality on most of these things. One of the largest subjects where we have agreed to disagree is on religion. I was raised Presbyterian and I am still largely orthodox; Chas on the other hand was raised in an irreligious home, though both his parents grew up marginally Christian. Chas is an agnostic deist who finds Christianity and most other religions logically incoherent but morally useful and psychologically beneficial. He has now graduated college and is working in the insurance industry close to where we grew up.

To be frank, Chas is a womanizer. When we both went to college we diverged completely in how we lived. For me, college was a renewing experience where I felt a need for God in my life that had not been present in this way before. I came to terms with who I was and what I wanted out of life. For Chas, college was an opportunity to escape the homogenous blue-collar middle-class white majority Southern Baptist community that we had grown up in. When he went to college he slacked on his grades, smoked marijuana, got drunk every weekend, and had sex with various women. Still, he and I remained friends despite our differences. We had a strong history together; each of us still enjoyed the company of the other. I felt that I tended to be guarded against coming across as judgmental, making it difficult to feel relaxed in his company.

Incident

Last summer I went to San Diego for eight weeks to do an extensive MCAT training course. This is the exam required to apply to medical school, and I wanted to do well. I was very busy and did not take most of my calls. But whenever Chas called I always answered because we don't talk enough. It was 11:00 p.m. in San Diego when he called. I'm from North Carolina, so it must have been about 2:00 a.m. at home, which is very strange because he never calls that late. I asked how he was and in a calm voice he explained his situation.

One of his classmates was pregnant, and he was the father. The phone call wasn't that long, maybe twenty minutes. We considered his circumstances and what he could do. He shared that he had a lot of influence on this woman and whatever he wanted her to do she would do. He was considering encouraging her to get an abortion. He asked me what I would do, and I felt trapped. I felt trapped because I knew what I would do, and he knew what I would do. I told him that if I were a woman I would not consider an abortion and as a man I would do everything I could to encourage her not to have one. We had always agreed about this until this conversation. He asked me why I felt this way. I said it was because I am Christian and Jesus showed God's love to the vulnerable, those on the margins of society or social outcasts. How could I believe that and not also believe that he cares for the unborn?

He then shared with me that the pregnant woman was an Asian American and that her parents are Chinese. She told him that they would disown her if they discovered she was pregnant. Chas said that he believed she had to have an abortion so she could stay with her family. He felt guilty about this, and at one point he wanted to feel guilty because he was causing this woman so much pain. The conversation ended pretty quickly. The woman we were talking about was calling him on the phone.

Rationale

I bring this up to talk about what I might have done after this phone call. We still talked by phone, but every time I steered the conversation toward these events, he would move in another direction. Gradually our friendship grew more strained and he stopped initiating any of the calls. I believe Chas needs to know the love of God, but I also believe he is right to feel guilty. His life wasn't all that different from other people his age, but it was pretty focused on pleasure and centered around himself. How might I have shared the gospel with him?

APPENDIX 3

Guidelines for Evangelization

Here is a recapitulation of guidelines covered in chapter 6:

Guideline: It is important to move beyond thinking about evangelism focused on a single point-in-time event in which a person is converted. Responding to Jesus's call and following him involves both significant moments of change and a longer process of coming to trust in him and follow in his way.

Guideline: The congregation is the first witness to the gospel. It points to Christ by loving as he did. The love of Christ must be embodied in its fellowship, its welcome of people into the community, and its outreach to the world. This is the context in which evangelization takes place. The church must embody visibly, if provisionally, the love of God in Jesus Christ for evangelization to share the gospel with others in a credible way.

Guideline: Evangelization must develop a variety of different ways of sharing the gospel to reach different people and groups. In doing this, it corresponds to the witness of Scripture.

Guideline: Evangelization involves entering into the suffering and pain of other people in order to share the good news of God's participation in and care for their plight. Salvation involves healing and consolation now, but also, hope in God's promised future for creation when the Spirit will manifest the healing and reconciliation of the world.

Guideline: The gospel celebrates the glory of God and God's beauty, splendor, and might in the form of self-giving love. Evangelization invites people to live in the light of God's glory right now, for life abundant begins in the present and continues into eternity. This is a life of partic-ipation in the Triune God, a life of joy, intimacy, and fulfillment as we live in one another through the Holy Spirit, who joins us to Christ and through him to the Father.

Guideline: New forms of evangelism will only emerge in congregations with missional orientations, whether these are church plants or estab-lished congregations in the process of revitalization. It is important for established congregations with financial resources to support church plants and to learn from their innovations. It is equally important for many church plants to move beyond their anti-establishment postures, which sometimes come across as more adolescent than innovative.

Guideline: Focusing on children's experience of church must become a priority for evangelization. It represents a long-term missionary strategy in a context in which many emerging adults move through a prolonged period of identity exploration and distance themselves from the institu-tional church but later are more open to returning if they had a positive experience of the church during childhood.

Guideline: Evangelism is the good news of God's salvation of the world in Jesus Christ. It is the story of God's love for the world, from election to reconciliation to the consummation. Our message is: God loves you; Christ has saved you out of love; if you trust this love your life will be transformed. Come and see.

Guideline: Evangelism does not begin by shaming people, mocking them, making them feel guilty, or trying to manipulate them because their very salvation is at stake. It communicates through attitudes and words the high cost and depth of God's love. God knows who we really are; God knows us better than we know ourselves. Yet God loves us as we truly are; God loves us better than we love ourselves. This profound sense of being known for who we are and still loved is a good place to start in evangelization.

Guideline: In evangelizing the unaffiliated and nominal Christians, un-derstanding who a person is, taking time to develop a relationship, and sharing the gospel in words and actions improves the likelihood that it will be given a hearing.

Guideline: People in all three of these groups (unaffiliated; nominal Christians; responsible, long-term Christians) experience times of crisis, triggering experiences of dislocation and the search for meaning. Evangelization that shares the love of God in Jesus Christ through words and deeds is one form of the church's ministry to people at such times. It should pay special attention to their desire to make sense of what they are experiencing, to find supportive relationships and communities that embody the way of life they are learning, and "techniques for living," practical tools to help them begin to live in a new way.

Guideline: Responsible, long-term Christians need to hear the gospel again and again—in times of crisis and as they move from one stage of life to another, but most importantly of all because they live in the tension of being simultaneously saved and sinful. The gospel breaks into their experience to wake them up and send them in a new direction. It also provides them a foretaste of joy, peace, and celebration in anticipation of God's promised future for creation.

INDEX

academic liberal theology, 136, 137–38.
See also Protestant liberalism
Ad Gentes (Vatican II decree, 1961), 143
altar calls, 11, 28, 161, 224
Anabaptists, 8, 21
*Anabaptist Story: An Introduction to
Sixteenth-Century Anabaptism, The*
(Estep), 17
*Analogy of Grace: Karl Barth's Moral
Theology, The* (McKenny), 167
antisemitism, 111, 241–42, 250–51
antistructuralism, 9
Appold, Mark L, 117n34, 131
Arrowsmith, Paula, 26–28, 30–32, 53, 69
atonement: and cultic sacrifice, 45–47;
John's universal imagery, 117–18;
Paul's imagery, 41–44, 45–47, 201–2;
representative, 173; substitutionary,
172–73
*Atonement: The Origins of the Doctrine in
the New Testament, The* (Hengel), 54

Balthasar, Hans Urs von, 136, 144
baptism: in case study of evangelistic
practice, 91–93, 110; and footwashing in John's Gospel, 121n40; Jesus's
baptism by John, 64; and Paul's
congregations, 47, 198; and Protestant evangelistic practice, 8, 169; and
Reformation theology, 149–50
Baptists, 3–4, 8, 9–12, 21
Barrett, Lois, 219
Barth, Karl, 133–40, 141–67, 168–91,

194, 205–19, 235–46; alternative to
conversionistic evangelism, 139–40,
168–69, 184–85, 194, 205–17; on the
"being of the church," 142–49, 196,
204; case studies of evangelistic
practice in dialogue with, 159–65,
186–90; the Chalcedonian pattern,
147–49, 150, 165, 170, 194, 204; on
Christ as Son of God, as Son of Man,
as the God-human, 178–79; Christ
in our place (theme), 134, 139, 169,
172–82, 204, 219; Christocentric
theology, 134, 238; on conversion and
sanctification, 181; critique of classic
view of the church's purpose, 150–52;
critique of Protestant liberalism, 134,
135–36, 144–46; critique of Roman
Catholicism, 135–36, 142–44; on the
cross, 180; on the diaconate, 154–55,
189; on dialectical inclusion in the
theological disciplines, 239–46; doctrine of reconciliation, 175–82, 237–39;
and evangelicalism, 133–35, 141; and
evangelization to nominal Christians,
157–59, 173–74, 184–85, 210–11; Holy
Spirit as mediator of communion, 134,
139–40, 170–71, 182–84, 190, 205; on
human freedom and agency in salvation, 171–72, 183, 245–46; on judgment
and evangelization, 174–75, 189–90,
209–10; on "lordless powers," 174,
207–8, 216; and Luther's understand-

topic of gospel, 31, 39–48, 52; topic of salvation (soteriology), 31, 52; use in courses in evangelism, 1, 61, 221–35; "a spiritual conversation in Brooklyn," 252–57; "can you evangelize a friend?," 265–67; "evangelism in a time of war," 159–65; "evangelizing a family member," 257–61; "from scratch" evangelism, 24–26, 28–31, 38, 51–52, 164; "I'm gonna do a bad thing," 186–90; "rainbow-sensitive evangelism," 261–65; "tongues of healing and unity," 26–32, 53; "too late for me," 56–61, 84–87, 200; "washed clean," 89–94, 108, 110–11, 112, 113

Chalcedonian Pattern, 147–49, 150, 165, 170, 194, 204

Charlemagne, 19–20, 143

Chitwood, Paul, 28n3

Chopp, Rebecca, 237

Christian Ethics as Witness: Barth's Ethics for a World at Risk (Haddorff), 247

Christian Life, The (Barth), 207

Christ in Our Place: The Substitutionary Character of Calvin's Doctrine of Reconciliation (van Buren), 172

Christ in Perspective in the Theology of Karl Barth (Thompson), 191

Church and the Crisis of Community, The: A Practical Theology of Small Group Ministry (Latini), 247

Church Dogmatics (Barth), 133, 135–36, 141–42, 148, 150, 155–56, 172, 175, 177, 238–40, 243, 245; *The Doctrine of Creation* (CD III), 150, 215; *The Doctrine of Reconciliation* (CD IV), 150, 155–59, 177

church planting, 202–4

Church Planting in the Secular West: Learning from the European Experience (Paas), 220

Confessing Christ for Church and World: Studies in Modern Theology (Bender), 166

Confessing Church, 133

Confirmation Project, 215–16, 217–18, 223

Continuing Conversion of the Church, The (Guder), 17

conversionistic evangelism. *See* evangelism as conversionism

Council of Chalcedon, 147. *See also* Chalcedonian pattern

Cousar, Charles B, 53

Creating a Missional Culture: Equipping the Church for the Sake of the World (Woodward), 220

cultural diffusion, evangelism as, 19–22

cultural toolkits, 8–12; religious toolkit of conversionistic evangelism, 9–12, 139–40, 224

Deddo, Gary, 190, 237

Defending Substitution: An Essay on Atonement in Paul (Gathercole), 54

diaconate, ministry of, 154–55, 189

dialectical inclusion of the theological disciplines, 239–46

Diaz, Ariana, 26–28, 30–32, 53, 69, 164, 200, 214

Disruptive Grace: Studies in the Theology of Karl Barth (Hunsinger), 167

Divided by Faith: Evangelical Religion and the Problem of Race in America (Emerson and Smith), 9–10

Divine Freedom and the Doctrine of the Immanent Trinity: In Dialogue with Karl Barth and Contemporary Theology (Molnar), 166

dogmatic theology, 12–17, 193–94, 196–97, 238, 239–46

Dominican Order, 20

Dufault-Hunter, Erin, 214n23, 230

Dulles, Avery, 143

Dunn, James D. G., 46, 54

ecumenical theology, 136–38

Edwards, Jonathan, 9

election, reconciliation and, 139, 175–78, 219

Emerson, Michael, 8–10

enclave theology, 136–37

Espinosa, Gaston, 30

Estep, William R., 17

euangelizō/euangelion (the gospel, good

news, glad tidings), 32–33, 34n12, 36–37, 133
Evangelical, Catholic, and Reformed: Doctrinal Essays on Barth and Related Themes (Hunsinger), 191
Evangelical Theology: An Introduction (Barth), 165
evangelicalism: Barth and, 133–35, 141; diversity of, 134–35; evangelical liberals, 147n22; and evangelism as conversionism, 8–12, 21, 139–40, 224; "from scratch" evangelism, 24–26, 28–31, 38, 51–52, 164; and Luther's understanding of justification, 42–43n36; religious toolkits, 9–12, 139–40, 224; and the sinner's prayer, 28–29, 52. *See also* evangelism as conversionism
evangelism: crossing boundaries in, 69–70; as cultural diffusion, 19–22; in dialogue with Barth, 133–40, 141–67, 168–91, 194, 205–19, 235–46; distinctions between insiders and outsiders in, 72–74; and the Gospel of Mark, 55–88; and the Gospel of John, 89–131; and the Holy Spirit, 16, 53, 183–84; initial definition (as invitation), 12–16, 196–99; mission of the church as witness, 16, 149–59, 163–65, 173, 182, 189, 196, 204; New Testament examples, 4–5, 6, 12–16, 197–98; and Paul the apostle, 23–54; and Roman Catholicism, 142–44; theme of calling, 12–16; traditional American Protestant practice of, 1–7; words and deeds, 68–69, 153, 155–56, 164. *See also* evangelism as conversionism; "new evangelization"
evangelism as conversionism, 3–5, 7–12, 21–22, 60, 193, 224; Barth's alternative to, 139–40, 168–69, 184–85, 194, 205–17; and case studies of evangelistic practice, 24–26, 28–31, 38, 51–52, 159–65; conversion as life-changing transformation, 11, 139–40; freedom to decide to convert, 10–11, 139–40; and "from scratch" evangelism, 24–26, 28–31, 38, 51–52, 164; hypothe-

sis for dominance of, 7–12, 224; lost/saved contrast, 10, 139–40; and the New Testament, 4–5; once-and-for-all conversion event, 184–85, 211; post-Reformation Christianity, 3–4, 7–12, 21, 149–50, 224; problems with/criticisms of, 5–6, 11–12, 21–22, 149–50, 209; religious toolkit of, 8–12, 139–40, 224; and revivalism, 2–4, 6–7, 28, 52, 174, 183; and salvation, 168–69, 224; and sin, 206–10; soteriological existentialism, 168–69; and white evangelicals, 8–12, 21, 139–40, 224
Evangelism in the Early Church (Green), 17
Evangelistic Love of God and Neighbor, The: A Theology of Witness and Discipleship (Jones), 17
Exercises in Sermon Preparation (Übungen in der Predigtvorbereitung) (Barth), 241–46
Exodus stories, 100–102, 105n15

Faith, Freedom and the Spirit: The Economic Trinity in Barth, Torrance, and Contemporary Theology (Molnar), 191
Finney, Charles, 28
Flett, John G., 191
Ford, David, 167
Four Gospels and the One Gospel of Jesus Christ, The (Hengel), 87
Fourfold Gospel, The: A Theological Reading of the New Testament Portraits of Jesus (Watson), 88
Franciscan Order, 20
freedom: Barth on human freedom and agency in salvation, 171–72, 183, 245–46; conversionistic evangelism and choice/decision to convert, 10–11, 139–40; freewill individualism, 9
Frei, Hans, 139n13
"from scratch" evangelism, 24–26, 28–31, 38, 51–52, 164

Galatians: A New Translation with Introduction and Commentary (Martyn), 54